Occupational Stress Management

OCCUPATIONAL STRESS MANAGEMENT

Editor

Prof. (Dr.) P. K. Dutta

First Edition : 2009

Himalaya Publishing House

MUMBAI • NEW DELHI • NAGPUR • BANGALORE • HYDERABAD • CHENNAI • PUNE • LUCKNOW • AHMEDABAD • ERNAKULAM

First Edition : 2009

Published by : Mrs. Meena Pandey
for **HIMALAYA PUBLISHING HOUSE PVT. LTD.,**
"Ramdoot", Dr. Bhalerao Marg, Girgaon, **Mumbai - 400 004.**
Phones: 2386 01 70/2386 38 63, Fax: 022-2387 71 78
Email: himpub@vsnl.com
Website: www.himpub.com

Branch Offices:

New Delhi : "Pooja Apartments", 4-B, Murari Lal Street, Ansari Road, Darya Ganj,
New Delhi - 110 002. Phone: 23270392, 23278631
Fax: 011-23256286

Nagpur : Kundanlal Chandak Industrial Estate, Ghat Road,
Nagpur - 440 018. Phone: 2738731, 3296733
Telefax : 0712-2721215

Bangalore : No. 16/1 (Old 12/1), 1st Floor, Next to Hotel Highlands,
Madhava Nagar, Race Course Road, **Bangalore - 560 001.**
Phone : 22281541, 22385461, Telefax: 080-22286611

Hyderabad : No. 3-4-184, Lingampally, Besides Raghavendra Swamy Matham,
Kachiguda, **Hydrabad - 500 027.** Mobile : 09848130433

Chennai : No. 85/50, Bazullah Road, T. Nagar, **Chennai - 600 017.**
Phone: 044-28144004/28144005

Pune : First Floor, "Laksha" Apartment, No. 527, Mehunpura, Shaniwarpeth,
(Near Prabhat Theatre), **Pune - 411 030.**
Phone: 020 - 24496323/24496333

Lucknow : C-43, Sector - C, Ali Gunj, **Lucknow - 226 024.**
Phone: 0522-2339329

Ahmedabad : 114, "SHAIL", 1st Floor, Opp. Madhu Sudan House, C.G.Road,
Navrang Pura, **Ahmedabad – 380 009.**
Phone: 079-26560126, Mobiles: 09327324149,09314679413

Ernakulam : 39/104 A, Lakshmi Apartment, Karikkamuri Cross Rd.,
Ernakulam, **Cochin – 622011**, Kerala.
Phone: 0484-2378012, 2378016, Mob- 09344199799

DTP by : **HPH, Editorial Office, Bhandup (Sunanda)**

Printed by : **A to Z Printers**
New Delhi

NATIONAL SEMINAR

ON

OCCUPATIONAL STRESS AND ITS REMEDIES IN THE 21st CENTURY

February 9, 2008

Conducted and Organised By

Dr. P. K. Dutta (Director)

Shri. Atmanand Jain

Institute of Management & Technology

(Affiliated to Kurukshetra University, Kurukshetra, Approved by AICTE)

Ambala City (Haryana)

Preface

This publication incorporates the paper to be presented at the National Seminar on "Occupational Stress And Its Remedies in the 21st Century" being organised by the Shri Atmanand Jain Institute of Management and Technology (AIMT) campus, Ambala city on 9th February, 2008. AIMT is affiliated to Kurukshetra University Kurukshetra and is approved by All India Council for Technical Education (AICTE), New Delhi. The papers presented at the conference have been classified under the following themes:

1. Psychological aspects of stress
2. Stress at work place and social environment
3. Stress and trauma pain
4. Stress and performance in organisation
5. Health and wellness programmes related to stress
6. Improvement in quality of work life
7. Future research on stress
8. Stress in IT Industry
9. Stress Management Strategies
10. Pain Management Related to Stress

The Director of AIMT express his gratitude to all the paper presenters, chairpersons and discussants, participants, speakers' guests of honour, keynote address presenters, presidents of various events, sponsors, members of committees for organising the national seminar, faculty and staff of the institute and media for their active engagement in planning and organising the seminar.

The institute is grateful to the Jain Management Society and all members of the Board for their encouragement and motivation to organise the seminar.

Prof. (Dr.) P.K.Dutta
Editor in Chief

Contents

About the Institute

Shri Atmanand Jain Institute of Management and Technology (AIMT) was established in 1996 to impart Quality Management Education to the budding managers for the modern corporate world. AIMT is affiliated to *Kurukshetra University, Kurukshetra* and approved by *All India Council for Technical Education (**AICTE**)*, New Delhi. Since inception, the institute has been an active member of *Confederation of Indian Industry (**CII**), Ludhiana Management Association (**LMA**)* and *All India Management Association (**AIMA**)*.

The institute is located in Ambala City, and well connected by road and rail to Chandigarh, Delhi and surrounding areas. The institute focuses on regular upgradation of its syllabi, in line with Kurukshetra University, Kurukshetra.

AIMT is the only institute that has been rated in 2005, AIMA B-School Survey, besides MDI Gurgaon.The Institute has been awarded with "Vidya Rattan Award" on April 10, 2003 by International Business Council Association with IIEM, New Delhi and recently honoured with "Academic Excellence Award" by Indian Solidarity Council, New Delhi on December 12, 2007.

Four batches of **MCA** & Ten batches of **MBA** course have already passed from the institute. More than 85% of the students who passed out from the institute are well placed in the corporate sector and academic field.

Introduction

Occupational stress has become a topic of great interest to academic researchers, managers in organisations, and to the general public as well. The negative impact of stress is often thought to be due to increases in healthcare costs. It is claimed that employee stress is costly to organisations in terms of reduced productivity, decreased quality of customer service, increased accident rates, and increased employee withdrawal.

The nature of work is changing at whirlwind speeds. Perhaps now, more than ever before, job stress poses a threat to the health of workers. Stress has long been associated with the onset of significant physical and mental health problems. Stress began to be implicated in areas beyond the bounds of physical and mental health as far back as the 1980s. In the organizational environment, stress has been implicated in the deterioration of performance efficiency by both managers and subordinates. When performance efficiency suffers the quality of the overall organizational environment and productivity deteriorates. A deterioration of the organizational environment is accompanied by deterioration in organizational communication.

The primary sources of occupational stress within an organization originate from four areas. These areas include task demands, physical demands, role demands, and interpersonal demands. "Any demand, either of a physical nature or psychological nature, encountered in the course of living is known as a 'stressor'. A stress response will occur as a result of an individual's interaction with and reaction to the stressor." Task-related stress is directly related to the specific characteristics of the job itself. This type of stress involves role ambiguity, conflicting task demands, work overload or work underload, inadequate resource support, no provision for meaningful participation in decision-making, and insecurity, among others. Physical demands of the workplace are another source to be considered. Environmental factors such as temperature variations, noise vibrations, and lighting may significantly affect individual stress. For example, "extreme lighting can cause stress, which often results in headaches and nervous tension." Role demands are external to the tasks associated with a job. This particular type of stress typically develops as a result of flawed organizational structures, ineffective organizational development, the inability of an individual to successfully pursue achievement goals within an organization, or some combination of all three. The individual's stress often results when his or her work role and responsibility has not been clearly defined. The final source area of occupational stress relates to interpersonal demands. "Interpersonal stress at work is concerned with the demands that are placed on us in developing working relationships with other people in our organizations." Leadership style of managers and supervisors is often a source of stress for their employees.

Stress outcomes the result of stressors commonly associated with occupational stress tends to vary widely. Workers may simply resort to daydreaming or fantasizing. Alternatively, employees may react more actively by creating interpersonal and intraorganizational conflicts involving escalating levels of communication problems. Workers may also experience effects in their psychological and physical health. Psychological consequences may include anxiety, boredom, low self-esteem, forgetfulness, depression, anger, apathy, or worry. Physical consequences may include, but are certainly not limited to, headaches, diabetes, fatigue, hypertension, chest and back pain, ulcers, or even infectious diseases. From the organizational aspect, stress has many consequences. Reductions in effectiveness, productivity, and communication are results that are not as easy to identify, however, such outcomes can be among the most debilitating for both the organization and for the individual. Other results may include accidents in the workplace, job turnover, low morale, poor work relations, poor organizational climate, and absenteeism.

Like many areas in the organisational sciences, the study of occupational stress is relatively new. In assessing the effects of job-related stressors over the years, however, a clear pattern has developed in terms of the various outcomes that researchers have investigated. Specifically, stress outcomes (called "strains") have typically been *psychological*, *physical*, and *behavioural* in nature. Common psychological outcomes that have been studied include anxiety, depression, and general psychological well-being. Physical outcomes have been popular due to the potential link between experiencing job-related stressors and ill health. Most researchers have opted to measure physical strain through self-reported physical symptoms, although some researchers have used more objective measures such as physiological indicators (e.g., blood pressure) or even healthcare utilization. Behavioural outcomes (e.g., job performance, absenteeism, and turnover) have been studied the least, due largely to the practical difficulties associated with obtaining these indicators.

Possible work place strategies include bringing in a nutritionist for a day of training, encourage employees to keep diet diaries for a week, offer nutritional foods at the worksite, form a healthy snacks club. Start a walking club at lunch time, look for group discounts at nearby health clubs, bring in a fitness trainer for an in-service day, and provide exercise equipment or facilities. Psychologists have known for some time that anxiety and deep muscle relaxation are mutually exclusive. That is, you can't be anxious and relaxed at the same time. This finding has been used to successfully treat many phobias, but it can also be a useful strategy for dealing with stress. The goal is to train your employees to be able to become relaxed on demand, thereby cutting the stress cycle short. One widely used relaxation technique was developed by Edmund Jacobsen. It is an effective method for training individuals how to relax their major muscle groups. There are other useful techniques available for employees working on computers. Individuals who are under a great deal of stress begin to self-medicate themselves in order to feel better. They may drink more, take more prescription medication, or take illegal drugs.

Every organization has individuals who may already have serious problems in this regard. These individuals probably need professional help. Substance abuse awareness is best used as a preventative measure. Obviously the work place isn't responsible for solving employee's domestic problems. But it is in your interest to have the healthiest possible workers. Transition time can be a useful technique in short circuiting the stress response at home.

The present book makes an attempt to dissect and analyse occupational stress and its remedies in the present era of globalization. This volume incorporates the papers presented and discussed at the national seminar held on 9th Feb 2008 at the Shri Atmanand Jain Institute of Management and Technology.

The thrust of the various papers has been presented here under:

Vidhu Mohan in her paper titled *Occupational Stress and its Remedies explain* that stress is the non-specific response of the body to a non-specific stimulus. In the process the entire body along with mind is roped in. Stress affects our total life. Whatever work we do, its quality depends to a great extent on whether we are having peace of mind, or a disturbed state. There is an intimate relation between the work load, work performance & experience of stress. The optimum work load differs from individual to individual. We should understand our own level of peak performance in relation to stress. This also means that in an organization the person at the helm of affairs must do various activities to minimize the stress.

Kapoor's paper titled *Stress Management: Strategy and Techniques* argues that a reasonable level of stress is necessary to propel a person too but excess of it can have disastrous consequences, physically, emotionally and socially.Time pressure, competition, financial problems, noise and disappointments are the major reasons for stress. Remedies can be found by building of physical reserves, supportive relationships, psyching up and proper planning.

Darolia in his paper titled *Stress At Work: Issues of Concern* explains that the stress occurs when resources of a person falls short of the demands made on him by the situation. Stress is complex phenomenon resulting from many environmental organizational and personal factors. A moderate level of stress stimulates performance However over a period of time, even a low level of stress can be detrimental to a person's energy resources. Psychological aspect of job stress still leaves much to be explained and research in this area is imperative.

Bodla and Divya in their paper titled *Winning over Stress .Some Strategies for Stress Management* explain that stress perceptions vary from person to person. An individual's reaction to particular event determines whether it is stressful or not. A single situation can make one person happy and another person sad. When a person feels that demands of the situation exceed his personal and social resources; Stress is the fall out. Stress can be managed if we understand the reasons behind it, and its level. Managing stress is all about taking 'Charge'. Take charge of your thoughts, emotions, schedules and environment and it departs.

Kulbhushan and Raj Kumar's paper titled *Managing Stress – A Survey of Macro Scenario* conclude that stress is a typical feature of the modern world. An individual should know where to draw a line (Lakshman Rekha) between negative and positive stress. Causes of stress are both external and internal. External factors are often beyond control but internal factors are by and large within one's control. Stress has negative as well as positive implications. It affects a person physically as well as emotionally. Stress management has two dimensions— Prevention and copying ability. Classical approach goes a long way to reduce stress. Raj yoga, Nishkam Kaorma propounded in the Gita and Guna theory can extricate us from this cesspool.

Rajender *et.al.* concluded in their paper entitled *Occupational stress & how to reduce its effects in Haryana* that occupational stress is a response that includes both physical and mental responses to what we experience in our day to day life. In this context, occupational stress may be defined as the collective physical and mental responses to an unacceptable disparity between personnal expectations and actual physical and/or imaginary personal experiences. Occupational stress is also increasing in India, as well in its Haryana state. Occupational stress is somehow an unavoidable consequence of life and life without stress is probably not worth. As long as some occupational stress can be a major cause of disease, the good news is that there are many types of good stress that may promote wellness. Winning a football match or a race can be just as stressful as losing one. In this article the views of Doctors (Psychiatrics) and Psychologists about various types of occupational stress and suggestions by Doctors (Psychiatrics) and Psychologists to reduce the effects of occupational stress in Haryana have been studied.

Sushil *et.al.* in their paper on *Good work life and relationships' conceptual study* explains that generally, people and society are not sufficiently enjoying the values of ties between families, community and their workplace these day, A critical change in the economic and social environment and attitudes of people weakens these ties. The present Paper examines relationships within the family; the community and the workplace, analyses the anticipated impact and state of these relationships, and some directions are offered to rebuild these relationships. The paper is divided into four sections: first section is on introduction; second section includes impact of weak relationship on work life, third section includes some important directions to improve relationship, and the last concludes these ties.

Rajan *et.al.* concluded in their paper titled *Organizational Stress: A silent killer on the prowl* that today, pursuit of ambitious goals by organizations have put a tremendous pressure on its employees. Behind the proud balance sheets of a company lie the mentally wrecked employees. With the advent of globalization, the traditional Indian industry has crumbled. Protectionism has given way to sense of insecurity. The employees are also finding it difficult to cope with the cultural and ethnic diversities, which they have face to face, in the fast changing scenario. Remedies for stress at individual level include cleaning up of homes, sprucing up of relationships and finding repose in automation moderation in habits also go a long way. Organizations can help the employees by introducing ethical cultural and a sense of belongingness.

Himani and **Sultan** in their paper entitled *of Stress management in information technology sector* explores the signs and symptoms of stress, major work related stressors, and their effect, and provides some tips for removing the stress in Information Technology sector. Various work related stressors are categorised under the main headings like, overload, work relationships, work-life balance and pay and benefits. The results indicate that job stress poses a threat to the health of workers, which, in turn, threatens the success of the organization. The results have been discussed and some suggestions for stress management summarized.

Esha and Sumeet's paper titled *Relax or Retire: Academicians at Stake!* concluded that the future of any country lies on academicians. They have the responsibility to shape up the society, come out with programmes which fulfils the changing demands of the present scenario. Apart from sharing knowledge they are expected to develop innovation, creativity and problem solving skills in all spheres of education, be it technical, social or psychological. The solution lies here! The expectations lead to stress, stress leads to tension, tension works as an obstacle for creativity and newness, which in turn gives more stress, and the cycle goes on....either relax or be prepared to retire!

Praveen *et.al.* in their paper titled *Stress Management: Strategy and Techniques* conclude that a reasonable level of stress is necessary to propel a person too but excess of it can have disastrous consequences, physically, emotionally and socially.Time pressure, competition, financial problems, noise and disappointments are the major reasons for stress. Remedies can be found by building of physical reserves, supportive relationships, psyching up and proper planning.

Anil *et.al.* in their paper titled *Adaptability Reduces the Stress* explore that there are thousands of reasons for generating stress. This stress may affect adversely the physique, psyche, social status, family environment and above all, congenial environment at work place. The effected person cannot control all the components of environment. But one thing which can be controlled only by him is – Perception. Perception reflects that one may be having, 'positive' as well as 'negative' attitude. The behaviour is the outcome of the a attitude, which is also no exception to the one of effected components of personality of an individual. It means a person who is suffering from stress should put maximum efforts to improve his personality, so that he is able to overcome the various shortcomings as well as complexes about himself. After this exercise one will be capable to compete and achieve the set targets.

Mehta and Sharma's Paper titled *Stress! What is that*? explains that work is the main source of stress in life but paradoxically it is also a healer. It is both a troublemaker and a troubleshooter. Practice the time tested mantra work is worship. All successful people do lots of work. They are always busy or working. So work more and get more out of life. And you can find a panacea for stress.

Sandhya and **Sandeep** in their paper on *Organizational role stress among teachers (a comparative study of technical and non-technical teachers)* reveal that educational researchers have long been concerned with role stress among teachers. The concept of role and its two related aspects, role space and role set, have a built-in potential for conflict and stress .The present study was carried out to compare and analyze the organizational role stress among the technical and non-technical teachers in Ludhiana district. The organisational role stress scale by Udai Pareek was administered(1971). The findings indicated that Inter-Role Distance, Role Stagnation, Role Expectation Conflict, Role Erosion, Role-Overload, Role Isolation, Personal Inadequacy, Self Role Distance and Role Ambiguity are acceptable at 5% level of significance and 1% level of significance.

Pawan and **Rajinder** in their paper titled *Stress at work place: a review article* conclude that work place stress has a negative impact on the business as well as on the individual employee. The increase in job stress creates emotional, financial, and safety concerns for employers and managers. The bottom line: workplace stress management and stress reduction make sense. Stress in the workplace is not a new phenomenon, but it is a greater threat to employee health and well-being than ever before. While technology has made aspects of many jobs easier, it has also added to the anxieties of office life through information overload, heightened pressure for productivity, and a threatening sense of impermanence in the workplace. In 1996, the World Health Organization labelled stress a "worldwide epidemic". Today, workplace stress is estimated to cost American companies more than $300 billion a year in poor performance, absenteeism and health costs. Among the general causes, some causes specific to the call centre industry and strategies to remove stress have been highlighted in this paper.

Anju in her paper titled *Technostress of library professionals' — the path for recovery* conclude that "Technostress" (computer-related stress), a common problem for reference librarians in the new millennium, is a combination of performance anxiety, information overload, role conflicts, and organizational factors. This article analyzes the phenomenon and suggests individual coping strategies and organizational management strategies.

Shivani and Kamaljeet in their paper titled *Stress in software industry and its remedies* explain that IT careers are generally more stressful than other careers. IT people are often characterized by hard work, long hours, tight deadlines. The purpose of this article is to assess the degree of the reported job stress among IS professionals. The Information Systems (IS) profession is a stressful profession. However, there is little theoretical or empirical research on the effects of occupational stress on IS professionals, probably because IS professionals and researchers are unaware of the consequences of occupational stress and unfamiliar with the occupational stress literature. The purpose of this paper is to propose a theoretical framework of occupational stress for IT professionals. With the advent of globalization, constantly evolving business models, progress in Information Technology, changing environment and lifestyles, the term 'stress' is so often used in our lives today, but is yet enshrouded in a thick veil of conceptual confusion and divergence of opinion. In this article we focus on the modern scourge of stress and professional burnout which plagues IT professionals.

Priyanka and Arti's paper titled *Teacher stress in the field of education and wellness programme* reveal that teacher's stress becomes problematic and potentially harmful, when the challenges the teachers face outpace their perceived ability to cope. Perhaps the most effective strategy for reducing stress is to know one's own stress points, and practice the coping techniques that work best.

Giridhar and **Rimpi**'s paper titled *Stress Avoidance Strategies from Shrimad Bhagvad Gita* argue that the pressures of modern life, coupled with the demands of a job, can lead to emotional imbalances that are collectively labeled 'stresses.' There are many stress management techniques and strategies which are basically remedial in nature. As we all know that prevention is better than cure, hence in this paper we have tried to find out some stress management strategies from Shrimad Bhagwad Gita, which are basically preventive in nature. The aim of this paper is not to discard the other stress management strategies but to provide the holistic attitude towards creating such an environment which can help to lead such life which itself is free from stress and does not require the need to manage stress. Hence these can be termed as basic stress avoidance strategies.

Sapna *et.al.* conclude in their paper titled *Occupational Stress and Its Management Strategies* that stress is a part of day-to-day living of every individual. The college students may experience stress in meeting the academic demands, people on the job, business men may suffer stress to reach office in time and to complete the projects on time and even the household ladies may experience stress in managing the home affairs and to look for a maid servant. The reasons for the stress differs from person to person. The stress people experience should not be necessarily treated as harmful. An optimum amount of stress can always act as an energizer or motivator, and propel people to make efforts and complete the work. But a high level of stress can be a serious threat to the personality traits of the individual, and can cause physiological and social problems.

Anjali and Monika in their paper titled *Occupational Stress in the Present Social Environment and its management Techniques* conclude that stress is both, the cause and result of pressure building in body and mind of an individual. Bullying, job insecurity, relationship difficulties and any situation or at home and work place generate stress.

Unfair treatment, run down conditions and feeling of being trapped invariably lead to stress. Women are better at coping with stress than men. They share their grievances with friends or partners and release pent up stress.

People usually turn self-help for managing stress.However sometimes help of psychologist or a psychiatrist is necessary. Nevertheless stress is necessary as it galvanizes into action. So stress management and not stress elimination is the answer.

Anjali in her paper titled *Work place stress: how to manage* explains that moderate levels of stress increase efforts, stimulate creativity and encourage diligence in one's work. Excessively high levels of stress can overload and breakdown a person's physical and mental system. Stress is an inevitable part of one's life and cannot be avoided. What can however be avoided is negative reaction to stress. Organizations are beginning to realize the importance of stress management. The US corporate giants have incorporated health education and wellness programmes, realizing that a healthy employee is a productive employee. Stress counselling and management in India, still has a low profile. It is high time that Indian Corporate giants take steps like their western counterparts, enabling their executives to absorb and by-pass stress and strain in their jobs, which are rapidly increasing.

Suparna in her paper titled *What is occupational stress?* explains working conditions that smother the capabilities and resources of workers bring the onset of stress. Job stressors include poor management, discrimination, sexual harassment, poor inter-personal relationships, work overload etc. Stress is difficult to diagnose, but once recognised, it can be successfully treated. Organizational and job re-designing are the most effective ways to reduce stress.

Sharma's paper titled *Stress As I see It* conclude that stress stems from a feeling of inadequacy – physical or mental. A person cannot share responsibilities to avoid stress. But one should realize his capacity to undertake a task otherwise, result will be stress.

A fixed time –table for work and leisure, healthy food, regulated life style , service to follow beings and lofty goals can give much relief from stress.

Stress – What is that? Work is the main source of stress in life but paradoxically it is also a healer. It is both a troublemaker and a troubleshooter. Practice the time tested mantra work is worship. All successful people do lots of work. They are always busy of work. So work more and get more out of life. And you can find a panacea for stress.

Vijay and Varun in their paper titled *Occupational Stress* argue that certain jobs that require a higher level of decision-making or have dangerous or unpleasant physical and emotional conditions are more stressful . Stress can be managed by understanding the factors responsible for stress.

Stress can be classified into four groups: Distress, Euphoric, Hyper and Hypo. Information Technology and business outsourcing firms are alive to the stress related problems and some have gone an extra mile to built up stress-copying strategies

1

OCCUPATIONAL STRESS AND ITS REMEDIES

** Prof. Dr. Vidhu Mohan*

* Ex.Prof.Deptt. of Psychology, Punjab University, Chandigarh.

Stress & Life

The ultimate goal of human life is to attain peace and live a happy life. "I am more and more convinced that our happiness or our unhappiness depends far more on the way we meet the events of life than on the nature of those events themselves."

—*Karl Wilhelm & Von Humboldt.*

But the tragedy is that the path adopted by most people does this goal. They enter a rat race in which there is considerable stress and struggle. By and large, people feel that "Life Is a Struggle." They accept struggle, which has a foundation in attachment and desires. Desires egg us on for further struggle and we move away from peace and happiness. Too much competition often lands us into a violent mode, and a mentality to hurt others. Struggle ought to be merely a fight against negative forces. But in race to achieve more and more, to struggle for desires, peace and happiness are the first casualties and stress walks in. "Stress comes from within; it is your reaction to circumstances, not the circumstances themselves." — *Brian Tracy.*

STRESS

Let us see what stress is:

- It is the non-specific response of the body to a non-specific stimulus. In the process the entire body along with mind is roped in.
- Usually Stress begins with a life situation. This life situation could be:
  - ✔ A sudden change in atmosphere, or one's psychological world,
  - ✔ A threat from outside,
  - ✔ The death of a loved one,
  - ✔ Some other sudden change in your life,
  - ✔ Or your own temperament & habits.

But is all stress bad? NO

There are three types of stresses: **Nustress** i.e., a kind of neutral state. Then there is:

- *Good stress like,* job promotions, to which we must adapt, termed as **Eustress**.
- *Bad stress* (death of loved one, or accident) to which we must adapt termed as **Distress**.

All types are experienced physiologically, one gives health the other ill health. Eustress & Nustress are connected with health, whereas Distress is connected with ill health.

How ANXIETY and STRESS Operate

- The more effectively our different systems are co-ordinated, the more effectively we function.
- Main sub-systems which need coordination are:

- ✔ Cognitive (perceptions, learnings & thoughts)
- ✔ Affective (feelings & emotions)
- ✔ Conation (actions, our responses to situations)
- ✔ Physiological (our total body muscles, skeleton, nervous system, glands)

- These Sub-systems respond according to the demands of a particular time and the circumstances. If there is a harmony & co-ordination amongst them, a person has a happy & peaceful life. Disturbance in one area disturbs our entire peace of mind.

Work & Stress

Stress affects our total life. Whatever work we do, its quality depends to a great extent on whether we are having peace of mind or a disturbed state. There is an intimate relation between the work load, work performance and experience of stress. The relation between work load and stress is graphically shown below:

The optimum work load differs from individual to individual. We should understand our own level of peak performance in relation to stress. This also means that in an organization the person at the helm of affairs must do the following:

- Try to understand work stress and its impact on the well-being and productivity of workers;
- Explore organizational climate and sources of stress;
- Seek to find behavioural interventions to reduce stress, illness, and injury in the workplace.

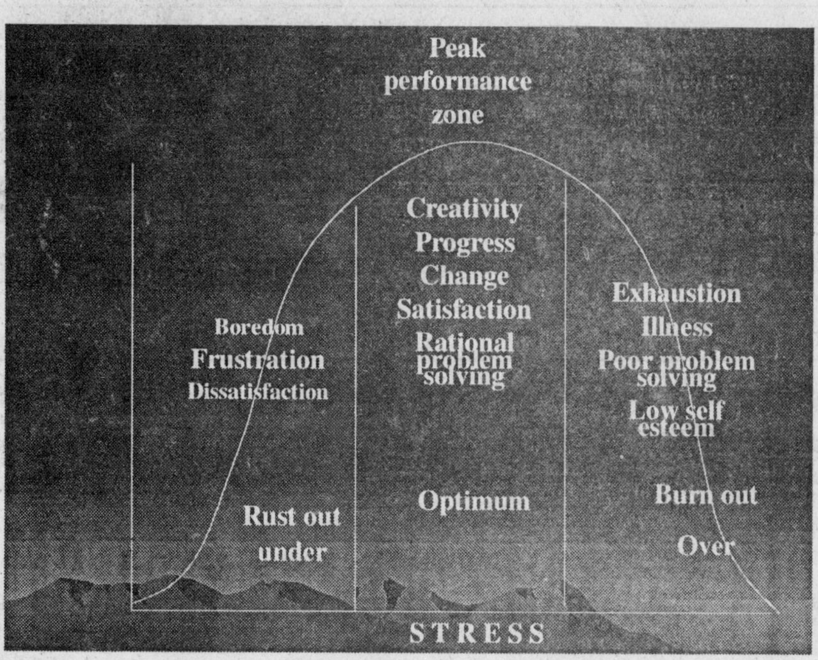

Work Stressors

A model of Organizational Role Stressors has been developed by Udai Pareek. He has identified 10 stressors in the work situation. These are given below:

Sources of Occupational Stress:

- Inter-Role Distance: the conflict arising out of various roles that an individual plays in life.
- Role-Stagnation: the feeling that "I am not growing in my career".
- Role-Expectation/Conflict: this is the conflict between your own expectation out of the job and that of others in your world.
- Role Overload: the feeling that your work is more than what you can cope with.
- Role Isolation: that you are left alone, others are clicking together.
- Personal Inadequacy: the feeling that you are not growing, or you have become a little obsolete.
- Self Role Distance: the conflict between your value system and the compromises you have to make to carry on in your job.
- Role Ambiguity: when your role has not been defined adequately.
- Resource Inadequacy: when sufficient resources are not available to be able to do the job satisfactorily.

Effect of Stress on Body and Mind

Stress has an effect on our entire being. Some of the prominent outcomes of stress are:

- Effects on the body- such as, psychosomatic disorders
- Behavioural outcomes- such as, use of defense mechanisms,
- Mental breakdown: such as psychosis, neurosis, distorted thinking, memory losses, suicidal ideation.

We will study the psychosomatic disorders in some details since they affect our total life.

Psychosomatic Disorders

There are four primary physiological systems which get affected by stress & anxiety.

- Respiratory system: the diseases that are typically associated are asthma, bronchitis, nasal catarrh, allergy
- Digestive system: the disorders which are typical as a function of stress are: constipation, irritative bowel syndrome, flatulence, ulcers.
- Blood circulatory system: typical diseases are high or low BP, heart problem, stroke.

- Skin is the covering of the body and stress makes it vulnerable & weak so that allergies & germs can enter our bodies. The typical disorders are artic aria, eczema, psoriasis & allergies.

Causes of Stress

In order to find remedies for stress we must learn the causes. There are four major sources of stress namely: Situational crisis, Environmental Pressures, Inherent pre-dispositions, and developmental crisis. We will deal with them one by one.

Situational Crisis

- Sudden trauma
- Accident
- Death of a dear one.
- Job trauma
- Family disaster

Environmental Pressures

- Ecological stressors like pollution.
- Social & cultural norms, changes and erosion.
- Job stressors like long working hours, overload, bad work climate, in group fighting etc.
- Economic stressors like escalation in prices.
- Nutritional imbalances like junk food preferences resulting various diseases.
- Psychological fears and apprehensions.

Inherent Predispositions

- Personality traits causing stress, such as, over suspiciousness, anger, anxiety, hurry.
- Conflict resolution styles i.e., do you face or avoid conflict in the situation it accumulates.
- Attitudes like pessimism.
- Belief systems like superstitions.
- Emotional predispositions like, anger, depressions.
- Habits like untidiness.

Developmental Crisis

This model has been developed by the author to explain various stages of development which if not coped with can lead to stress.

Stages	*Counselling Needs*
1. Birth	The birth trauma is experienced, not only by the mother, but also by the new-born. The longer the labor pains, the more the trauma experienced by the neonate. Not only this, but also the reception the child is given by the parents and others who matter is an important landmark in the growth of a child. Attitudes of rejection or over- protection can affect the individual's personality.
2. Early discipline	Toilet training and the process of weaning the child are two areas of discipline, which can leave a long impact on the child. Very few parents know the right way to deal with these issues.
3. Transition from home to school	The first experience of being without the comfort of known faces can be quite traumatic for the child. Many parents take going to school as a threat to the child.
4. Adolescence	This is the period of storms and stress. Hardly any preparation is made for this stage. Neither schools nor parents try to guide the pre-adolescents, with sex education.
5. School leaving	The adjustment of ten years or more comes to an end, and now the individual has to choose a way of life—whether he/she wants to go for higher studies or choose a vocation. How to go about doing this can be a major issue in one's life.
6. Adjustment to new environment	Whether one goes to institutions of higher learning, or one goes to the world of work, many new adjustments have to be made. Interaction with new people, taking up new responsibilities, even facing hostility sometime, can be issues that need help.
7. Entering 'Grahasth Ashram'	Settling in life, seeking a life partner getting married and adjustment to the new status requires many skills and now-how. Bringing up a family is a task of great responsibility and at many points requires counselling and help.
8. Child bearing and rearing	Giving birth to a child, and its satisfactory rearing. Hardly any training is imparted for doing this tedious job.
9. Middle age crisis	This is the period of a greater responsibilities and making important decisions. This is also the period of female and male menopause, and orientation to the onset of ageing process as well as its acceptance.
10. Retirement 'Vanprasth' Ashram	This is the stage for the heartache of leaving active life, power, status, and withdrawal into the family bounds.
11. Old age & death	If one is not prepared for this stage, it can be very traumatic.

Stress Leading to Burnout

Overload or frequent frustration at work can lead to a syndrome of physical and emotional exhaustion. This syndrome is called Burnout: An adverse work stress reaction with Psychological, Psycho-physiological and Behavioural components. Burnout has many outcomes which can disturb life.

Some Consequences of Burnout are:

- Social withdrawal:
- Pulling away from: colleagues, peers, friends & family members:
- Self medication:
- Increased use of smoke and alcohol; intake of tranquilizers and other mood altering drugs, falling a prey to toxins. Many people start self-medicating to reduce their stress but these are short-term solutions for anxiety. Self-medication with alcohol, caffeine, nicotine or drugs, only creates more problems in the long run. It becomes a vicious cycle.
- Skipping rest and food breaks: Continually having no time for coffee or lunch breaks to restore stamina

Some Major Symptoms accompanying Burnout

Internal changes in the personality: such as emotional exhaustion, loss of self-esteem, epression, frustration a "trapped" feeling.

- Feeling of pessimism, paranoia or vague fears & apprehensions, loneliness and guilt and hopelessness

Attitude of rigidity, callousness, difficulty in making and explaining decisions. Increased physical complaints like fatigue, irritability, muscle tension, stomach upset, susceptibility to illness. Changed job performance: like increased absenteeism, lethargy in doing work, increase in the use of sick leave, decreased efficiency or productivity, faulty coping etc.

Coping with Stress and Burnout

- Now that we know enough about the debilitating effects of stress, anxiety & burnout, we must understand some strategies to cope with it. Some on the spot coping strategies are: Walk Away, Close Your Eyes, Find Some Solitude, Go Outside in nature, Find Some Water either to drink or swim or watch Blue Sky. "In the Midst of movement and chaos, keep Stillness Inside of you." — Deepak Chopra.

Apart from these on-the spot strategies, there are five areas in which coping has to be done for long range effects:

- physical
- mental
- emotional
- social
- spiritual

We will briefly discuss each area and its coping strategies.

Physical:

- An exercise is one of the best self-treatments for anxiety available. You may go for a walk, join a water aerobics class, dance, play tennis or any other sports.
- Yoga asana,
- Pranayam: Breathe deeply as follows:
  1. Breathe in slowly to a count of four.
  2. Hold the breath for a count of four.
  3. Exhale slowly through pursed lips to a count of four.
  4. Rest for a count of four (without taking any breaths).
  5. Take two normal breaths.
  6. Start over again with number one.
- Healthy nutrition
- Deep muscle- relaxation

Mental: Do stress-inoculation by giving self-instructions for positive thoughts or by using coping imagery practice.Practice mind expansion through imagery, as has been used by the author in some of her research work.

- Indulge in positive activities, see this quote: "My mind is a garden. My thoughts are the seeds. My harvest will be either flower or weeds." – *Mel Weldon*
- Develop long-range goals in life, with highly specific short-range sub-goals. Develop realistic means to achieve these sub-goals.

Psychological Means:

- Bringing about a change in one's attitude – develop positive thinking. For a healthy and wholesome life one has to develop a realistic optimism and positive attitude in life. Some people tend to look at the dark side of the picture & others live in an unrealistic euphoria. These persons, through their foolhardiness get hurt badly and then start blaming others. "If you are distressed by anything external, the pain is not due to the thing itself but your own estimate of it; and this you have the power to revoke at any moment." – *Marcus Aurelius.*
- The other type are the ones who are perpetually pessimistic, fault finding, suspicious, and blaming others or situations.
- One has to learn to appreciate the assets of others and one's own.
- Also, one should learn to cope with one's limitations, liabilities and contain them or convert them into assets.
- One should cultivate a belief that 'failures are never final & success is never ending.'
- Learn techniques of time management.
- Try to cope with one's conflicts by facing them, and not procrastinate.

- Learn better inter-personal skills.
- Learn to relax and try out new alternatives.
- The best way to succeed in difficult life situations is not by accepting the emotional challenges but through Samarpan (surrender), which is based on a logical control system. Samarpan of your rigid ego. SAMARPAN YOG (Non-judgmental Acceptance)

Social Support Systems

- Try to cultivate your "Social Support Systems".
- Take the help of family members - they are your allies.
- Seek the help of sincere friends.
- For in-job situation, seek the help of honest and sincere colleagues.
- Even religion can help in reducing stress.
- Make friends.

Coping with Stress: Emotional

- Mind expansion & relaxation.
- 'Flooding' or giving full exposure to the emotion causing disturbance and getting rid of it. For example, if one is afraid of some thing, give a full exposure to that thing or situation.
- Use 'catharses' or giving vent to your feelings, as a strategy to rid yourself of unwanted feelings.
- Forgive yourself for mistakes, sins, failures and past embarrassments.
- Dealing with Anger springing from stress.
- Lower down your own expectations and demands out of others. When these are not fulfilled one feels angry and frustrated.
- Lack of interpersonal skills and ability to deal with a situation, often causes a great deal of irritation and anger, sometimes even mixed with a little apprehension. So learn these skills.
- Once we understand this, we can control and modify our anger. Stress & anger go hand in hand.
- Seek 'Formal Help' when ever necessary. Go to a trained counselor for help; Join formal groups where training is imparted for coping strategies; Join courses imparting self development skills.
- Do not allow others to criticize you as a person.
- Use soft meditation and music therapy,
- Stop being so over-protective about your ego; it is tougher and more resilient that you imagine. It bruises but never breaks.
- "A ruffled mind makes a restless pillow". – *Charlotte Bronte*
- Make constructive use of the released emotional energy

Spiritual

- Nurture Your Spirit.
- Cultivate humanism and decide what you value, what you believe in, what you realistically would like your life to be like.

  Have control over desires
- Mediate & Pray: They trigger the relaxation response, helping calm the mind and body. Give yourself the time to relax, to listen to yourself, to enjoy hobbies and activities you can do alone. In this way, you can get in touch with yourself.

Coping with stress: from different religions

- Fulfillment of desire is an illusion; desire leads to more desire, not satisfaction.

  – Kathleen McDonald, "How to Meditate" (Buddhism)
- "Take to compassion and abstain from oppression and obscenity. Compassion is grace and the lack of it a disgrace."

  – The Prophet Muhammad (SAW), as reported by Aisha bint Abu Bakr
- If you detach yourself from identification with the body and remain relaxed in and as Consciousness, you will, this very moment, be happy, at peace, free from bondage.

  – Ashtavakra Gita
- I seek refuge in Allah from knowledge that brings no wisdom, from a heart that lacks kindness, from desires that bring discontent, and from supplications that go unanswered.

  – The Prophet Muhammad (SAW), as reported by Abu Hurairah
- It is my own firm belief that the strength of the soul grows in proportion as you subdue the flesh.

  – Mahatma Gandhi, 1924
- "To make a man happy, fill his hands with work, his heart with affection, his mind with purpose, his memory with useful knowledge, his future with hope, and his stomach with food."

  – Frederick E. Crane

✡✡✡

2

STRESS MANAGEMENT

* *V. K. Kapoor*

* Ex-ADGP V K Kapoor,Director, Institute Of Stressmanagement & Research (Regd), 1058, Sector 7, Panchkula.

"The birds of worry and care fly over your head, this you can't change, but they build nests in your hair, this you can prevent".

Anxiety and Stress are our total Psycho-Biological responses to a situation in which we feel vulnerable to as a threat or a danger.

- Stress begins with a life situation that knocks you (gently or abruptly) out of balance.
- This life situation could be:
  - ✔ A change in temperature
  - ✔ A threat from another person
  - ✔ The death of a loved one
  - ✔ Some other sudden change in your life
- You are nudged or shoved into disequillibrium and need to correct yourself.

Change is stressful whether it is happy or unhappy.

That means

- ✔ ***Good things*** (job promotions) to which we must adapt (termed Eustress) and
- ✔ ***Bad things*** (death of loved one) to which we must adapt (termed Distress)

Both are experienced physiologically.

The Difference between Pressure and Stress Pressure

- Refers to those features of a situation that may be problematic for an individual.
- The situation demands for adaptation of some kind.
- Pressure exists in the situation

Stress

- Refers to a specific set of biochemical conditions within a person's body.
- These conditions reflect the body's attempt to make the adjustment.
- Stress lies in the person

A Working Model of Stress

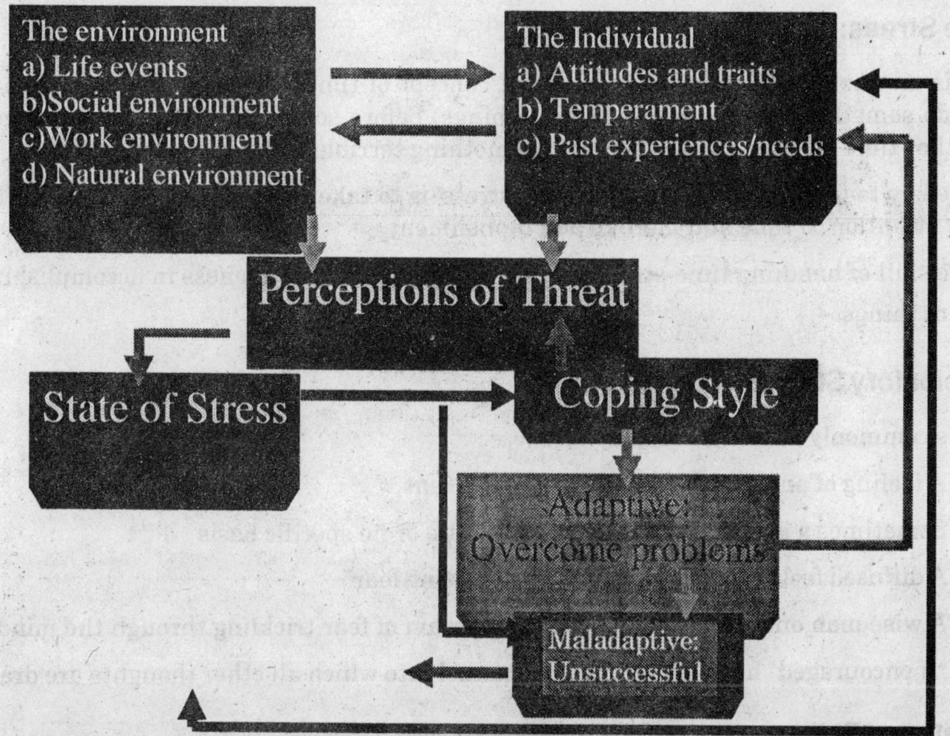

What Causes Stress?

- ✔ Part of the answer is "a stressor".
- ✔ The other part is "stress reactivity."

A stressor is a stimulus with the potential of triggering the fight-or-flight response.

Types of Stressors

- Environmental

  (Toxins, Heat, Cold)
- Psychological

  (Threats to Self Esteem, Depression)
- Sociological

  (Unemployment, Death of a loved one)
- Philosophical

  (Use of time, Purpose of life)

Regardless of the stressor, body's reaction will be the same.

Self-Induced Stress

1. Time Stress:

It is an anxiety reaction to the abstract concept of time, including the feeling that one "must" do something (or a number of somethings) before some deadline. There is a general feeling that time is "running out" and that something terrible will happen when it does.

The key to freeing one's self from 'time-stress' is to take a new view of time or, rather, to pay less attention to time and more to accomplishment.

The skill of handling time-stress is in improving one's effectiveness in accomplishing the important things.

2. Anticipatory Stress:

It is commonly known as "Worry"

- A feeling of anxiety about an impending event
- Sometimes a generalised anxiety, with little or no specific basis
- A diffused feeling of dread called "free-floating fear"
- A wise man once said "worry is a thin stream of fear trickling through the mind".
- "If encouraged" he added, "it cuts a channel into which all other thoughts are drained".

3. Situational Stress:

- It is anxiety, as a result of finding one's self in a situation that is threatening and at least partially beyond one's control.
- The expected terrible happening may involve physical injury or danger.
- More often, it involves loss of status, significance or acceptance, in the eyes of others.

HASSLES

Relatively unimportant events characterised as "Hassles" have an even greater impact on our well being.

- Hassles range from getting stuck in a traffic jam to becoming involved in a dispute at work, to misplacing our address book.
- Hassles are constant, everyday stressors.
- Greatest stress often comes from the daily routines.

How Colour Affects Stress

The color of your surroundings can both create stress and ease stresses in your life, often in ways so subtle that you are influenced subliminally.

Yellow

Yellow reduces boredom.

Students seated in areas painted yellow described themselves as more alert than those seated in areas painted in nine other colors.

Black

Looking at a black surface lowers oxygen levels than any other color.

Blue

Blue elevates mood.

Students tested in a room lined with blue fabric described themselves as calm and happy than those tested in rooms lined with red, yellow and neutral fabrics.

Pink

Studies indicate that pink has tranquilizing effects and it lowers blood pressure, pulse rate and anxiety levels.

Red

Red is an arousing, stimulating color. In a study on risk taking, students who sat under red lights gambled more and made "riskier" bets than those who sat under blue lights.

Stress and the Male Role

- Men experience the harmful effects of 'playing the Male role'. Manliness carries a chronic burden of stress and anxiety.
- The traditional Male sex role, characterised by Stoicism and Isolation is fraught with stress and anxiety.

Stress at the Workplace

With increasing working hours and new technology such as:

- ✔ lap-top computers
- ✔ e-mail
- ✔ mobile phones executives are never really switching off.

Downsizing and increased productivity goals mean longer work hours and higher stress for many.

It is not how long you work, it is how you are working that causes stress.

The impact of working hours was dwarfed by factors related to the job itself, such as schedule flexibility and autonomy. Many researchers believe that this increased time at work leads to work-family conflicts and increased stress.

Every day we are faced with multiple deadlines, meetings, and all the other demands of putting out a quality product — demands which in his case led to some destructive coping mechanisms.

Burnout

Burnout is an adverse work stress reaction with psychological, psycho-physiological and behavioural components.

Major symptoms are:

- Internal changes:
  - ✔ Emotional exhaustion
  - ✔ Loss of self-esteem
  - ✔ Depression, frustration
  - ✔ A 'TRAPPED' feeling
  - ✔ Susceptibility to illness
- Social withdrawal:
  - ✔ Pulling away from colleagues
  - ✔ Peers
  - ✔ Family members
- Changed job performance:
- Increased physical complaints
  - ✔ Fatigue
  - ✔ Irritability
  - ✔ Muscle tension
  - ✔ Stomach upset
  - ✔ Increased absenteeism
  - ✔ Tardiness
  - ✔ Use of sick leave
  - ✔ Decreased efficiency or productivity

How to manage

High Performance & Low Stress

1. The Relation between Pressure, Stress and Performance

- ✔ Many managers feel that the way to get a lot of work out of their employees is to "keep the pressure on." This kind of thinking leads to coercive style of management rather than the facilitative style.
- ✔ Employees who are subjected to continuing levels of pressure that go beyond their "challenge" levels into their "discomfort" levels will sooner or later show the effects of the pressure in stress-reactive behaviour.

2. Pressure *Yes* - Stress *No*

- ✔ Human beings in any organisation need a certain level of pressure to function together.
- ✔ Without some reason for action, some common purpose, sense of necessity, or sense of obligation, they do not really constitute an organisation.

3. Constructive Pressure

- ✔ One of the functions of an effective manager is to impose a carefully controlled amount of constructive pressure on the members of the organisation so that they have a well- defined sense of necessity and mission.
- ✔ Very few people resent being held accountable for reasonable performance, within reasonable constraints of time and resources.

4. Authority Dynamics

- ✔ A more enlightened method of deploying authority is to apply and maintain a comfortable level of pressure — a level that the employees find demanding and challenging but not threatening or overly stressful.
- ✔ Remember, that no matter how carefully one tries to put the employee at ease, he seldom forgets one key fact: You are the boss.

Humanizing the Workplace / Organisation

The organisation will look something like the following:

- A very large number of its members express overall satisfaction with their jobs and roles.
- Its members enjoy relatively high quality relationships with one another.
- Its members work effectively and productively, according to definitions of job-related productivity.
  - ✔ Its members are in good health with the incidence of stress disease and occupational health problems at a practical minimum.
  - ✔ The top managers make themselves visible and approachable and they respond sensitively to the feedback they get about their performance as managers.
  - ✔ The top managers are well informed about the current attitudes of the employees. They account for these factors in their decision making and planning.

Stress-Interventions

Faith

- Human beings are engineered for religious faith. Our genetic blueprint has made believing in an Infinite Absolute — a part of our nature.
- The research has shown that Temple/Gurudwara/Churchgoers have lower blood pressure than non-goers.
- Those who are both religious and socially involved have a fourteen fold advantage over those who are isolated or lack faith.
- Prayer operates along the same bio-chemical pathways as the relaxation response.

Family

Family is a unique set of intimate relationships.

Predominant family is the Breadwinning Father, Home Making Mother and Resident Children.

Friends

- The absence of stable social relationships affects our minds and biology as few other events can.
- Being lonely is a major risk factor of heart disease.
- Loneliness tends to raise blood pressure and disrupt sleep.
- Loneliness is not just being alone. It involves feelings of isolation, of disconnectedness and of not belonging
- Lonely people perceive their world as less reinforcing and more threatening.
- Form at least one or two high-quality relationships with people you trust.

A few more tips:

- Don't worry alone
- Add structure to your life
- Do something you like
- Don't drink excessively
- Take physical exercise
- Let music play in life
- Have a good cry

So when I am downcast and feeling sad,

- I repeat over and over again,
- Things are far from being as bad
- As they easily might have been.
- Take time to love and be loved
- It is a Godgiven privilege
- Take time to be friendly
- It is a road to happiness
- Take time to give
- It is too short a day to be selfish

✩✩✩

3

STRESS AT WORK: ISSUES OF CONCERN

* *Dr. C. R. Darolia*

* Professor, Deptt. of Psychology, Kurukshetra University, Kurukshetra.

The modern world which is said to be a world of achievements, is also a world of stress.One finds stress everywhere, whether it be family, business organization, enterprise, or any other social or economic activity. Right from the time of birth, till the last breath drawn, an individual is invariably exposed to various stressful situations. Thus it is not surprising, that interest in the issue has been rising with the advancement of the present century, which has been called the age of anxiety and stress.

Stress is epidemic in the modern world. In developed countries over two thirds of office visits to physicians are for stress-related-illness. Stress is a major contributing factor, either directly or indirectly, to coronary-artery disease, cancer, respiratory disorders, accidental injuries, cirrhosis of the liver and suicide; the six leading causes of death throughout the world. In United States, only stress costs industry approximately 150 billion dollars per year, in the form of increased health insurance outlays, burnout, absenteeism, reduced productivity, costly mistakes in the office and on the shop floor, poor morale, high employee turnover, as well as family, alcohol and drug related problems.

In general, stress is described as a condition that results when person's environmental transactions leads him/her to perceive a discrepancy, whether real or not; between the demands of situation and the resources of a person's biological, psychological and social system. Stress has been conceptualized in three different ways. One of these approaches focuses on the environment describing stress as a stimulus. According to Selye (1975), any external event or any internal drive, which threatens to upset the organism equilibrium is stress. Events or circumstances, that we perceive as threatening or harmful, thereby producing feelings of tension; are called stressors. Researchers, who follow this approach, study the impact of wide range of stressors including:

(a) catastrophic event; such as tornadoes and earthquakes

(b) major life events; such as the loss of loved one or job and

(c) More chronic circumstances such as living in crowded or noisy conditions.

The second approach treats stress as a response, focusing on people's reaction to stressors. Psychiatrists have identified four phases in the reaction to stress. The intial phase is of anticipatory threat, the impact of stress, the recall phase and the post traumatic phase. The third approach describes stress as a process that includes stressors and strain, but also adds an important dimension, the relationship between the person and the environment (Cox 1978; Strelau 2001). . This involves continuous interactions and adjustments, a kind of transaction between the person and the environment, with each affecting and being affected by other.

In Selye's view, stress is not always bad or harmful; it is necessary and useful for person's growth, when in optimum quantity. When the optimum level, which varies from person to person is exceeded, than it costs much to the individual and the system. According to him the nation of stress can be broken down further into positive stress (i.e., eustress) and negative stress (i.e. distress). The term eustress derived from the Greek 'eu', which means good is positive and pleasent side of stress caused by good things. Distress is caused by something bad that people experience as a result of external or internal stressors. External stressors include adverse physical conditions such as, pain or hot or cold tempratures or stressful psychological environments (such as poor working conditions or abusive relationships). Stressors can also be described as short-term (accued) or long-term (chronic). Acute stess is the reaction to an immediate threat commonly known as, the fight or flight response. The threat can be any situation that is experienced, subconsciously or falsely, as dangerous. The common acute stressors include noise crowding, isolation, hunger, danger, infection and imagining a threat or remembering a dangerous event. Under most circumstances, once the acute threat has passed, the response become inactivated and levels of stress hormones return to normal, a condition called the relaxation response. Chronic stress is a result of stressful situations that are not short -lived and when the urge to act (to fight or to flee) must be suppressed. Here stress becomes chronic common chronic stressors including highly pressured work, long term relationship problems, loneliness and persistent financial worries.

Job and work place are two important aspects of individual's life that inherently involve stess. Sress at work, like stress in other setting, is a matter of great concern. Job stress may be viewed as "a condition arising from the interaction of people that forces them to deviate from normal functioning" (Beehr and Newman, 1978). Many environmental, organizational and personal factors are the important sources of stress. For example, economic uncertaintes are the important sources of stress for our organization, as well as for the employees, when economy contract people become increasingly anxious about the security of their jobs. Tasks demands and role demands are the common causes of stress in organizations. Interpersonal demands pressurize individuals to do things in certain specific manners. Poor interpersonal relationships with co-workers and supervisors, and lack of social support from colleagues and seniors can cause considerable stress, especially to those who need it more than others.

Substantial evidence is available to show that, in an organization, workers are likely to experience the stress of low status, shortage of resources, high demands for a large volume of work (Parsuraman and Alutto, 1981) and poor representation in the decision making policies. It seems that any situation, which is monotonous, or unchallenging, is generally considered stressful. Likewise job with little influence, motivation and participation have been associated with stress (French and Caplan 1972). Managerial style characterized by excessive controls to perform, and to perform it well in a short span of time, always causes tension, fear and anxiety in the employees.

Occupational stress is not a single isolated variable. It is complex phenomenon that may be the result of interaction of many environmental, organizational and personal factors. Contracted financial resources could be one of the important causes to distract worker's attention from his work which may lead to drastic results. Uncertainity and newness of the situaton creates stress for many individuals.But as they proceed with experience in job, the related stress either disappears or reduces to a significant degree study conducted in organizational settings show, that voluntary turnover is more problem among people who experiance intense and persistent job stress. On the other hand,the individuals who continue to stay in the organization longer, are often those who have more stress resistent traits.The other way to say it is, that such individuals have developed more benefiting coping mechanisms to deal with constraints and demands of the job (Motowidlo,Packard, and Manning,1987)

Attributing causes to occurrences, individuals with internal locus of control believe that they can control their own destiny and perceive their job comparatively more stressful, and in the situation of excessive stress,they are more likely to be passive and defensive rather than to do something constructive to eliminate or reduce it (Murphy 1986).

Type-A persons are charactersized by a chronic sense of time urgency and an excessive competitive drive. They are agressively involved in a chronic incessant struggle to achieve more and more in less time, even against all the opposing forces. Studies show that type-A persons are likely to experience more stress, on and off the job, than their type-B counterparts who also believe in progress and success but at a steady progressive pace and speed. It is the work - alcoholic, rushing around to important and competitive temperament of type-A persons that makes them more susceptible to stress. But more important is their being chronically angry, hostile, suspicious and socially mistrustful, that increases their vulnerability for the negative effects of stress including coronary heart disease and burnout.

The mediating role of social support in meeting occupational stress, and buffering its ill effects on the health of employees, has a great significance. Relationships with co-workers or supervisors can always act to palliate and mitigate strain even of high stress jobs. In the absence of supportive relationships at work place, involvement in and interaction with the family members, relatives and friends make job stressors less tolerable (Ammings, 1990;; House 1981; Jayaratne, Himle & Chess, 1988)

Individual's perception of stress and its sources are all the more important than any other factor. Stressors are differently perceived by different individuals and even by the same individual on different occasions (Pestonjee, 1987) This perception depends upon the importance of the stressor for the individual, threat element which the stressor poses, and how the individual perceives it; personal and social support systems available to him; selection of the coping strategy likely to be used, and above all, the ego strength and willingness of the individual to combat with the stressors.

Manifestations of stress: Manifestations of the negative effects of the stress could be physiological, psychological and behavioural, unmediated stress may manifest itself in many physiological symptoms, such as, blood pressure, insomnia headache, and bodyaches, loss of appetite, increased accident proneness, tremors, ulcers and the like.

Psychological and behavioural consequences of stress are important for all health and behavioural scientists. Job dissatisfaction is "the simplest and most obvious psychological effect of stress (Steffy and Jones, 1986). Job stress is an unpleasant emotional experience at work associated with elements of anxiety, irritability, difficulty in making decisions, tensions, annoyance, sadness and depression etc.

Multiple and conflicting job demands on the part of the employees may result in increased stress and dissatisfaction (Cooper and Marshall, 1976). Research evidence shows that jobs providing low level of variety, significance, autonomy, feedback and identity to incumbents create stress, and reduce their satisfaction and involvement in the job (Hackman and Oldhman, 1975). Behaviour related stress symptoms include, changes in eating habits, rapid speech, fighting and sleep disorders; and increased use of alcohol or smoking. Research has shown the stress performance relationship in almost all organizations, and has suggested that it is an inverted u-type-curve which also depicts that low to moderate levels of stress stimulate the body and increase its ability to react.Thus Individuals often perform their task better, more intensely or more rapidly. But too much stress characterized by unattainable demands or constraints on them, results in lowering performance. However, even the moderate levels of stress can have a negative influence on performance over the long term as the continued intensity of stress wears down the individual, and saps his or her energy resources.

In the main, stress is a common phenomenon of life's growing complexities, and pressures of modern living are severely taxing. Today, stress relating to job has become a predominant feature of all psychological research. This is one reason that systematic studies on stress in all organizational settings are dramatically increasing. But more and more studies have been conducted on physically hazardous conditions and their impact on work life. Psychological aspect and their impact on work life.It seems that occupational stress is inevitably present in all sectors of organisational set up and because of many contradictions and complexities of human behaviour; research in this area seems to be quite pertinent.

4

WINNING OVER STRESS: STRATEGIES FOR STRESS MANAGEMENT

** Prof. B. S. Bodla*

*** Ms. Divya Malhan*

* Director, Institute of Management Studies, Kurukshetra University, Kurukshetra.

** Lecturer, Institute of Management Studies, Kurukshetra University, Kurukshetra.

Introduction

Never put off till tomorrow, what you could have done today.

Anonymous Proverb

Stress is a part of day-to-day living of every individual. The college students may experience stress in meeting the academic demands, people on the job business men may suffer stress to reach office in time and to complete the projects on time. And even the household ladies may experience stress in managing the home affairs. The reasons for the stress differs from person to person. The stress, people experience should not be necessarily treated as harmful. An optimum amount of stress, can always act as an energizer or motivator, and propel people to apply the efforts and complete the work. But a high level of stress can be a serious threat to the personality traits of the Individual, and can cause physiological and social problems. We generally believe that stress is caused by external events and dynamics of the environment. But we need to emphasize the fact that, stress is caused by our reaction to the external environment. The manner in which we perceive and understand a particular event, varies from person to person and can bring happiness or cause stress in two different people depending upon how they react to it. When students are asked to prepare a presentation, some may take it to be an opportunity to reveal their talents, and to improve upon their weaknesses while the other students may fear revealing weakness. So, stress is our reaction to external events, and it can be positive or negative, depending upon how we react. It is the general wear and tear of the body machine that takes place due to extra demands put on it.

"Out of clutter, find simplicity.

From discord, find harmony.

In the middle of difficulty lies opportunity."

– Albert Einstein

Understanding Stress

Stress is defined as an adaptive response to an external situation that results in physical, psychological, and/or behavioural deviations for organizational participants (Luthans, 1989).

Hans Selye was one of the founding fathers of stress research. His view in 1956 was that "stress is not necessarily something bad – it all depends on how you take it. The stress of exhiliarating, creative successful work is beneficial, while that of failure, humiliation or infection is detrimental." (http://www.mindtools.com/pages/article/newTCS_00.htm). The most commonly accepted definition of stress (mainly attributed to Richard S Lazarus) is that stress is a condition or feeling experienced, when a person perceives that "demands exceed the personal and social resources, an individual is able to mobilize." In short, it's what we feel, when we think we've lost control of events (http://www.mindtools.com/pages/article/newTCS_00.htm). We can define stress as body's non-specific response to any demand made on it. Stress is not by definition, synonymous with nervous tension or anxiety. On one side, stress provides the means to express talents and energies, and pursue happiness; on the other side, it can also cause exhaustion and illness, either physical or psychological.

Many people delay the start or completion of tasks, often feeling uncomfortable and anxious about the delays. This phenomenon in psychological research and clinical interventions has been labeled procrastination. The Romans provided the roots of the present form of the word "procrastination"—*pro* = "forward" + *crastinus* = "of tomorrow" (Ferrari, 2001).

Donovan and Kleiner (1994), in their study, give an overview of events in the field of stress management. They describe the relationship of stress to the human autonomic nervous system, and investigate the sources and methods of detection of stress. They also examine methodologies for stress management, the design of stress management programmes for industry application, and the results which selected corporations have achieved.

Symptoms of Stress

Stress is caused by, or is a reaction to the external events and brings about changes in our response and our general behaviour. The presence of stress can be estimated by the analysis of certain symptoms that an individual shows. These symptoms can be divided into three different categories. They are feelings, behaviour and physiology. When an individual experiences stress, one or more of the following symptoms can be exhibited.

Feelings

- The individual becomes anxious about the outcomes and is scared. The person feels that he has got something to loose or something wrong will take place.
- In an anxious state the person does not want to be corrected or interrupted. He looks out for other areas where he can forget about the stress-causing event for a while. The person becomes irritable and moody.
- During high level of stress, an individual develops a negative frame of mind and suffers from low self-esteem. The person looses faith in his capabilities, and is afraid of the failures. The individual does not have a focused approach, and is not able to concentrate, and is involved in his own plans and thoughts.

Physiological and Behavioural Changes are as follows:

Speech problems, impulsive behaviour, crying for no apparent reason, laughing in a high pitch, and nervous tone of voice, grinding of teeth, increased smoking, use of drugs and alcohol, being accident-prone, perspiration /sweaty hands, increased heart beat, trembling, nervous ticks, dryness of throat and mouth, tiring easily, urinating frequently, sleeping problems, diarrhoea/ indigestion/vomiting/nausea, butterflies in stomach, headaches, premenstrual tension, pain in the neck and/or lower back, susceptibility to illness, loss of appetite or overeating, etc.

Causes of Stress

Both positive and negative events in one's life can be stressful. However, major life changes are the greatest contributors of stress for most people.

- If people have to travel a lot, and have to move from place to place, it can cause stress.
- Individuals can also be under stress, if they are about to enter some new environment. They may be going to a new colony, a new college, or they may be joining a new organization.

- Some events, which are generally once in a lifetime can also cause stress. The social institutions of marriage or divorce can cause stress. Pregnancy can also generate stress.
- Some of the untoward incidents like critical illness or death of a relative, can also cause stress in individuals.

These are some of the major events in the life of the individual that cause stress. It is also supplemented by the environmental factors that act as catalyst to stress. They are time pressure, competition, financial problems, noise, disappointments etc.

Managing Stress

If you're living with high levels of stress, you're putting your entire well-being at risk. Stress wreaks havoc on your emotional equilibrium, as well as your physical health. It narrows your ability to think clearly, function effectively, and enjoy life. The goal of stress management is to bring your mind and body back into balance. By adopting a positive attitude, learning healthier ways to cope, and changing the way you deal with stress, you can reduce its hold on your life (http://www.helpguide.org/mental/stress_management_relief_coping.htm). Stress can be managed, if we understand the reasons that cause stress, and the level of stress. We should also try to estimate, if we could bring about any change in the environment that can subsequently reduce stress.

Stress Management Involves at the simplest level:

1. recognising the symptoms of stress
2. identifying the causes
3. taking action to address the causes and thereby reduce the symptoms
4. where necessary, taking interim steps to relieve the symptoms until the underlying causes have been addressed (http://www.teamtechnology.co.uk/tt/t-articl/stress.htm).

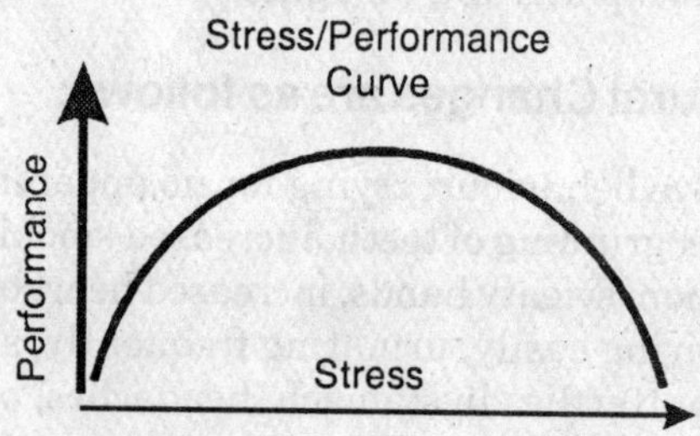

Some Strategies for Managing Stress

Managing stress is all about taking charge: taking charge of your thoughts, your emotions, your schedule, your environment, and the way you deal with problems. The ultimate goal is a balanced life, with time for work, relationships, relaxation, and fun—and the resilience to hold up under pressure and meet challenges headon (http://www.helpguide.org/mental/stress_management_relief_coping.htm)

1. **Avoid unnecessary stress**

Not all stress can be avoided, and it's not healthy to avoid a situation that needs to be addressed. You may be surprised, however, by the number of stressors in your life that you can eliminate.

- **Learn how to say "no"** – Know your limits and stick to them.
- **Avoid people who stresses you out** – If someone consistently causes stress in your life and you can't turn the relationship around, limit the amount of time you spend with that person or end the relationship entirely.
- **Take control of your environment** – If the evening news makes you anxious, turn the TV off. If going to the market is an unpleasant chore, do your grocery shopping online.
- **Avoid hot-button topics** – If you get upset over religion or politics, cross them off your conversation list.
- **Pen down your to-do list** – Analyze your schedule, responsibilities, and daily tasks. Drop tasks that aren't truly necessary to the bottom of the list, or eliminate them entirely.

2. **Alter the situation**

If you can't avoid a stressful situation, try to alter it. Often, this involves changing the way you communicate and operate in your daily life.

- **Express your feelings instead of bottling them up.** If you don't voice your feelings, resentment will build up, and the situation will likely remain the same.
- **Be willing to compromise.** When you ask someone to change his/her behaviour, be willing to do the same.
- **Be more assertive.** Don't take a backseat in your own life. Deal with problems headon, doing your best to anticipate and prevent them.
- **Manage your time better.** Poor time management can cause a lot of stress.

3. **Accept the things you can't change**

Some sources of stress are unavoidable. You can't prevent or change stressors such as the death of a loved one, a serious illness, or a national recession. In such cases, the best way to cope with stress is to accept things as they are.

- ✓ **Don't try to control the uncontrollable.** Many things in life are beyond our control. Rather than stressing out over them, focus on the things you can control, such as, the way you choose to react to problems.
- **Look for the upside.** As the saying goes, "What doesn't kill us makes us stronger." When facing major challenges, try to look at them as opportunities for personal growth.
- **Share your feelings.** Talk to a trusted friend or make an appointment with a therapist.
- **Learn to forgive.** Accept the fact that we live in an imperfect world, and that people make mistakes.

4. **Adapt to the stressor**

If you can't change the stressor, change yourself.

- **Reframe problems.** Try to view stressful situations from a more positive perspective.
- **Look at the big picture.** Take perspective of the stressful situation. Ask yourself how important it will be in the long run.
- **Adjust your standards.** Perfectionism is a major source of avoidable stress.
- **Focus on the positive.** When stress is getting you down, take a moment to reflect on all the things you appreciate in your life, including your own positive qualities and gifts.

5. **Adjusting Your Attitude**

How you think, can have a profound affect on your emotional and physical well-being. Each time you think a negative thought about yourself, your body reacts as if, it was in the throes of a tension-filled situation. If you see good things about yourself, you are more likely to feel good; the reverse is also true. Eliminate words such as "always," "never," "should," and "must." These are tell-tale marks of self-defeating thoughts.

6. **Managing Your Support Networks- Getting help when you need it** http://www.mindtools.com/stress/Defenses/SupportNetworks.htm

We all have networks of people, who can help us solve problems. This network extends professionally and socially, as well as, includes our family and public services. These people can give help, and support in a wide variety of ways, including:

- **Physical assistance:** This can be financial or direct help, or provision of useful resources.
- **Political assistance:** Other people can use their influence and personal networks on your behalf to cope with the situation.
- **Information:** People may have information that helps in the situation or solves the problem, or may have personal experience that can help you.
- **Problem solving:** Similarly, they may be able to help you to think on how to solve the problem.
- **Reassurance:** People can also give emotional support and reassurance, when you may be starting to doubt yourself. Others can cheer you up, when you are feeling down.

Rest, Relaxation and Sleep

When many people are faced with a stressful situation at work, they respond with complete commitment, by working intensely hard at resolving it. To do this, they may work all hours, cancel vacations and cut back on sleep, all to make more time to tackle the problem.If this is short-lived, then negative effects will be minimal and success will often be spectacular. However, if this level of hard work is sustained for a long time without relief, people increasingly risk ill-health and burnout (http://www.mindtools.com/stress/Defenses/Rest.htm). Doing fun things that we enjoy in our leisure time, compensates us for the stress we experience at work, bringing some balance back into life. This is particularly important, if we routinely experience unpleasant levels of stress. A good way of getting rest and reducing long-term stress is to take up an enjoyable, non-rushed sport or hobby. If you spend all your working day competing, then, it can be very pleasant to be completely non-competitive for some of your free time. Slow physical activities such as, sailing or walking, are good for this, as are where there is little or no pressure for performance. Reading novels, watching television or socializing can also be very restful. Vacations are particularly important, and you really do need to take these. Whenever possible, take two weeks off, rather than just one week: A common observation that people make is, that they really do not start to relax properly until the end of their first week of vacation. Make sure that you take your vacations, and that you use them to relax. Also, make sure, that you get enough good quality rest during the week, so that you can keep on enjoying life to its fullest.

Sleep

On average, people need around eight hours sleep at night (although this can vary between three hours and eleven hours, depending on the person and his or her age).If we are regularly short of sleep, then our concentration and our effectiveness suffer, and our energy levels decline.This diminishes our effectiveness in our job, and can therefore increase stress: As our concentration wanders, we start to make mistakes. As our energy declines, we become less proactive in what we do, reducing our control over events. This means, that a situation that is already difficult and stressful can become worse, needing even more sacrifice to bring it back under control. Make sure you get enough sleep. If you have become used to being tired all the time, you will be amazed by how sharp and energetic you will feel, once you start sleeping normally.

Managing Chemical Stress

The chemicals (food, drink, pills, etc) we put in our bodies, can cause a surprising amount of stress.Similarly, if we are eating an unbalanced diet, we may be stressing our bodies by depriving them of essential nutrients. And eating too much for a long period causes obesity: This puts your heart and lungs under stress, overloads your organs and reduces your stamina.

You should be aware of the effects of the following:

- **Caffeine:**

  Caffeine is a stimulant. One of the reasons we drink it is to raise our levels of arousal, particularly at the start of the day. If you drink many cups of coffee a day, then you may become twitchy, hyperactive and irritable.

- **Alcohol:**

  In small amounts, alcohol may help you relax. In larger amounts, it may increase stress, as it disrupts sleep, reduces your effectiveness, and possibly harms working relationships.

- **Nicotine:**

  For a while nicotine can cause its users to relax, its toxic effects raise your heart rate and stress your body.

- **Sugar:**

  Sugar-rich foods can raise energy in the short term. The problem with this is that your body copes with high levels of sugar by secreting insulin, which reduces the amount of sugar in your blood stream. Insulin can persist and continue acting, after it has controlled blood sugar levels. This can cause an energy dip.

If you eat a good, well-balanced diet, you should be able to minimize this sort of chemical stress. With a little forethought, you can make sure that your body receives all the nutrients it needs to function effectively (http://www.mindtools.com/stress/Defenses/ChemicalStress.htm).

7. Managing Stress With Regular Exercise

Taking frequent effective exercise is one of the best physical stress-reduction techniques available. Exercise not only improves your health and reduces stress caused by unfitness; it also relaxes tense muscles and helps you to sleep.

Exercise has a number of other positive benefits you may not be aware of:

- It improves blood flow to your brain, bringing additional sugars and oxygen that may be needed when you are thinking intensely.
- When you think hard, the neurons of your brain function more intensely. As they do this, they can build up toxic waste products that can cause foggy thinking (you may have experienced the feeling that your brain has "turned to cotton wool"). By exercising, you speed the flow of blood through your brain, moving these waste products faster.
- Exercise can cause release of chemicals called endorphins into your blood stream. These give you a feeling of happiness and positively affect your overall sense of well-being (http://www.mindtools.com/stress/Defenses/Exercise.htm).

Stress reduction tips

Beyond a take-charge approach and a positive attitude, you can reduce stress in your life by making healthy lifestyle choices and taking care of yourself. If you regularly make time for rest and relaxation, you'll be in a better place to handle life's stressors when they inevitably come.

- Set aside relaxation time
- Connect with others
- Do something you enjoy every day
- Keep your sense of humor
- Go for a walk.
- Spend time in nature.
- Talk to a supportive friend.
- Sweat out tension with a good workout.
- Do something for someone else.
- Write in your journal.
- Play with a pet.
- Opening up (Aquinas, 2006).
- Learned optimism (Aquinas, 2006).
- Self-hypnosis (Suri and Verma, 2005).
- Auto-suggestion (Suri and Verma, 2005).

- Work in your garden.
- Get a massage.
- Curl up with a good book.
- Take a yoga class.
- Listen to music.
- Watch a comedy.
- Take a long bath.
- Exercise regularly.
- Eat a healthy diet.
- Reduce caffeine and sugar.
- Avoid alcohol, cigarettes, and drugs.
- Get enough sleep

Living a healthy lifestyle and well-built defenses against stress can help you to be happy and in control, even when under long-term stress. (http://www.mindtools.com/stress/Defenses/StressIntro.htm).

Conclusion

"Smiling is infectious; we catch it like the flu.
When someone smiled at me today, I started smiling, too.
I passed around the corner and someone saw my grin
When he smiled, I realized I'd passed it on to him
I thought about that smile and then realized its worth,
A single smile, just like mine, could travel round the earth."
So, if you feel a smile begin, don't leave it undetected,
Let's start an epidemic quick, and get the world infected".

References

1. Luthans, F. (1989) Organizational Behaviour, New York, McGraw-Hill.
   http://www.mindtools.com/pages/article/newTCS_00.htm
   http://www.mindtools.com/pages/article/newTCS_00.htm
2. Ferrari, J. R (2001) Getting Things Done On Time: Conquering Procrastination in C. R. Snyder (edn) "Coping with Stress: Effective People and Processes". Oxford University Press, New York.
3. Donovan, S. B. and Kleiner, B. H (1994) Effective Stress Management, Managerial Auditing Journal, Vol. 9, No. 6, pp 31-34.

http://www.helpguide.org/mental/stress_management_relief_coping.htm

http://www.teamtechnology.co.uk/tt/t-articl/stress.htm

http://www.mindtools.com/stress/Defenses/StressIntro.htm

http://www.mindtools.com/stress/Defenses/ChemicalStress.htm

4. Suri, R. K and Verma, S. (2005) Organizational Behaviour: Text and Cases, Delhi, Wisdom Publications.

5. Aquinas, P. G (2006) Organizational Behaviour: Concepts, Realities, Applications and Challenges, New Delhi, Excel Books.

6. Sharma, U (2005) Stress Management: through ancient wisdom and modern science, New Delhi, Excel Books.

7. Robbins, S. P (2003) Organizational Behavior, Prentice-Hall of India Private Limited, New Delhi.

✡ ✡ ✡

5

MANAGING STRESS – A SURVEY OF THE MACRO SCENARIO

*Dr. Kulbhushan Chandel

** Dr. Raj Kumar

* Assistant Professor, Department of Commerce, Himachal Pradesh University, Shimla-5.

** Head, Department of Commerce, Government College, Theog, Shimla.

The phenomena of stress have become very common in the modern complex world. In the fast changing world of rapid technological advancement, more and more people are becoming victims of stress and this is true of people in all organization and at all levels. The victims of stress are more in the developed countries particularly in the urban areas whereas in the rural areas, where the pace of life is slow, problems of stress are minimal. A study conducted by the W.H.O in 2001 reveals that every fourth person in the world is suffering from high level of stress, and by 2020, depression will be the world's the second largest cause for urban disease after heart ailments.

Etymologically, the word stress is derived from the Latin word stringer which means to draw tight. The word stress expresses the mental image of an individual with a situation of uneasiness and distress that is gradually tightening its hold, taking all in its grip till it eventually strangulates the individual. In a very simple way, stress can be defined as the mental strain that an individual experiences as a result of coping with some environmental factors. In the wisdom literature of ancient India, the word stress is close to the word Bishad. It has been explained in the 1st chapter of the Gita titled Bishad-Yoga, when Arjun under the extreme stress in the battle field. In the Sankhya yoga, two concepts are highlighted, namely, Klesha and Dukha. Kalesha refers to stressor aspect and Dukha to the phenomena of stress itself. Hence, stress signifies an intense, adverse and painful emotion that an individual experiences in the course of his/her interaction with the world. Stress involves an experience of painful emotion and is characterized by powerlessness and helplessness inspite of an urge to escape from the situation causing up the stress. There is a very old saying that "healthy body leads to healthy mind" whereas the reverse is rather more true "healthy mind leads to healthy body."

The role of stress in everyday life therefore needs hardly to be over emphasized. Stress as well as its prevention and management has now become an integral and essential part of modern life.

Objectives

The following are the main objectives of the present paper:

(i) To examine the cause and implications of stress.

(ii) To suggests remedial measures to manage the stress.

Research Methodology

In order to carryout the present study, a desk research and delphy method (Expert Opinion) is applied. The interview and observation method has also been applied to analyse and to reach the conclusion. Various books, journals, magazines, newsletters and newspapers, etc., were consulted to collect and evaluate the various facts. The help of electronic media like internet etc., has also been sought.

Causes of Stress

Stress is a situation that provides external and internal stimuli. These stimuli or stress causing factors are stressors. An individual may come across pleasant stress that may lead to the situation of distress and turn under the experimental psychology. Stress is always considered to be negative.However, some positive elements are also perceived in stress that may be called as challenge. An individual has to draw threshold line or Lakshman Rekha to differentiate between negative and positive stress. The threshold level varies not only from person to person but also varies for the same person under extremely varying situations. The followings have been noted as the main causes of stress in the era of modern Information Communications and Technology (ICT) society or say Knowledge Society.

External Factors:

These causes are called *ipso-facto* that means, causes are out of the control of an individual, at least in the short run. When nothing can be done, one has to live with the problems of stress. The following have been noted as the causes of eternal stress:

- Rapid obsolescence of skills
- Poor time management of others
- Unreasonable boss/superiors at workplace
- Uncongenial work environment
- Target chasing & continuous target enhancement
- Sudden transfer from one work place to another
- Stock market crash
- Economic factors
- Socio-political factors.

Stress Generating Events and Situations:

The empirical study has been carried out to identify the list of such stressors that produce stress. The following are the cause of stress generating events and situation.

- Death of a member in the family
- Sick member in the family
- Wedding
- Death of spouse
- Partition of property
- Physically handicapped child in the family
- Loss of job
- Change of job
- Shifting residence
- Noise pollution
- Major personal failure
- Loss in business

- Financial problem
- Major theft in the house
- Significant increase in income.
- Loneliness
- Leaving home for spiritual pursuits.

Internal Factors:

The presence of internal factors also makes one stressful, and these are by and large within one's control. These factors are listed as follow:

- Strong negative emotions, like, anger, arrogance, ambitions etc.
- Materialistic world view like, selfishness, greed, jealousy, social rivalry etc.
- Leading an impure life it includes illegal and unethical life ruled by senses, for example, extra marital relations etc.
- Personality composition.
- The Dwandik theory of stress which means interplay of duality.

Implications of Stress

Stress has both negative as well as positive implications for an individual under the varying circumstances. Stressful person will either become by functional, or he cannot perform upto his full potential. Under the extreme stressful circumstances, an individual may become lunatic, may commit suicide, may meet sudden demise and may become a criminal. The followings implications of stress have been revealed.

The implications of the stress may be physiological in nature which implies adverse effect: increased heart rate, respiratory disorder, blood pressure, indigestion, thrombosis, cancer, headache, etc.

Emotional Implications

It includes anxiety, anger, ambition, apprehension, etc. The behavioral implication includes, over dependence, unpredictability, uncommunicativeness, unreasonableness, argumentativeness, and haphazard daily routine, withdrawal of law and lack of interest or over-interest in sex.

The cognitive implication has adverse effects on mental functions; such as, reasoning, thinking, concentration memory and decision-making.

Managing the Stress

Prevention and management of stress has now become an essential and integral part of modern life. The management of stress is to some extent related to the management of time, since the basic prerequisite for both is management of self. If one monitors stress he can notice three stages; such as, alarm, resistance and exhaustion, while using the fight and flight strategy.

The management of stress has two aspects. One, how an individual can prevent becoming stressful and remain in the challenge state and second, once a person gets into stress-state, how soon he can revert back to the challenge state. Hence, two dimensions of managing stress are prevention and coping ability.

Methods of Stress Prevention

In the first stage, the efforts should be made to monitor and prevent the stress. There are various methods of managing the prevention of stress. These are discussed as follows:

Effective management of anger, arrogance, anxiety, ambition and apprehension, i.e. management of 5A's. To manage 5 A's, there is modern and classical approach but there is almost complete unanimity among the psychologists, that the classical approach is valid. The Raj Yoga also helps to prevent stress.

The theory of Nishkam Karma as given in the Gita also helps to prevent stress. In the Gita, Shri Krishna Arjun's that you surrender to me and I will bear the burden of your Yoga Ksema.

Conscious efforts towards developing a healthy personality, based primarily upon the Guna Theory, which consists of Satwa, Rajas and Tamas.

The Gita offers two alternative method of dealing with Dwandick, Nirdwanda and Samattwa are the operationalising methods of Gyan Yoga and Bhakti Yoga respectively.

The ethico-moral law of cause and effect is the appropriate method of dealing with stress.

Method of Coping with Stress

Vedantic Model:

The vedantic model of higher-self, also known as Astang yoga of Maharishi Patanjali, helps to cope with the stress. The following is the model of Astang yoga.

Yama: It comprises (1) Ahinsa (2) Satya (3) Astay (4) Aprigrah (5) Brahamcharya.

Niyam: It includes (1) Shoach (2) Santosh (3) Tup (4) Swadhyay (5) Ishwar Pranidhan Assan

Pranayam: Regulation of energy.

Pratyahar: To concentrate on inner self.

Dhayan: To meditate.

Dharane: To merge in state of Dhyan

Smadhi: State of higher self and merging with supreme soul by being aware of the existence of higher self, and trying to awaken the same through the above methods of yoga.

The Pancha Kosha model of the Taittiriya also makes an individual capable of coping with the stress. The five Kosha's are Annamya Kosha, Pranamaya Kosha, Monomaya Kosha, Vijnanmaya Kosha, and Anandmaya Kosha. The two innermost Koshas i.e. Wisdom and Bliss are stress free. Stress can touch only the first three Koshas.

The Purusha Prakriti model in the Sankhaya Philosophy.

Similarly, the Prakriti state in our being is Guna-driven and is therefore, stress-prone, stress being the outcome of the interplay of the three Gunas. But the Purusha dimension being beyond Gunas (i.e.'Gunatita') is stress free. One can revert back from a stressful to a stress-free situation.

A Few Vital Guidelines

Stress is a reality of modern life; there is no escape from if. The following are the few vital guidelines to prevent stress.

Enhance the level of tolerance and patience.

Control anger by all means

Control jealousy by all means

Have a daily time schedule for all activities

Practice regularly some physical exercise

Practice regularly some mental exercise

Change your food habits

Change your reading habits for proper nourishment of the mind

Always keep your mind occupied — in meaningful work

Develop a spirit of contentment

Share frankly your limitations and inabilities with your boss and near and dear ones.

Aspire within the framework of your capabilities.

Avoid comparing yourself with others.

Work efficiently but avoid competition with others.

Strive for excellence through 'work is worship'— follow the spirit of 'Nishkam Karma'— alongside kartavyam karma, i.e. the work is done as duty for the sake of duty only.

Don't be a workaholic — don't forget there are so many finer aspects of life

Do not be rigid in your ways of functioning and dealing

Do your best to get out of a provocative situation.

Spend time with children in the 'age of innocence'

Always thank the Almighty for whatever He has given to you

Look forward to opportunities to serve the needy and unfortunate people.

Finally, in order to operationalise the given set of practical guidelines, for both prevention and coping with the stress it would be extremely useful to adopt the state of quality mind process that is called meditation.

References

1. Sri Aurobindo, The message of the Gita, Sri Aurobindo Ashram, Pondicherry.
2. C. Northcote Parkinson, The World's Great Achievements and Failures in Management, India bookhouse Pvt. Ltd.
3. S.K. Chakraborty, Managerial Effectiveness and Quality of Work life, Indian Insights, Tata McGraw Hill.
4. Stephen P. Robbins, Organizational Behaviour, Prentice Hall of India Pvt. Ltd.
5. Swami Vivekanand, Complete Works, Vedanta-The Voice of Freedom.
6. B.K. Chatterjee, Organizational Behaviour and Beyond, Asian Books Pvt. Ltd.,

✡✡✡

6

Occupational Stress & How to Reduce its Effects in Haryana

** Dr. Rajender Kumar*
*** Dr. Sanjeet*
**** Smt. Sharmila*
***** Chander Parkash*

* Lecturer, Deptt. of Education, Chaudhary Devi Lal University, Sirsa.

** Lecturer, Department of Business Admn. , Chaudhary Devi Lal University, Sirsa.

*** Lecturer, Department of Business Administration, Chaudhary Devi Lal University, Sirsa.

**** Lecturer, Shah Satnam Ji College of Education, Sirsa.

Occupational Stress is a response that includes both physical and mental responses to what we experience in our day to day life. In this context, occupational stress may be defined as the collective physical and mental responses to an unacceptable disparity between personnal expectations and actual physical and/or imaginary personal experiences. Although stress has been around us since the very beginning of our existence on planet earth, there is probably more stress today than there has even been in human history. Stress in America is number one health problem and occupational stress in particular is widely believed to be the major culprit. The occupational stress is also increasing in India as well in Haryana state also. Occupational Stress is somehow an unavoidable consequence of life and life without stress is probably not worth. As some occupational stress can be a major cause of disease, the good news is that there are many types of good stress that may promote wellness. Winning a football match or race can be just as stressful as losing one.

Reducing occupational stress levels is generally advantageous to one's emotional and probably physical stability, and some tips for reducing occupational stress levels include being more organized, planning well, listing the "to do things" and prioritizing them.

Occupational stress management can improve the quality of life, health, job and can avoid the problem of exhaustion, depression, ill health, burnout and breakdown which are associated with long term occupational stress.

Objectives Of The Study

1. To study the views of Doctors (Psychiatrics) and Psychologists about the various types of Occupational Stress found in Haryana State.
2. To study the suggestions and opinions given by Doctors (Psychiatrics) and Psychologists to reduce the effects of Occupational Stress in Haryana State.

Methodology of the Study

The sample of the study was purposefully selected. The Ten Doctors (Psychiatrics) and Ten Psychologists of Haryana were selected for the study of Occupational Stress in Haryana and the various suggestions given by them to reduce its effects in Haryana.

Tools Used For Data Collection

An Interview of Ten Doctors (Psychiatrics) of Haryana and Ten Psychologists of Haryana were conducted regarding the various types of Occupational Stress found in Haryana and their suggestions to reduce its effects. The Interview had twentyfive (25) structured and open-ended questions to collect the knowledge of various types of Occupational Stress found in Haryana and suggestions of the Experts to reduce its effects.

Procedure and Data Collection

Data were collected by the researchers through personal visits to ten, eminent and expert doctors (psychiatrics) of Haryana and ten famous psychologists of Haryana asking Twenty five (25) structured and open ended questions regarding various types of Occupational Stress found in Haryana and suggestions or opinions given by them to reduce its effects.

[I] Views of Doctors (Psychiatrics) and Psychologists of Haryana regarding various types of occupational stress found in the state.

- What are the **Survival Stress** cases found in Haryana?

  In views of Doctors (Psychiatrics) and Psychologist the **Survival Stress** cases found in Haryana are 12%. It may occur when your survival and health is threatened when you are put under pressure or when you experience some unpleasant and challenging event. Adrenaline is increased in your body and you experience all the symptoms of your body preparing for fight and flight.

- What are your views regarding **Internally Generated Occupational Stress in Haryana ?**

  According to Doctors (Psychiatrics) and Psychologists, cases of internally generated Occupational Stress cases found in Haryana are 10%. Internal generated Occupational Stress cases have anxious worry about the events which are beyond their control from a tense hurried approach of life or from relationship problems caused by one's behaviour. It can also come from an "addiction to" and enjoyment of occupational stress.

- What are your views regarding **Occupational Environmental Stress** cases in Haryana?

  In views of Doctors (Psychiatrics) and Psychologist regarding occupational environmental stress, cases found in Haryana are 10%. They explained that it may come from noise, crowding, pollution, untidiness, dirt or other distraction which may come from events at work.

- What are your views regarding **Fatigue and Overwork causing Occupational Stress** cases in Haryana ?

  In views of Doctors (Psychiatrics) and Psychologists regarding fatigue and overwork occupational stress, cases found in Haryana are 10%. It develops over a long period. This can occur where you try to achieve too much in too little time over, or when you are not using effective time management strategies.

- What are your views regarding **Physical and Emotional Occupational Stress** cases in Haryana?

  Doctors (Psychiatrics) and Psychologists say that physically and emotionally occupational stress cases in Haryana are 8%. It may occur when your body adapts to help it react more effectively to meet the threat. This is controlled mainly by release of adrenaline, which mobilizes sugars, reduces blood supply to skin and other organs and it can cause nausea and diarrhoea. Threat causes fear which help to survive or perform better but prolonged exposure to adrenaline can cause ill health.

- What are your views regarding **Anxiety Occupational Stress** cases in Haryana ?

  In views of Doctors (Psychiatrics) and Psychologists,anxiety occupational stress cases found in Haryana are 15%. It may occur when you feel concerned that circumstances are out of control. In some cases, being anxious and worrying over a problem may generate a stress hormone which results in negative thinking.

- What are your views regarding **Chemical and Nutritional Occupational Stress** cases in Haryana ?

In views of Doctors (Psychiatrics) and Psychologists, chemical and nutritional occupational stress cases found in Haryana are 20%. The food you eat may contribute to stress experience. Examples are (1) **Caffeine**:- This raises the levels of Stress Hormones,thereby making it more difficult to sleep and can make you more irritable. (2) **Excessive sugar from sweets and chocolate**:- This can make you feel more energetic in the short term, however, your body reacts to stabilize abnormally high sugar levels, by releasing too much insulin This causes a serious energy dip shortly after a sugar high. (3) **Too much salt:-** This raises your blood pressure, and puts your body under chemical stress.Doctors suggested that if you take an unbalanced or unhealthy diet, some dietary deficiency or excess may occur causing discomfort and illness which generates stress.

- What are your views regarding **Occupational Lifestyle Stress** cases in Haryana ?

According to Doctors (Psychiatrics) and Psychologists regarding occupational lifestyle stress cases found in Haryana are 15%. Such type of occupational lifestyle stress cases may come from your occupation and lifestyle, which includes (1) Too much or too little work (2) Having to perform beyond your experience (3) Having to overcome unnecessary obstacles (4) Time pressure deadlines (5) Keeping up with new developments (6) Changes in the procedures and policies (7) Lack of relevant information, support and advise (8) Lack of clear objectives (9) Under promotion- Frustration (10) Lack of job security (11) Personal and family stresses (12) Financial problems (13) Relationship problems.

- What are your views regarding **Short Term Physical Symptoms of Occupational Stress cases** in Haryana?

Views of Doctors (Psychiatrics) of Psychologists regarding short term physical symptoms of occupational stress cases in Haryana are that it causes physical threat / fear, releases adrenaline and assists in survival or high performance, which includes (1) Faster heart beat (2) Increased sweating (3) Cool skin (4) Cold hands and feet (5) Nausea (6) Rapid breathing (7) Tense muscles (8) Dry Mouth (9) Desire to urinate (10) Diarrhoea.

Various Types of Occupational Stress Cases (%) found in Haryana

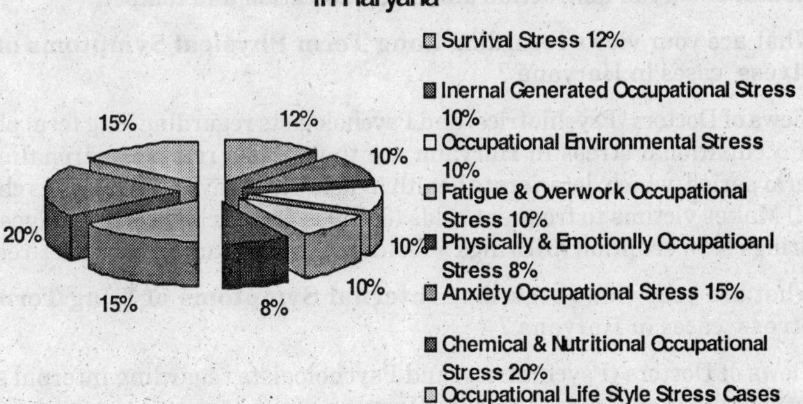

Various Types of Occupational Stress Cases (%) found in Haryana

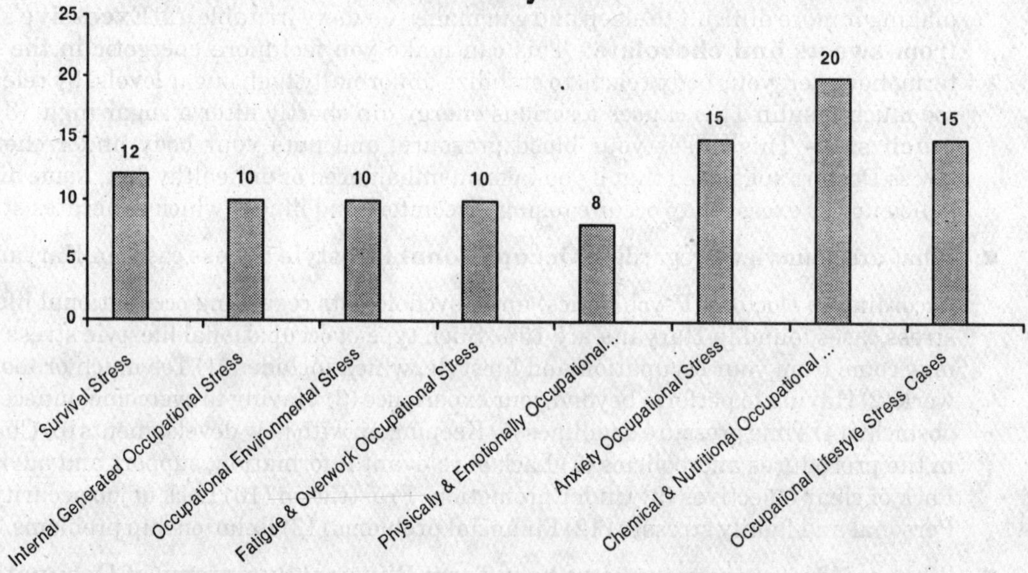

- What are your views regarding **Short Term Performance Effects of Occupational Stress** cases in Haryana ?

  Views of Doctors (Psychiatrics) and Psychologists regarding short term performance effects of occupational stress cases in Haryana are that it releases adrenaline which help you to cope with a "Fight or Flight "situation and it has negative effects in such situations which include (1) Interference with clear judgment (2) Promotes negative thinking (3) Damages self - confidence (4) Affects focus and concentration (5) Consumes mental energy in distraction anxiety, frustration and temper.

- What are your views regarding **Long Term Physical Symptoms of Occupational Stress** cases in Haryana ? .

  Views of Doctors (Psychiatrics) and Psychologists regarding long term physical symptoms of occupational stress in Haryana are that it also releases adrenaline for over a long term period, which deteriorate health in following ways :- (1) It brings changes in appetite (2) Makes victims to frequent colds (3)Gives headache (4) Gives digestive problems (5) Brings skin eruption (6)Brings a feeling of intense and long term tiredness.

- What are your views regarding **Internal Symptoms of Long Term Occupational Stress** cases in Haryana ?

  Views of Doctors (Psychiatrics) and Psychologists regarding internal symptoms of long term occupational stress cases in Haryana are that any person under a stress for a long period, is less able to think clearly and rationally about problems which can lead to the following internal emotional upsets:(1) Worry or anxiety (2)Confusion (3) Feeling ill (4) Feeling out of control (5) Mood changes (6) Frustration (7) Hostility (8) Restlessness.

- What are your views regarding **Behavioural Symptoms of Long Term Occupational Stress** cases in Haryana ?

  Views of Doctors (Psychiatrics) and Psychologists regarding behavioural symptoms of long term occupational stress cases in Haryana are that when a person is under pressure dealing with long term Occupational Stress, he can show following behavioral changes: (1) Talking too fast or too loud (2) Yawning (3) Nail biting and grinding teeth (4) Bad aggressive mood (5) Reacting emotionally (6) Unreasonably negative (7) Being unable to concentrate (8) Difficulty in making decisions (9) More forgetful (10) Making mistakes (11) More absenteeism.

- How **Long Term Occupational Stress become out of control** in Haryana ?

  Views of Doctors (Psychiatrics) and Psychologists regarding long term occupational stress becoming out of control in Haryana are that the effects of long term Occupational Stress can be out of control if Occupational Stress is more severe and you do not take any action to control it, which can lead to (1) Fatigue (2) Exhaustion (3) Depression (4) Burnout or Breakdown.

[II] Suggestions or Opinions given by Doctors (Psychiatrics) and Psychologists to reduce the effects of Occupational Stress in Haryana State.

- What are the **Occupational Stress Reduction Techniques for Anticipation & Avoidance** for Haryana stressors.

  Views of Doctors (Psychiatrics) and Psychologists regarding occupational stress reduction techniques for anticipation and avoidance in Haryana are: (1) Anticipation :- By anticipation, you can prepare for it and work out how to control it when it happens.(2) Avoidance :- Where a situation is likely to be unpleasant and will not yield any benefit to you, you may avoid it . There are other ways like (1) Rehearsal (2) Planning to reduce the Occupational Stress.

- What do you understand by **Reducing the Importance of Event to Reduce Occupational Stress** in Haryana?

  Views of Doctors (Psychiatrics) and of Psychologists regarding reducing the importance of event to reduce occupational stress in Haryana are that there are number of factors which can make an event a high level of significance depending upon (1) The importance and size of event (2) The prospect of large financial award (3) The presence of family, friends or important people.

- How **Negative Thinking can be made into Positive Thinking** to reduce Occupational Stress in Haryana?

  Views of Doctors (Psychiatrics) and Psychologists regarding change of negative thinking into positive thinking can be adopted to reduce occupational stress. Negative thinking which causes Occupational Stress and damages your confidence, and paralyses mental skills can be arranged into positive thinking by following ways :- (1) Eliminate negative thoughts. (2) Review them rationally. See whether the thoughts have basic reality or truthfulness. (3) Make positive affirmations: (a) I can do this work (b) I can achieve my goals (c) I am in complete control of my life. (d) I can learn from my mistakes.

- **Occupational Stress can be reduced by Self Hypnosis** in

Views of Doctors (Psychiatrics) and Psychologists regarding reducing occupational stress by self hypnosis in Haryana is that with affirmation and suggestion, the unconscious mind can get rid of occupational stress and induce relaxation.

- How **Suggestions and Affirmations can reduce** occupational stress in Stressors?

Views of Doctors (Psychiatrics) and Psychologists are that before you enter a hypnotic state , it is useful to think about suggestions that you want to apply. Suggestions can be simple affirmations that undo the damage caused by negative thinking.

- How **Meditation is helpful in reducing Occupational Stress** in Haryana?

Views of Doctors (Psychiatrics) and Psychologists regarding role of meditation in reducing occupational stress is that meditation quickens your thoughts by focusing completely on just one thing. It seeks to exclude thoughts by concentrating all mental faculties on the subject of meditation. In meditation lotus position or sitting in a comfortable chair or lying in a bed for 20-30 minutes in an effective posture and number of different postures may be used

How **Anger Management is helpful in reducing Occupational Stress** in Haryana?

Psychiatrists and Psychologists advise that to reduce both our emotional feelings and the physiological arousal that anger causes, we can learn the various methods to control our angry reactions.

- **What are the Physical relaxations Techniques for reducing Occupational Stress in** Haryana?

Psychiatrists and Psychologists recommend this type of Occupational Stress reduction technique when occupational stress is caused by physical processes in your body where muscles are tense or where you are experiencing the effects of adrenaline: (1) Taking Exercise (2) Breathing Control. These can reduce stress.

- What are the **Techniques for reducing Long Term Occupational Stress in** Haryana?

Long term Occupational Stress can be reduced by adjusting your working methods - your lifestyle. Formal relaxation techniques are part of it but equally important are (1) Time management skills (2) A positive attitude (3) A healthy or balanced diet (4) Sufficient exercise (5) Adequate rest (6) Pleasant environment (7) Pleasant environment includes (a) Good air quality (b) Lighting (c) Decoration (d) No noise

- What are the **Suggestions for Treatment of Severe Depression cases** in Haryana Stressors ?

In Views of Doctors (Psychiatrics) and Psychologists regarding treatment of severe depression, severely depressed patients should be properly examined by expert psychologists and their detailed reports or summary of patient should be properly analyzed and confirmed by the medical investigations and finally the patients of depressions should take the treatment under the guidance of expert Doctors (Psychiatrics) and not on their own or from quacks.

Conclusion

The various suggestions given by Doctors (Psychiatrics) and Pschyologists reveal the following key points :-

That the Occupational Stress you experience is something that is largely under your control.

Occupational Stress can come from a range of different sources.

Short Term Occupational Stress occurs where you find yourself under pressure in a particular situation.

A certain level of short term occupational stress is needed to feel alert and alive.

Too much is unpleasant and can seriously damage performance.

Short term occupational stress occurrences is best handled using mental or physical stress management techniques.

Long term occupational stress comes from a buildup of stress over a long period.

Sustained high levels can lead to serious physical and mental illness if not controlled.

Long term occupational stress is best managed by changes in lifestyle, attitude and environment.

By using a stress report you can monitor and understand the causes of occupational stress in your life. The complete report can help you to evaluate your performance under occupational stress.

Once you understand what is causing you occupational stress, you can make an action plan for Occupational Stress Management. This gives you positive goals to work towards.

References

1. How to enjoy your life and your job : Selections from How to Win Friends and Influence People and How to Stop Worrying and Start Living (1986), Dale Carnegie/Mass Market Paperback.
2. The Book of Stress Survival – How to Relax and Live Positively (1986), Alix Kirsta/Thorsons.
3. 60 Second Stress Management : The Quickest Way to Relax and Ease Anxiety (1992), Andrew Goliszek.
4. The Wellness Book : The Comprehensive Guide to Maintaining Health and Treating Stress Related illness (1993) Herbert, M.D., Benson, *et. al.*
5. The Big Book of Relaxation : Simple Techniques to Control the Excess Stress in You (1994) Larry Blumenfield (Editor), *et. al.*
6. Adrenaline and Stress/the Exciting New Breakthrough That Helps You Overcome Stress Damage(1995), Archibald D. Hart.
7. Instant Calm : Over 100 Easy – To- Use Technique for Relaxing Mind and Body (1995), Paul Wilson.
8. Relaxation and Stress Reduction Workbook (1995), Matthew McKay, *et. al.*

9. Conscious Breathing : Breath work for Health, Stress Release and Personal Mastery (1997), Gay Hendricks/Audio Cassette.

10. From Panic to Power : Proven Techniques to Calm Your Anxieties, Conquer Your Fear, Put you in Control of your life (1997), Lucinda Bassett.

11. Stress Relieving Techniques- Written by Thedy Harrill Article Submitted 15 Nov., 2006.

12. Understanding and Managing Stress – Written by Denise Lammi and David Wojtowicz – Article Submitted on 10th March 2006.

13. Reduce your stress and be Happier – Written by Kathryn Beach- Article submitted on 18th May 2006.

14. Ultimate Stress Management- Written By Cathy Gariety, RN, Professional Life Coach- Article Submitted date on 21st September 2006.

15. Unique Stress Relievers- Written by Kathy Thompson Article submitted on 30th December 2006.

16. Audio Cassette of Interview of Ten expert Doctors (Psychiatrics) & Ten Psychologists of Haryana made by researcher in Nov. 2006

http://stress-guided.com.

http://www.mindtools.com

http://www.springer-sbm.com

✲ ✲ ✲

7

GOOD WORKLIFE AND RELATIONSHIPS: A CONCEPTUAL STUDY

** Mr. Sushil Kumar*
*** Mr. Rohtas Kumar*
**** Dr. D. P. Warne*

* Research Scholar, Department of Commerce, Chaudary Devi Lal University, Sirsa.

** Lecturer, Department of Business Economics, Chaudary Devi Lal University, Sirsa.

*** Chairperson & Reader Department of Commerce, Chaudary Devi Lal University, Sirsa.

Introduction

The behaviour of family members is becoming more individualized, and in the community people are becoming at odds with their neighbours, many people playing very little part in the activities of neighbourhood or resident associations. Relationships outside work are also declining and the extent to which people are identified by the company in which they work for, is starting to move away. There are many possible reasons for these changes, and some of these may be the following. First is transformation in the economic and social environment. Increase in the numbers of employees and single households are weakening community ties and changes in traditional employment practices are weakening ties in the workplace; Second is improvements in quality of life. For example, with one television set per person and the evolution of home gaming machines, it is possible that family members are becoming more individualized.

It is also likely that the progress of information technology such as e-mail is leading to more chances for people to work alone

In today's world people do not want close relationships within the community and workplace, the recent tendency is to have such relationships which lead to a less degree of disturbance. So in the present paper we have decided to study about the impact of these weak relationships on improvement of work life and possible directions to rebuild these relationships.

Impact of Weak Relationship on Work Life

Weakening of relationships may influence the work and personal life in various ways. The ways in which the weak relationship can affect the work life can be divided into the following parts.

Impact on Spiritual Comfort

There are various type of relationship that brings spiritual comfort and a sense of fulfillment, such as the peace of mind afforded by being with one's family or the feeling of achievement at having participated in a community activity Due to weak relationships, mind can be adversely affected. Weakening of ties now prevents people from enjoying the effects of relationships that existed in the past. Though there has been an emphasis on spiritual well-being in recent years, people will not feel any richness in their daily lives if they are unable to obtain mental comfort and a sense of fulfillment because of the weak relationships.

Impact on Social Values

Weak relationship can effect the creation of certain set of values required by society through help and cooperation with other people. These include disciplining children, guarding against fires and crime with other local people or making a concerted effort with one's colleagues to complete a project at work. If, discipline in households is inadequate, it is possible that it will affect the personalities and abilities of the next generation; if community's ability to provide the expected education, parental support, crime prevention and safety are impaired, this may also have an impact on the quality of life of the local people. In the workplace too, it is possible that people will feel more stressed out and this will effect the companies' results and the nation's economic vitality .

The inadequate provision of opportunities to form relationships

Lack of opportunities and information about participation in activities.Keep many people away from participating in community activities. For example part-timers and temporary workers may not have a strong urge to form relationship as they do not get many opprutunities to come together.

Directions for Rebuilding the Relationships

Considering the fact that the weakening of relationships is impacting people's lifestyles in various ways, the relations have to be rebuilt in order that the public can adequately enjoy their benefits. The following may be some important directions toward this end.

Remove The Restrictions On Maintaining Relationships

In reality, relationships are even weaker than what people are aware of. If the limitations placed upon relationships, the reasons due to which people cannot enter into relationships even if they want to do so, are be removed there is a hope that overall relationships can be improved. One important reason is time restrictions. Due to long working hours of fathers, the time spent by children on after-school studies and in front of their individual television sets is too long, the behaviour of family members is becoming individualized, and they are able to enjoy less time together. Salaried workers, whose time is restricted, are becoming particularly distanced from community activities. There must be opportunities to meet and develop new relationships for those who want. It is highly likely that the latent number of people wishing to participate in activities will increase greatly as the baby-boomer generation approaches retirement age. Currently, however, many older people who want to take part in local activities are not actually doing so because of barriers to participation such as, lack of friends to join in with or inadequate information about the details of activities. It is important that they be given opportunities to gradually build up relationships in the community before they approach retirement age. Against a background of increasing healthy life expectancy in the future, if all those who wish to do so become involved in community work, it may lead to the realization of communities that are even more attracted and in line with the needs of residents. In order to provide people with the sort of relationships that they are seeking, the restrictions indicated above must be removed.

Creation of Relationship in Harmony with Current Situations

Devising ways for relationships in harmony with the current situation within families, the community, and at the workplace is imperative. Changes in the economy and society, and improvements towards better quality of life and greater convenience are reasons responsible for these weakening relationships, but it is unrealistic to expect these contemporary trends to immediately change. This means that wisdom that can help to strengthen relationships has to be expended, even in the midst of these current trends. New forms of relationships suited to the current economy and society and to contemporary lifestyle patterns need to be created. There are examples of homes being designed in ways that prevent family members from becoming isolated, and provide them with chances to spend more time with each other in a natural way and promote a sense of solidarity according to their individual conditions. In the community, local activities that include the participation of professionals, who cannot take part on weekdays or during working hours, can also be observed.

Work-Life Balance Programmes

In order to support a balance between working and parenting, some companies have introduced work-life balance programmes such as childcare vacation schemes and shorter working hours. The introduction of such systems to support balance such as these are now recognized not only as being helpful in securing more time to devote to child-rearing at home, but for reviews on how jobs are carried out in the workplace and in the long term, to an atmosphere in which colleagues help each other, feel attached to their company and workplace and make a favorable effect on employee's sense of unity. There are also examples of cases in which encouraging people to take paid vacations has enabled them to secure more time to spend with their families. At the workplace too, some companies are offering those who wish to learn, regardless of their employment status, with opportunities for self development, and providing chances for employees to mix with each other, in order to encourage the vitalization of better working practices and communication. Elsewhere, efforts are being made to involve the community in child-rearing and care, rather than leaving these tasks entirely to families, and there are also some companies that are supporting parenting through work-life balance programmes.

Use of Information Technology

The growth of IT is removing the limitations of time and distance, and contributing to the provision of opportunities for new relationships. For example, people living far away from home can share information using mobile phones and e-mail, thus feeling a sense of togetherness with their families. In the community too, there are cases in which the use of social networking services (SNS) and other services is enlivening local activities.

Create an Environment to Maintain Relationships

There is need to create an environment in which relationships can be maintained. Relationships between people will not be formed unless individuals make their own choices. The type of relationships that people choose in order to enrich their lives is, in the final analysis, an individual choice. The government must not try to foist particular types of relationships upon people. However, since there are people who would like to but cannot have relationships, the government should put the following measures into practice and create an environment in which it is easier for people to maintain the relationships that they need.

Raising the People's Awareness about Relationships

Another measure to improve the relationship is to raise the people's awareness about relationships. In many cases, it is only when they enter into relationships that people first realize their true values. It is possible that some people have yet to realize the value of relationships and are reluctant to enter into them. It is therefore essential that steps are taken to raise awareness and enable people to appreciate the value of relationships so that they can enjoy comfortable work life on the basis of good relationship with each others.

Conclusion

Thus in the end, we can say that by creating a comfortable work life for the people through relationships in a society, in which each and every citizen enjoys pleasant relationships, gets opportunities to relax and spend life in comfort social bonds can be solidified. Interaction with the family can bring tranquility to people in the community too, ties between people and activities can provide services that precisely meet the needs of residents and this surely brings security and peace of mind. Furthermore, if the relationships and communication sought after in the workplace are achieved, people will probably be able to continue working with a renewed vigor. It is also thought that creating an environment in which people can have the relationships they want and sharing the importance of relationships, could lead to a stemming of the trend towards individualism and moves towards this are already underway. And it is to be hoped that this will lead not only to enjoyment of life, but also to improvement in mindset of our workforce which lead to better productivity which is beneficial for both companies and society both.

References

1. Martino (2003) **'Relationship between work stress and workplace violence in the health sector'** v.dimartino@worldonlinc.fr
2. Chris and Smith (2005) **'Extending working life: A review of the research literature'** Department for Work and Pensions Research Report No 299.
3. Mahi (2006) **'Increasing Availability and Take Up In New Zealand'** Discussion Paper.
4. Hartley Dean and Alice Coulter (2006) **'Work-Life Balance in a Low-Income Neighbourhood'**, Centre for Analysis of Social Exclusion, London School of Economics.
5. Tad W. Patzek (2007) **'How Can We Outlive Our Way of Life?'** Department of Civil and Environmental Engineering the University of California Berkeley, CA 94720 patzek@patzek.berkeley.edu

✡ ✡ ✡

8

Organizational Stress: A Silent Killer on the Prowl

** Rajan Sidhar*

*** Dr. Bimal Anjum*

**** Girish Nayyar*

* Sr. Lecturer, GNIMT. Model town, Ludhiana.

** HOD Management Department (AP), RIMT (Institute of Management & Technology), Mandi, Gobindgarh.

*** Sr. Lecturer, RIMT (Institute of Management & Technology), Mandi, Gobindgarh.

Business world is buzzing today with economic activities at their best. In our modern history, we have neither expected, nor seen such a great economic scene, ever. Indian business is at its best. There is a lot of expansion of business within the boundaries as well as beyond the boundaries. Manufacturing as well as Service industry, is operating at the best possible efficiency. Indian market was known to be cost effective in the previous era, but today multinational companies are establishing their bases in India, not only due to cost benefits but also because they are well aware of the fact that Indians are highly efficient in achieving their goals.

In the pursuit of perfection and to optimally use the resources, employees in the organizations are under tremendous stress. Some kind of stress is always welcome to bring out the best from the workers, but it has been observed that east is falling in the same trap, where west has fallen and trying to free itself in vain.

Stress can have other reasons as well, like environmental and individual stress. But unlike west, the resources with our organizations are scanty, and generally this aspect is either ignored or overlooked. Balance sheets of an organization would never mention the manhours lost, health auditing of employees, and loss of interest of the workers at work. But truth behind these healthy balance sheets is, low morale of employees, over stressed workers, poor family life and poor health, which is resulting in national loss, in terms of spending of savings by these workers, on the stress related disorders. Some times, these disorders results serious ailments, and the end results are disastrous.

Various studies done in BPO and service related industry have established the fact that young people who are working in these organizations are suffering from various ailments, and the situation is worsening with every passing day. Some of the companies are taking remedial measures, but these are insufficient and are not helping the employees. Situation in the case of Small Scale Industry and Small and Medium enterprises is still more alarming.

The Irony is that these workers are either semi-skilled or unskilled and working in the unorganized sector. They are migratory in nature and hardly able to meet their ends. Government and NGOs are not reaching them and the result is that they are left with no other choice but to end their life in despair.

This paper is an attempt to find the causes behind stress in the industry and suggest the remedial measures to get the best out of the workers and make their working place a second home, where they can enjoy and earn their livelihood with peace, calm and tranquility.

Symptoms of Stress

As stated earlier, stress is caused by or reaction to the external events and brings about changes in our response and general behaviour. The presence of stress can be estimated by the analysis of certain symptoms an individual shows. These symptoms can be divided into three different categories. They are Feelings, Behaviour and Physiology. When an individual experience stress, one or more of the following symptoms can be exhibited.

Feelings

- The individual becomes anxious about the outcomes, and is scared. He feels that he has got something to loose or something wrong will take place.

- In an anxious state, a person does not want to be corrected or interrupted. He looks out for other areas where he can forget about the stress-causing event for a while. The person becomes irritable and moody.
- During high levels of stress, the individual develops a negative frame of mind and suffers from low self-esteem. He loses faith in his capabilities, and is afraid of failures. The individual does not have a focused approach, is unable to concentrate and is involved in his own plans and thoughts.

It is necessary to understand the reasons as well as the dynamics behind the generation of stress in the organizations. Organizations are just like our second home, where we spend maximum time. If the work place is the source of stress, then one cannot hope to get best out of the employees. Various reasons that have been identified by the various researchers are:

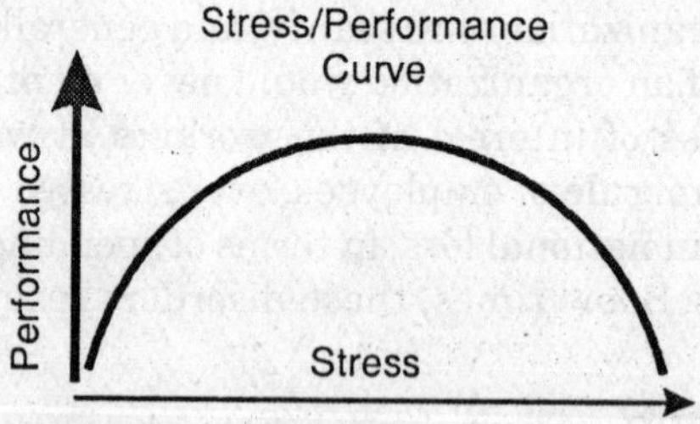

Organizational Factors Causing Stress

Dynamic nature of organization and ever changing environment

Message is obvious : change or perish. Business landscape is changing with every passing day. India has become the hub of BPOs, private banks are giving tough competition to the public sector banks, government is planning to privatize the non-essential services and some parts of the essential services are being privatized as well. FIIs are the major investors in India and service industry is becoming stronger. All this makes Indian scenario a tough one and the brunt is being borne by the employees working at various positions. Every person is running faster to save himself and to win this race. Under such conditions stress in the lives of people is clearly visible.

Rise of globalization is resulting in diversity and increased uncertainty in the business. Traditional Indian organizations have worked long under the license raj and protection, but suddenly, opening up of the economy and entrance of MNCs, bringing in new culture of quality and innovativeness, has shaken the industry from inside. Market is free for all now. Globalization has brought new culture and people from the diverse cultures in India. There is going to be a demand of 4000 pilots in India by 2010. Already, there are around 800 pilots from other countries, working with Indian air carriers. It is true about the various IT companies of India. All this makes Indian employees to work harder, to match the efficiencies of these people.

Business has become very uncertain these days due to open boundries. China and other developing economies are performing really well and they can give fierce competition to the Indian companies. This stress has percolated down to the employess as well. The state of Indian sports industry is an example how Chinese companies have destroyed this industry and made employees of this industry unemployed. Certain products in the sports industry are being only imported and not manufactured in India now. Same is true about some other products at Jalandhar and hosiery industry at Ludhiana.

Gender bias in the Indian organizations

Indian society is a traditional society and it was generally male dominated. But in the past, women power has increased due to their financial independence by working in the industry. Still in SSI and SMEs, not many women are heading the organizations. There is frequent uproar about the glass ceiling for the women executives in the organizations. Women workers are under tremendous stress in the organizations due to this factor and there is lack of motivation.

High-Stress Times with No "Down" Times: Many jobs and industries have "crunch times", where workers must work longer hours and handle a more intense workload for a time. This can actually help people feel invigorated if the extra effort is recognized, appropriately compensated and is in limits. It starts becoming problematic when "crunch time" occurs year-round and there's no time for workers to recover.

Overwork and Resistance to Change

People working in the organizations are either overworked or do not have time to complete the tasks. Some times they are in too much of multi-tasks. This creates a web of stress for them.

Poor Leadership: Company leadership can go a long way toward preventing or contributing to burnout. For example, depending on the leadership, employees can feel recognized for their achievements, supported when they have difficulties, valued, safe, etc. Or they can feel unappreciated, unrecognized, unfairly treated, not in control of their activities, insecure in their position and unsure of the requirements of their jobs

Individual Factors

- **Unclear Requirements:** When it's not clear to workers *how* to succeed, it's harder for them to be confident, enjoy their work, and feel they're doing a good job. If the job description isn't explained clearly, if the requirements are constantly changing and hard to understand or if expectations are otherwise unclear, workers are at higher risk of burnout.
- **Impossible Requirements:** Sometimes it's just not possible to do a job as it's explained. If a job's responsibilities exceed the amount of time given to complete them properly, for example, it's really not possible to do the job well. Workers will put in a lot of effort and never feel quite successful.
- **Big Consequences for Failure:** People make mistakes, it's part of being human. However, when there are dire consequences to the occasional mistakes (like the risk of a lawsuit, for example), the overall work experience becomes much more stressful, and the risk of burnout goes up. (This is part of why nurses have such a high rate of burnout.)
- **Lack of Personal Control:** People tend to feel excited about what they're doing, when they are able to creatively decide what needs to be done, and come up with ways of handling problems that arise. Generally speaking, workers who feel restricted and unable to exercise personal control over their environment and daily decisions tend to be at greater risk for burnout.

- **Lack of Recognition:** It's difficult to work hard and never be recognized for one's accomplishments. Awards, public praise, bonuses and other tokens of appreciation and recognition of accomplishment, go a long way in keeping morale high. Where accolades are scarce, burnout is a risk.
- **Financial Problems:** India economy is at its best these days. It has resulted in launching of product and services which were available in only western world few years ago. Indian service class is in a dilemma to cope with this change. Cost of living has increased manifold. This has resulted in financial problems.

Remedies to avoid Stress

Clear Clutter

Many stressed people live in cluttered homes. But, house clutter is both an effect and a cause of stress. Clutter can bring a general feeling of uneasiness and can literally drain your energy, but getting rid of it is difficult for stressed people with busy schedules. One strategy to simplify life, by clearing clutter, is to take 15 or 30 minutes each night to tackle one pile at a time, decluttering your house, space by space. Another strategy is to take several hours, one weekend and just be done with it. Either way, you'll remove a subtle but significant energy drain from your life, and replace it with the feelings of relaxation that comes from having your home as a haven of peace.

Cut Out Negative Relationships

You may already be aware of the value of solid, supportive relationships in your life — the friend who picks you up when you are down, celebrates with you when you're happy and shares events in your life as they happen. You may not be aware of the effects of conflicted relationships — the critical, unpredictable, or nagging friends; It turns out that these 'toxic friendships' actually drain us more than purely negative relationships. This is because we don't always have strong defenses against the people who are sometimes nice to us, so we can be taken off-guard. If you're wondering how to simplify life, save yourself from grief, frustration and drama, if you take an honest look at the relationships in your life and decide which are **worth maintaining** and which you should **let go**.

Automate What You Can

Getting some of the daily, weekly and monthly work of your life into an automated system can help simplify life and relieve stress in two ways: You don't have to take time to do the work and you don't have to clutter your mind by remembering to do the work. Setting up automatic timers to water your plants or turn off your lights, signing up for automatic bill pay options or getting off junk mail lists can be an easy way to simplify life. By putting in a little initial work, you can then forget about it.

Live Within Your Means

To say that money can't buy happiness is cliche, and research has supported it as well. The truth, is that money can't even buy you out of **financial stress** if you don't spend less than what you make. Many people who make large amounts of money simply spend more and carry large amounts of debt, leading to feelings of stress rather than abundance. The key to avoiding this type of financial stress is simple, but not always easy: Live within your means. This can be a difficult change at first, but one that will bring great rewards and can significantly lower your stress levels if you're not living within your means already.

Learn To Say No

While many people spend as much money as they possibly can, leaving themselves feeling stretched to the limit, too many of us also budget our time this way. With demands from work, school and life in general, it's easy to become overscheduled these days. However, if you're always rushing from one place to another, you may find yourself exhausted, but with no time left to relax. While most of us have busy schedules these days, it's important to schedule in time for exercise, hobbies and other stress relievers, as well as time for our relationships. One way to find this time is to get better at **saying no** to time demands that aren't serving you. After you trade some of your more taxing obligations with some more self-nurturing ones, you should see a lasting change in your stress level and find yourself living a more simplified life.

Become aware of your stressors and your emotional and physical reactions

Notice your distress. Don't ignore it. Don't gloss over your problems. Determine what events distress you. What are you telling yourself about meaning of these events? Determine how your body responds to stress. Do you become nervous or physically upset?

Recognize what you can change

Can you change your stressors by avoiding or eliminating them completely? Can you reduce their intensity (manage them over a period of time instead of dealing on a daily or weekly basis)? Can you shorten your exposure to stress (take a break, leave the physical premises)?

Can you devote the time and energy necessary to making a change (goal setting, time management techniques, and delayed gratification strategies may be helpful here)?

Reduce the intensity of your emotional reactions to stress

The stress reaction is triggered by your perception of danger...physical danger and/or emotional danger. Are you viewing your stressors in exaggerated terms and/or taking a difficult situation and making it a disaster? Are you expecting to please everyone?

Learn to moderate your physical seactions to stress

Slow, deep breathing will bring your heart rate and respiration back to normal. Relaxation techniques can reduce muscle tension. Electronic biofeedback can help you gain voluntary control over such things as muscle tension, heartbeat and blood pressure.

Medications, when prescribed by a physician, can help in moderating your physical reactions. However, they alone are not the answer. Learning to moderate these reactions on your own is a preferable long-term solution.

Build your physical reserves

Exercise for cardio-vascular fitness, three to four times a week (moderate, prolonged rhythmic exercise is the best, such as, walking, swimming, cycling, or jogging). Eat well-balanced, nutritious meals. Maintain your ideal weight.

Avoid nicotine, excessive caffeine and other stimulants. Mix leisure with work. Take breaks and get away when you can. Get enough sleep. Be as consistent with your sleep schedule as possible.

Maintain your emotional reserves

Develop some mutually supportive friendships/relationships. Pursue realistic goals that are meaningful to you, rather than goals others have for you that you do not share. Expect some frustrations, failures, and sorrows. Always be kind and gentle with yourself — be a friend to yourself.

Get a hobby or two, relax and have fun: Talk with friends or someone you can trust about your worries/problems.

Choose the right job During interviews, ask the questions that help you make sure the job's right for you. Get a realistic picture of the company or department's culture, working relationships, problems and hidden agendas.

Maintain a sense of personal power A study of high-pressure work environments by Essi, a San Francisco research firm, shows one factor that predicts, which employees would become ill and which stay healthy: people's perception of their personal power or lack of it. Personal power is defined as how much control you feel you have over your life, your ability to function and express yourself.

Be flexible Recognize and accept that things change. If you need to hold on tightly to the status quo, you need to loosen up. Think of your organization as a space ship. It's constantly correcting its course "to go where no man has gone before" in the marketplace. You have to change with it. Be pro-active. You're in a better position to maneuver if you are primed and ready.

Adjust your attitude Your attitude—how you make others feel about you and how you make them feel about themselves—can make or break your future

Organizational Efforts to reduce Stressful Conditions in their Premises

Starting Employee recognition programmes : Good work must be appreciated and employees who are contributing more towards the organization must be recognized and awarded.

Employee involvement programmes

Employees should be involved in the policy making and particularly in the change strategies.

Conflict handling machinery

Very active and mature executives should handle the conflicts efficiently and effectively.

Career development programmes

Companies may arrange career development for the employee which will send positive signals to them.

Spirituality in the organization

In the organization, spirituality should be promoted in different forms. Yoga is known for its stress removing abilities.

Proper organization structure

Clearly laid authority, responsibility and accountability would help the organization to destress its employee and there will be less scope for cribbing and conflicts.

Uniform and strong ethical organization culture

Every organization should develop a strong organization culture and it will help the employees to understand the expectations of the organization and they will be better adjusted in the environment. More stress should be given on ethics.

Stimulating Innovation

There are always some employees in the organization who are highly energetic and creative. Organization must provide them innovative and novel ways to express themselves. Injection of innovation in the organization will help in spreading a positive energy in the organization. It can help the employee to be in the up-mood, even in the times of stress.

Transparency and openness

Senior executives should work with transparency, and they should be open to the suggestions and ideas from the subordinates. An environment of mutual trust and faith should prevail in the organization.

✫ ✫ ✫

9

STRESS MANAGEMENT IN INFORMATION TECHNOLOGY SECTOR

*Mrs. Himani Sharma
** Dr. Sultan Singh

* Lecturer, Department of Business Administration, Ch. Devi Lal University, Sirsa.

** Reader, Department of Business Administration, Ch. Devi Lal University, Sirsa.

Introduction

Stress is a psychological and physiological response to events that upset our personal balance in some way. These events or demands are known as stressors. We usually think of stressors as being negative, such as an exhausting work schedule or a rocky relationship. However, anything that forces us to adjust can be a stressor. This includes positive events such as getting married or receiving a promotion. Regardless of whether an event is good or bad, if it strain our coping skills and adaptive resources, the end result is the subjective feeling of stress and body's biological stress response. While stress is readily acknowledged to be a common feature of modern life, defining stress, its causes, symptoms and effects is a very complex matter. It is often characterized as a primitive stone-age reaction to modern organizational and social factors, known as stressors. Stress, the responses our bodies and minds have to the demands placed on them, is a normal part of life and a normal part of any job.

Without stress, we wouldn't meet deadlines, strive to hit sales or production targets, or line up new clients. Meeting the demands and challenges of a job is part of what makes work interesting and satisfying, and it's often what allows people to develop new skills and advance in their careers. In the workplace, we regularly experience stress-causing situations, react to them with heightened tension and then return to a more relaxed state when the crisis, big or small, is resolved. However, problems occur when stress is so overwhelming or constant that the tension never abates and we never get to relax.

What we think of as "job stress" in I.T. sector is what happens when the challenges and demands of work become excessive. The pressures of the workplace surpass workers' abilities to handle them. When stress crosses the line from normal to excessive, it can trigger physical and emotional responses that are harmful to employees and businesses alike. And unfortunately, for many people "stress" has become synonymous with "work".

The paper consists of four sections. Section-I discusses the Review of Literature. Section-II presents research methodology. Section-III presents signs and symptoms of stress. Section-IV is on analysis and interpretation. Section-V suggests tips for stress reduction and Section-VI offers conclusion.

Section I: Review of Bygone Studies

Sandra, Hartington, Mills, Angela, G. Stern (1989) has drawn attention towards factors which create stress for women managers; it is essential that companies do recognise these specific stresses and create a policy to deal with them. The authors look at the role of stress management courses, and what stress management policies should include, for example, seeing the company as a source of stress and addressing issues, such as communications, to combat this.

Peter (1989) hypothesised that there is an increasing gap between organisations' concerns about stress at work and what the standard stress management training courses provide. To tackle this hypothesis, two questions are asked. Why do organisations demand interventions to help manage stress, and what interventions do the stress management suppliers provide? It is tentatively concluded that what is required is, to deal directly with organisational issues, such as workaholic expectations and changes at work, which are not often dealt with by stress management programmes. Three approaches are suggested to confront these sorts of issues directly: team building, management action groups and one to one development counselling.

Tanya, Arroba, Kim, James (1990) presented a model of organisational stress management, as a four stage process, comprising: getting the organisation to recognise stress; training individuals in stress management; providing helping skills; and providing a stress audit. It is argued that each of these stages involves a series of interesting tasks that can be either facilitated or hindered by a range of organizational supports or constraints. The management of stress is of major importance to all management functions – not only personnal – in the light of its heavy potential costs.

T. Foot (1991) discusses the nature of stress and methods of stress management. He considers behaviour and lifestyle as factors causing stress and provides a questionnaire to test managerial skill in recognizing stress. He states that stress management is the re-education of people to use existing coping strategies, rather than a substitute for those strategies.

Marie, McHugh, Shirley (1992) stresses that if organization development is to achieve the objective of improving organizational effectiveness, it is essential that companies adopt a proactive and preventive approach to stress management. Such an approach would reduce the costs of stress which result directly from organization development, and additionally, the costs of previously existing stress factors such as high labour turnover, absenteeism and reduced productivity. A practical all-encompassing model has been presented which brings the organization towards a philosophy of "total stress management" (TSM).

Lawrence, R., Murphy (1995) starts from the premises that stress at work is a significant and costly problem, and that the challenge for companies is to manage work stress, in order to reduce health-care costs and improve productivity. He suggests that this challenge can be met, with greater collaboration among company departments, and by bringing expertise from different areas to bear on the problem. He describes the conceptual basis for such collaboration and presents a case study of an ongoing partnership between an employee assistance programme and a human resource management group.

Bryan, S (1996) asserts that the central controversy in considering work-related stress is the extent to which it stems from the organization or from the individual. He suggests that the costs of preventing stress need to be seen in the context of not doing so, and looks at causes of occupational stress, such as factors intrinsic to the job, role, relationships, career development, and organizational structure and climate. He also examines who can manage occupational stress, outlining three approaches: individualism, collectivism and an integrated organizational approach, He concludes that the key areas for an ethical employer to tackle are primarily good management communication, human resources development, clarity of roles and expectations.

Williams, J (1996) outlines three reasons for the increase in stress-related training and brings out the purpose of the employee training in stress management. He discusses factors like raising awareness about stress, identifying causative factors, coping skills and prevention, before turning to the core content of a stress management course and its length. He also notes some of the difficulties and debates on the qualities of a stress management trainer.

Victor M. Rojas, Brian H. Kleiner (2000) looks at the nature of stress and the need to ensure that employees do not suffer excessive levels of stress. He also considers the different types of stress and focuses on detrimental stress. Techniques for stress management such as breathing methods, meditation, exercising and massaging have been suggested. The learned writer outlines the most common stressors in the workplace and suggests some ways in which these can be alleviated.

Philip Dewe, Michael O'Driscoll (2002) presented a report of research which surveyed managers' views on stress, their beliefs about stress interventions and who should be responsible for addressing job-related stress problems. Both qualitative and quantitative techniques were used to explore the issues, using a sample of 540 New Zealand managers. The results draw attention to a number of issues including: Do managers' views of stress reflect acknowledged definitions? Who should assume responsibility for managing stress? What do managers mean when they indicate that an intervention is effective? Are stress interventions any different from standard human resource practices, and is there a role for theory in stress interventions?

Sonja, Treven, Vojko, Potocan (2005) presented the problem of stress, employees might encounter; the individual inclination to stress; the individual methods for reducing stress; and the authors' model of training for stress prevention. The paper uses both descriptive and analytical approaches to research and dissemination. Within the descriptive approach various methods have been applied, including compilation, descriptive and comparative techniques; the analytical approach involves inductive and deductive methods. It emerges that individuals vary considerably in their ability to manage stress. Self-perception, locus of control, type A or B behavioural patterns and flexibility or rigidity, all appear to influence stress management abilities.

Vempati, R.P.,Telles Shirley conducted a study to evaluate psycho-physiological responses to a two day, yoga based stress management programme, and to study psycho-physiological changes based on levels of occupational stress at baseline. The paper evaluated the physiological changes of a yoga based stress management programme on 26 symptomatic, male, middle age managers. The Occupational Stress Index (OSI) and autonomic parameters were measured. Data of subjects with OSI greater or less than the median were analyzed separately. The't' test for paired data was used for pre-post comparisons.

Section II: Research Methodology

Objectives of the Study:

- To examine the symptoms and effects of stress,
- To examine the major work related stressors and their effects and
- To suggest some tips for removing the stress in Information Technology sector.

Research Design: The study is explorative cum descriptive in nature. Surveys of individuals who are apt to have ideas on the subject were consulted before finalizing the line of action.

Sample Design: The respondents are the employees of the I.T. Sector including both H.R. people and the technical people. 65 respondents were selected in the sample using the technique of judgment and convenience sampling. Of them, 15 are the HR people and 50 are the technical people.

Nature and Sources of Data: The present paper is of analytical nature and makes use of primary and secondary data. The primary data has been collected by self administered questionnaire and relevant secondary data has been collected from, www.ssrn.com. Different journals have also been referred to obtain the relevant information.

Data Analysis: Both descriptive and inferential statistics were used in analyzing the data collected. The responses have been presented in tables according to the variables being examined. The paper calculated the total score for each work related stressor for each category and after that the work related stressor which got the highest score in each category was selected. The software package SPSS was used to determine the mean, percentage etc. which is used to analyze the data.

Section III: Signs and Symptoms of Stress

Stress affects the mind, body and behaviour in many ways. The specific signs and symptoms of stress vary from person to person, but all have the potential to harm your health, emotional well-being and relationships with other. Below is a partial list of stress signs and symptoms that a person undergoing stress might experience.

Signs and Symptoms of Stress

Intellectual symptoms:How stress can affect your mind	***Emotional symptoms:How stress can make you feel***
Memory problems Difficulty in making decisions Inability to concentrate Confusion Seeing only the negative Repetitive or racing thoughts Poor judgment Loss of objectivity Desire to escape or run away	Moody and hypersensitive Restlessness and anxiety Depression Anger and resentment Easily irritated and "on edge "Sense of being over whelmed Lack of confidence Apathy Urge to laugh or cry at inappropriate times
Physical symptoms:How stress can affect your body	***Behavioural symptoms:How stress can affect your behaviour***
Headaches Digestive problems Muscle tension and pain Sleep disturbances Fatigue Chest pain, irregular heartbeat High blood pressure Weight gain or loss Asthma or shortness of breath Skin problems Decreased sex drive	Eating more or less Sleeping too much or too little Isolating yourself from others Neglecting your responsibilities Increasing alcohol and drug use Nervous habits (e.g., nail biting, pacing) Teeth-grinding or jaw clenching Overdoing activities such as exercising or shopping Losing your temper Overreacting to unexpected Problems

Section IV: Analysis and Interpretation

The various work related stressors are categorized under the main headings like overload, work relationships, work-life balance, pays and benefits and effects of work related stressors as described below.

Overload

Work related stressors due to workload, in order of their importance, are exhibited in Table-I which shows that unrealistic deadlines occupies the first position with a (total score of 238) followed by technology overload, unmanageable workload and work related time table.

Table-1: Overload

Sr. No.	*Work related stressors*	*Ranks (Score)*					*Total Score*	*Overall Ranks*
		1	*2*	*3*	*4*	*5*		
1.	Unrealistic deadlines	0 (0)	7 (14)	22 (66)	27 (108)	10 (50)	238	1
2.	Technology overload	0 (0)	6 (12)	25 (75)	31 (124)	3 (15)	226	2
3.	Unmanageable workloads	2 (2)	8 (16)	15 (45)	38 (152)	2 (5)	225	3
4.	Work related time table	8 (8)	6 (12)	17 (51)	24 (96)	10 (50)	217	4

Source: **Primary data**

Work Relationship

Work related stressors due to work relationship, in order of their importance, are exhibited in Table-2 which shows that aversive behaviour from superiors, aggressive management style, lack of effective management leadership, finding fault attitude of the superiors, others take credit for personal achievements, poor relationships with colleagues, non cooperation from other employees, lack of support form other colleagues and isolation at work are the main reasons of stress.

Table-2: Work Relationship

Sr. No.	*Work related stressors*	*Ranks (Score)*					*Total Score*	*Overall Ranks*
		1	*2*	*3*	*4*	*5*		
1.	Aggressive management style	0 (0)	0 (0)	7 (21)	17 (68)	41 (250)	294	2
2.	Lack of support from other colleagues	22 (22)	26 (52)	11 (33)	2 (8)	4 (20)	85	9
3.	Isolation at work	35 (35)	21 (42)	5 (15)	4 (16)	0 (0)	108	8
4.	Aversive behavior of superiors	0 (0)	0 (0)	4 (12)	21 (84)	40 (200)	296	1
5.	Lack of effective management leadership	0 (0)	4 (8)	8 (24)	21 (84)	32 (160)	276	3

6.	Finding fault attitude of the superiors	2 (2)	19 (38)	17 (51)	23 (92)	4 (20)	203	4
7.	Non cooperation from other employees	0 (0)	46 (92)	14 (42)	4 (16)	1 (5)	155	7
8.	Others take credit for personal achievements	0 (0)	13 (26)	45 (135)	5 (20)	0 (0)	181	5
9.	Poor relationships with colleagues	3 (3)	27 (54)	21 (63)	11 (44)	3 (15)	179	6

***Source:* Primary data**

Work-life Balance

Work related stressors due to work-life balance, in order of their importance, have been exhibited in Table-3 which shows that long hours at work, excessive travel time and work interfering with personal life are the main reasons of stress.

Table-3: Work-Life Balance

Sr. No.	*Work related stressors*	*Ranks (Score)*					*Total Score*	*Overall Ranks*
		1	*2*	*3*	*4*	*5*		
1.	Long hours at work	0 (0)	2 (4)	46 (138)	15 (60)	2 (10)	212	1
2.	Excessive travel time	3 (3)	16 (32)	21 (42)	16 (64)	9 (45)	186	2
3.	Work interfering with home/ personal life	9 (9)	19 (38)	20 (60)	13 (52)	4 (20)	179	3

***Source:* Primary data**

Pays and Benefits

Work related stressors due to pays and benefits, in order of their importance, have been exhibited in Table-4 which shows that salary/wages, lack of financial rewards associated with the job, excessive overtime, government taxation policies are the main reasons of stress.

Table-4: Pays and Benefits

Sr. No.	Work related stressors	Ranks (Score) 1	2	3	4	5	Total Score	Overall Ranks
1.	Lack of financial rewards associated with the job	0 (0)	0 (0)	4 (12)	57 (228)	4 (20)	260	2
2.	Salary/Wages	0 (0)	0 (0)	2 (6)	52 (208)	11 (55)	269	1
3.	Excessive overtime	0 (0)	13 (39)	13 (39)	46 (184)	4 (20)	247	3
4.	Government taxation policies	2 (2)	44 (132)	44 (132)	8 (32)	0 (0)	188	4

Source: Primary data

Effects of Work Related Stressors

Major physical-effects of work related stressors have been exhibited in Table-5 which shows that depression constitutes the major physical effect of stress, followed by headache, back pain, restlessness and frustration. Other work life stressors are tense muscles, dry mouth, aches and pain, faster heart beat etc..

Table-5: Effects of work related stressors

Sr. No.	Major physical effects	Frequency	Percentage
1	Faster Heart beat	39	60
2	Increased Sweating	28	43
3	Cool skin, hands, feet	24	37
4	Rapid breathing	21	32
5	Tense muscles	47	72
6	Dry mouth	45	69
7	Frequent colds	16	25
8	Asthma	02	03
9	Back pain	55	85
10	Digestive problems	17	26
11	Headache	55	85
12	Skin eruption	23	35
13	Sexual disorders	05	08
14	Aches and pain	44	68

15	Frustration	54	83
16	Depression	56	86
17	Restless ness	55	85

Source: **Primary data**

Section V: How to Reduce Stress in Workplace

Stress may affect performance. Many respondents feel stress due to various reasons and ultimately the performance level of the employees goes down because of the various work related stressors. It is very difficult to eliminate the work related stress completely, though we can try to manage the stress by using various stress management techniques.

Positive job factors can play an important part in keeping stress in check. Having supportive co-workers, managing time effectively, being active in social groups, and not taking work home with you, are effective ways to minimize stress. Management can provide invaluable assistance to employees (and themselves) by setting effective stress management techniques. Some of the vital ways to do this are:

- **Set realistic goals and priorities**: Encourage employees to be a part of the priority setting process. When they feel they are part of the decision makers, they are more likely to take responsibility rather than grumble about"my nasty boss" and "this terrible place".
- **Encourage good time-management technique:** Plan for important activities, schedule them in advance.
- **Job Security:** Up with others and keeping good records help people get things accomplished on time and realize their value. Take time to make notes on successes and projects accomplished.
- **Take short breaks after a particularly stressful event:** Encourage employees to take a 5 minute walk around the block or a few minutes of quiet meditation to re-balance their energies. Several short breaks throughout the day can keep employees working at peak performance.
- **Don't procrastinate:** Procrastination and delay breeds stress! Eliminate items which won't get done and do those that are important first.
- **Change your attitudes:** Think of stressful situations as a challenge to your creative thinking. Know that eventually, everything will either get done or it won't –worrying won't make it better.
- **Learn to say "no":** When your schedule is full, say "no" to activities you don't enjoy, to unrealistic demands, to responsibilities that aren't yours. Doing this with tact and diplomacy, takes some practice and may require special training.
- **Encourage positive self-talk:** Use positive self-reinforcement affirmations, like "I can handle this, one step at a time" and "Somehow the whole team will work this out".
- **Give positive reinforcement:** Make sure that all managers and supervisors tell people, when they do a good job, complement them on their neat offices or good work habits.

- **Set up employee recognition programmes:** "Employee of the Month" or "Creative Suggestion" systems, encourage people to do a good job. Everyone needs a pat on the back and a sense of being a valuable person. Constant criticism is counter-productive and causes hard feelings. A daily positive comment goes a long way, at no cost!
- **Provide a sympathetic ear:** Often stressful situations can be managed, if there is someone willing to listen to the employee's concerns and provide positive encouragement, to get through the problem. For many people, 15 minutes of a sympathetic listener can cancel out many days of otherwise unproductive worry.
- **Most important, maintain a sense of humour:** As a wise philosopher said, "Don't take life so seriously, it's only a hobby". Try to remember what was stressful in your life six months ago or a year ago. Chances are you can't. know that this day will be just another day in history and whatever seems traumatic now, will fade into oblivion as time passes.

Section VI: Conclusion

Most people experience stress on a daily basis. However, occupational stress is one issue that is rarely discussed. A lot of people may not want to admit that their job is causing them stress,or their work environment is a somewhat nerve wracking experience for them. Although rarely admitted or talked about, workplace stress is an issue that must be addressed avidly by HR Personnel and Managers. It is pertinent that this be discussed, because it is stress and anxiety that creates barriers to escalating productivity and high motivation among employees. The purpose of the current study is to examine the symptoms, and effects of stress, to examine the major work related stressors and to suggest some tips for removing the stress in Information Technology sector.

From the above analysis, it can be said that the top work related stressors, which have policy implications for the company under study in particular, and the industry in general are unrealistic deadlines, lack of control over aspects of the job, aversive behavior of superiors, job in security, long hours at work, inadequate training to do the job, salary/wages, lack of enjoyment of job, etc. The results of the study also showed that the most common physical affects which the I.T. people feel most due to stress are depression, headaches, restlessness, back pain, frustration, etc.

References

- Bryan S, "Work-related stress: an ethical perspective", Business Ethics: A European Review (UK), Volume 5, Issue 2, 1996.
- Cook R, "Is stress becoming an industry killer?", Campaign (UK), 1996.
- Douglas Paton, Rhona Flin, Disaster stress: an emergency management perspective, Disaster Prevention and Management, Volume 8, Issue 4, pp 261 – 267, 1999.
- Gatrell, Caroline J.; Cooper, Cary L., "Work-life balance: working for whom?" European J. of International Management,Volume 2, Number 1, pp. 71, 2008.
- Lawrence R. Murphy "Managing job stress: an employee assistance/human resource management partnership", Personnel Review, Volume 24 Issue 1 pp 41 - 50, 1995.

- Marie McHugh, Shirley Brennan, "Organization Development and Total Stress Management", Leadership & Organization Development Journal, Volume 13, 1992.
- Marie McHugh, Shirley Brennan, "Organization Development and Total Stress Management" Leadership & Organization Development Journal, Volume 13, 1992.
- Philip Dewe, Michael O'Driscoll, "Stress management interventions: What do managers actually do?" , Personnel Review, Volume 31 Issue 2 pp 143 – 165,2002.
- Peter, Callender, "Stress Management Training: Has the Bubble Burst?", Journal of European Industrial Training, Volume 13, 1989.
- R.P. Vempati and Shirley Telles, "Baseline Occupational Stress Levels and Physiological Responses" Two Day Stress Management Programme,Vivekananda Kendra Yoga Research Foundation, Bangalore, India.
- Stress at work, United States National Institute of Occupational Safety and Health, Cincinnati, 1999.
- Sandra, Hartington, Mills, Angela, G. Stern, "Should Stress Management be Company Policy?", Women In Management Review, Volume 4, Issue 2, 1989.
- Sonja, Treven, Vojko, Potocan, "Training programmes for stress management in small businesses" Education + Training, Volume 47 Issue 8/9 pp 640 – 652, 2005.
- Susan G. Forman, Occupational stress management: Cognitive-behavioural approaches , University of South Carolina, USA www.sciencedirect.com
- Tanya Arroba, Kim James, "Reducing the Cost of Stress: An Organisational Model" Personnel Review, Volume 19 Issue 1, 1990.
- T. Foot, "Stress Management" Work Study, Volume 40, Issue 3, 1991.
- Williams J, "Stress management training", Training Officer (UK), Vol 32 Issue 3, 1996.
- Victor M. Rojas, Brian H. Kleiner, "The art and science of effective stress management", Management Research News, Volume 23, Issue 7/8, pp 103 – 106, 2000.

✫✫✫

10

RELAX OR RETIRE: ACADEMICIANS AT STAKE!

*Dr. Esha Sharma
** Prof. Sumeet Gupta

* Faculty IBS-Jaipur
** Faculty IBS-Jaipur

Introduction

Stress is the "wear and tear", our bodies experience as we adjust to our continually changing environment; it has physical and emotional effects on us and can create_positive or negative feelings. As a positive influence, stress can help us to action; it can result in a new awareness and an exciting new perspective. As a negative influence, it can result in feelings of distrust, rejection, anger, and depression, which in turn can lead to health problems such as headaches, upset stomach, rashes, insomnia, ulcers, high blood pressure, heart disease and stroke. With the death of a loved one, the birth of a child, a job promotion or a new relationship, we experience stress as we readjust our lives. In so adjusting to different circumstances, stress will help or hinder us depending on how we react to it.

Causes of Stress

Attitude: Listing the causes of stress is tricky. There can be innumerable stress factors since different individuals react differently to the same stress conditions. Extreme stress situations for an individual may prove to be mild, for another person the situations might not qualify for stress symptoms at all. Stress is often termed as a twentieth century syndrome, born out of man's race towards modern progress and its ensuing complexities. For that matter, even simple causes such as a flight delay, managing a teenage child at home can put anyone under stress.

A stress condition can be real or perceived. Yet, our brain reacts in the same way to both the causes of stress, by releasing stress hormones equal to the degree of stress felt. The brain doesn't differentiate between real and imagined stress. It could happen while watching a horror movie or when one is apprehensive of some imminent danger. It is said that life acts and you react. Our attitude is our reaction to what life hands out to us. A significant amount of stress symptoms can be avoided or aroused by the way we relate to stressors. Stress is created by what we think rather than by what has actually happened. For instance, handling adopted children, adolescents, students, academic failures, retirements, tax audits or sudden loss of money need a relaxed attitude, focused will and preparedness to face the quirks of life positively. Otherwise one tends to feel stressed and reacts in anger and frustration. With a better control of attention, one can feel that the world is a more congenial place to live in.

Again, in case of a marital conflict, instead of adopting an accusing and frustrating attitude such as—"You made my life hell" or "You are not meeting my emotional needs," the American clinical psychotherapist Willard F. Harley suggests that accepting—" Yes, we have a problem", helps to clear the clouds. Failure in adopting a realistic attitude to events creates symptoms of depression and aggravates stress situations."

Attitude, is more important than facts. It is more important than the past, than education, money, circumstances, failures, successes, or what other people think or say or do. Life is 10 per cent what happens to oneself, and 90 per cent how he/she reacts to it. And so it is with you..." says Charles Swindoll, an author and public speaker. A right attitude can make a resilient person relaxed in the face of stressful situations.

Life's situations: Major life events such as divorce, death, midlife crisis, financial worries, persistent strain of caring for a chronically sick child, nagging health problems or managing a physically or mentally challenged family member can act as potential stressors. Even conditions such as, prolonged unemployment or a sudden lay-off from a job can leave you under tremendous stress. One just can't wish away a situation. Moreover, one has to live through these situations in the right spirit. Stress also comes from our personal and social contexts, and from our psychological and emotional reactions to such conditions Here, our mental and emotional disposition, built over the years, decides whether to accept these situations with a fighting or a fleeing spirit. Accordingly, we may either be under harmful influences of stressors or be out of them Children and women subjected to mental or physical abuses are known to suffer from tremendous stress symptoms of depression, constant anxiety and burnout.

Though anger, fear and other negative emotional reactions are natural and necessary we need to channel them constructively to create a balanced state in our body and mind.

Genetic Reasons: Do "stressed out" parents necessarily have stressed out kids? To this query Dr. Roxanne Dryden-Edwards, a senior Psychiatrist and Assistant Professor of Psychiatry at John Hopkins University School of Medicine, answers: "While no parental issue guarantees that the same issue will be duplicated in their children, parental stress certainly places the children at a great risk of becoming stressed as well. Besides being at higher genetic risk for stress, children of stressed parents can also learn the tendency to get stressed out in reaction to life's challenges from their parents." A research article published in the British Medical Journal, suggests: "The psychological state of the mother may affect fetal development." It could be caused by stress induced, reduced blood flow through the arteries that feed the uterus. It could also create a mental as well as physical predisposition to certain diseases, and behavioral patterns in the later life of a child. It's identified that specific genes govern three endorphin groups, which constitute our stress hormones. Hence, our reactions to physical and emotional stress could also be "genetic." In other words, how our parents or great-grandparents responded to stressful situations, may in part, determine how we handle ourselves today!

Children of stressed out parents are more likely to be ill equipped to handle stressors positively. They may suffer from emotional disturbances, depression, aggressive behavior or confusion, besides chances of weak physical constitutions, which again can be a source of anxiety.

Effect of smoking on stress ? The relationship between tobacco smoking and stress has long been an area for controversy. The paradox is, although adult smokers state, smoking helps them feel relaxed, they report feeling more stressed than non-smokers. Research shows that nicotine dependency actually increases stress levels in smokers-adults and adolescence alike. Adolescent smokers report increasing levels of stress as they develop regular patterns of smoking. They gradually become less stressed over a time when they manage to quit smoking. Whatever may be the personal accounts of smokers, clinical evidence reaffirms that smoking is associated with heightened stress.The majority of smokers recognize that smoking is physically unhealthy, but mistakenly believe, it has positive psychological functions. However, smokers need to become aware of why these beliefs are incorrect.

Causes of Workplace stress Job stress may be caused by a complex set of reasons. Some of the most visible causes of workplace stress are:

Job Insecurity: Organized workplaces are going through metamorphic changes under intense economic transformations and consequent pressures. Reorganizations, takeovers, mergers, downsizing and other changes have become major stressors for employees, as companies try to live up to the competition to survive. These reformations have put demands on everyone; from a CEO to a mere executive.

High Demand for Performance: Unrealistic expectations, especially in the time of corporate reorganizations, which, sometimes, puts unhealthy and unreasonable pressures on the employee, can be a tremendous source of stress and suffering. Increased workload, extremely long working hours and intense pressure to perform at peak levels all the time for the same pay, can actually leave an employee physically and emotionally drained. Excessive travel and too much time away from family also contribute to an employee's stressors.

Technology: The expansion of technology—computers, pagers, cell phones, fax machines and the Internet—has resulted in heightened expectations for productivity, speed and efficiency, increasing pressure on the individual worker, to constantly operate at peak performance levels. Workers, working with heavy machinery, are under constant stress to remain alert. In this case both the worker and their family members live under constant mental stress. There is also a constant pressure to keep up with technological breakthroughs and improvisations, forcing employees to learn new software, all the times.

Workplace Culture: Adjusting to the workplace culture, whether in a new company or not, can be intensely stressful. Making oneself adaptive to the various aspects of workplace culture, such as ,communication patterns, hierarchy, dress code if any, workspace, and most importantly working and behavioural patterns of the boss, as well as the co-workers, can be a lesson of life. Maladjustment to workplace cultures may lead to subtle conflicts with colleagues or even with superiors. In many cases office politics or gossips can be major stress inducers.

Personal or Family Problems: Employees going through personal or family problems tend to carry their worries and anxieties to the workplace. When one is in a depressed mood, his unfocused attention or lack of motivation affects his ability to carry out job responsibilities.

Job Stress and Women: Women may suffer from mental and physical harassment at workplaces, apart from common job stress. Sexual harassment in workplace has been a major source of worry for women, since long. Women may suffer from tremendous stress such as 'hostile work environment harassment', which is defined in legal terms as 'offensive or intimidating behavior in the workplace'. This can consist of unwelcome verbal or physical conduct. These can be a constant source of tension for women in job sectors. Also, subtle discriminations at workplaces, family pressure and societal demands add to these stress factors.

Symptoms of Stress

The signs of job stress vary from person to person, depending on a particular situation, how long the individual has been subjected to the stressors, and intensity of the stress itself. Typical symptoms of job stress can be insomnia, loss of mental concentration, anxiety, stress, absenteeism, depression, extreme anger and frustration, family conflict, and physical illnesses such as, heart disease, migraine, headaches, stomach problems, and back problems.

Can stress be managed better? ....

Identifying unrelieved stress and being aware of its effect on our lives is not sufficient for reducing its harmful effects. Just as there are many sources of stress, there are many possibilities for its management. However, all require work toward change: changing the source of stress and/or changing your reaction to it.

It is important to recognize whether you are under stress or out of it. Many times, even if we are under the influence of a stressful condition, and our body reacts to it internally as well as externally, we fail to realize that we are reacting under stress. This also happens when the causes of stress are there long enough for us to get habituated to them. The body constantly tries to tell us, through symptoms such as, rapid palpitation, dizzy spells, tight muscles or various body aches, that something is wrong. It is important to remain attentive to such symptoms and learn to cope with the situations.

One copes better with stressful situation, when he/she encounter them voluntarily. In cases of re-location, promotion or layoff, adventurous sports or having a baby, we tend to respond positively under stress. But, when we are compelled into such situations against our will or knowledge, more often than not, we wilt in face of unknown and imagined threats. For instance, stress may mount when one is coerced into undertaking some work against one's will.

How shall one proceed to manage? ....

Become aware of stressors and emotional and physical reactions. One needs to understand few things: Notice the stress. Don't ignore it. Don't gloss over your problems. Determine what events lead to distress. What is one telling to his own self about meaning of these events? Determine how the body responds to stress. Does one become nervous or physically upset? If so, in what specific ways?

Recognize what could be changed. Can one change the stressors by avoiding or eliminating them completely? Can one reduce their intensity (manage them over a period of time instead of a daily or weekly basis)? Can one shorten the exposure to stress (take a break, leave the physical premises)? Can one devote time and energy necessary to making a change (goal setting, time management techniques, and delayed gratification strategies may be helpful here)?

Reduce the intensity of your emotional reactions to stress.

The stress reaction is triggered by one's perception of danger i.e. physical danger and/or emotional danger. Is an individual viewing the stressors in exaggerated terms and/or taking a difficult situation and making it a disaster? Is one expecting to please everyone? Are people overreacting and viewing things as absolutely critical and urgent? Does one feel that he/she must always prevail in every situation? Work at adopting more moderate views; try to see stress as something one can cope with, rather than something that overpowers oneself. Try to temper the excess emotions. Put the situation in perspective. Do not labour on the negative aspects and the "what if's."

Learn to moderate physical reactions to stress.

Slow, deep breathing will bring the heart rate and respiration back to normal. Relaxation techniques can reduce muscle tension. Electronic biofeedback can help one gain voluntary control over such things as, muscle tension and blood pressure. Medications, when prescribed by a physician, can help, in the short term, in moderating the physical reactions. However, they alone are not the answer. Learning to moderate these reactions on one's own, is a preferable long-term solution.

Build the physical reserves.

Exercise for cardiovascular fitness three to four times a week (moderate, prolonged rhythmic exercise is best, such as, walking, swimming, cycling, or jogging).Eat well-balanced, nutritious meals. Maintain the ideal weight. Avoid nicotine, excessive caffeine, and other stimulants. Mix leisure with work. Take breaks and get away when you can. Get enough sleep. Be as consistent with the sleep schedule as possible.

Maintain emotional reserves.

Develop some mutually supportive friendships/relationships. Pursue realistic goals which are meaningful, rather than goals others have for you that you do not share. Expect some frustrations, failures, and sorrows. Always be kind and gentle with yourself — be a friend to yourself.

Balance between Career and Family life.

Balancing the family with professional life is tricky and often a frustrating challenge. It is important to consider the priorities and evaluate the choices, so that one can have time to work, time to play and time to make sure that life is as fulfilling as it can be. Stress often results from a conflict between work and family responsibilities. According to Stephen F. Duncan, Family and Human Development Specialist, your ability to cope successfully with work-family stress depends on three things: Resources (such as income, education, intelligence, determination), individual coping strategies (how you use your resources), and individual point of view or perception (for example, thinking: It's normal for me to feel this way)

The more resources you have and use well, the healthier your attitude, the more successful you will be at coping with stress.

Effects of stress on Academicians

Stress management is the need of the hour. However hard we try to go beyond a stress situation, life seems to find new ways of stressing us out and plaguing us with **anxiety attacks.** Moreover, be it our anxiety, mind-body exhaustion or our erring attitudes, we tend to overlook **causes of stress** and the conditions triggered by those. In such unsettling moments we often forget that stressors, if not escapable, are fairly manageable and treatable.

Stress, either quick or constant, can induce risky body-mind disorders. Immediate disorders such as, dizzy spells, anxiety attacks, tension, sleeplessness, nervousness and muscle cramps can all result in chronic **health problems**. They may also affect our immune, cardiovascular and nervous systems, and lead individuals to habitual addictions, which are inter-linked with stress.

Like "stress reactions", "relaxation responses" and stress management techniques are some of the body's important built-in response systems. As a relaxation response, the body tries to get back balance in its homeostasis. Some hormones released during the 'fight or flight' situation prompt the body to replace the lost carbohydrates and fats, and restore the energy level.

The knotted nerves, tightened muscles and an exhausted mind crave to loosen. Unfortunately, today, we don't get relaxing and soothing situations without asking. To be relaxed, we have to strive to create such situations. Stress management is a decision-making process. When we are under stress, there are three major ways we can deal with it.

The AAAbc's of Stress

A – Alter it. For e.g. Removing the source of stress by changing something. Problem solving, direct communication, organizing, planning, and time management are common techniques for altering stress

A – Avoid it. For e.g. Removing oneself from the stressful situation. To conserve stress energy, people sometimes need to walk away, say 'No', delegate, withdraw, and know their limits

A – Accept it i.e. equipping oneself physically and mentally for stress.

b – building resistance

- ✔ Physically– proper diet, regular aerobic exercise, and systematic relaxation techniques.
- ✔ Mentally- positive affirmation, taking time for mental health, and getting clear about goals/values/priorities.
- ✔ Socially- by building and maintaining support systems, investing in relationships, clear communication, and intimacy.
- ✔ Spiritually- meditation, prayer, worship, faith, and commitment, strengthen people.

c – Changing our perception. Change the way you perceive the situation or yourself. Changing unrealistic expectations and irrational belief is a good start. Building self-esteem and cultivating a positive attitude. Redefining the situation in a less stress-provoking way i.e., "isn't it funny" or "isn't it grand" instead of "isn't it awful," increases stress resistance.

The academicians who indulge in brain related work are prone to stress related problems. For them unattended stress may result in the following:

- **Problem solving skills are impaired**. Stress which leads to sleep loss impairs our ability to comprehend rapidly changing situations, increases likelihood of distraction, makes us think more rigidly and reduces our ability to produce innovative solutions to problems
- **Communication skills suffer**. High stress reduces the words in one's vocabulary both verbally and in writing, resulting in stilted conversations.
- **Learning and memory suffer**. Research studies show that the cerebral cortex is the part of the body, most affected by inadequate sleep. A direct connection has been shown between sleep loss and our abilities to concentrate and remember. This could be very dangerous for the academicians as the core strength of their life is at stake.
- **Motor skills are impaired**. Numerous studies, from both England and the US National Highway Traffic Safety Administration, have demonstrated a direct connection between heavy stress, sleepiness and impaired hand-eye coordination. The degree of impairment has led researchers to compare it, in severity, to drunkenness. The combination of impaired judgment and diminished hand-eye coordination leads to at least 100,000 MVA's per year in the U.S., and numerous home and industrial accidents

Summarized net results of stress: The combined effects are impaired judgment, diminished creativity and productivity, inability to concentrate, reduced language and communication skills, slowed reaction times, and decreased abilities to learn and remember.

All of these will increase the stress level!

Relaxation activities

Everyone needs a good laugh now and then. It's free, it's contagious, and it's good for you! Here are some suggestions to help add humor to the life.

- Keep a journal, diary, or dream notebook
- Play with children or animals
- Spend leisure time in the park
- Listen to quiet music
- Practice yoga
- Enjoy a snow or water sport
- Ride a bicycle for pleasure
- Run, jog, or take a long walk
- Eat only natural, healthy food
- Enjoy an aerobic sport
- Get or give a massage
- Practice gymnastics or dancing
- Use a hot tub steam room, or sauna
- Work in the yard or garden
- Enjoy a craft of manual hobby
- Read for pleasure
- Spend time in the woods, mountains, desert, or a beach
- Take a nap or sunbath
- Meditate
- Go hiking or camping
- Attend theatre, concerts, or shows
- Play a musical instrument or sing
- Practice martial arts
- Do breathing exercises

Conclusion

The academicians go through lot of changes throughout their lives. One needs to learn to cope up with them. Otherwise the results could be illnesses, physical as well as mental. Stress when dealt effectively, could give miraculous positive results. One just needs to understand the relaxation process. One may adopt any one style from the above list or may develop one's own style. The list is endless.

To cope up with the pressurizing demands from the industry, as well as students, one needs to relax and succeed, they don't work in isolation.

References

[1] Bartholomew, L.K., Parcel, G. S., Kok, G., & Gottlieb. (2001). Intervention mapping: Designing theory- and evidence-based health promotion programs. New York: McGraw-Hill.

[2] Darcy, J. (2000). Families are experiencing more stress than ever. Hudson Valley Business Journal, December 4, 2000, pg. 23; Wappingers Falls, New York.

[3] National Centers for Disease Control and Prevention (CDC), (2003). Behavioral Risk Factor Surveillance System Trends Data. Retrieved October 12, 2006 from http://apps.nccd.cdc.gov/brfss/Trends/TrendData.asp.

[4] National Centers for Disease Control and Prevention (CDC). (2004). The state of aging and health in America, 2004. Retrieved September 20, 2006 from http://www.cdc.gov/hrqol/community.htm

[5] Stephen P. Robbins, Organization Behavior, Pearson Education, New Delhi

[6] S. K. Chakraborty, Ethics in Management, Oxford University Press, New Delhi

[7] Selye, H.," The Stress of Life" New York: McGraw-Hill, 1956

[8] Times Accent, October 14, 2004

[9] Ader, R., & Cohen, N., "Psychoneuroimmunology: Conditioning and stress", Annual Review of Psychology,

44, 53-85, 1993

[10] Cannon, W.B., "Stresses and strains of homeostasis", American Journal of the Medical Sciences, 189(1), 1-14, 1934

[11] Chesney, M.A. & Rosenman, R.H., "Specificity in stress models: Examples drawn from type A behavior. In C.L. Cooper (Ed.). Stress research: Issues for the eighties", Chichester: John Wiley, 1983

[12] Cooper, C.L. & Cartwright, S., "Stress-management interventions in the workplace: Stress counseling and stress audits. British Journal of Guidance and Counseling", 22(1), 65-73, 1994

[13] Hobfoll, S.E., "The ecology of stress", New York: Hemisphere, 1988

[14] Law, J., "Technology and heterogeneous engineering: the case of Portuguese expansion. In W.E. Bijker, T.P.

[15] Hughes & T.J. Pinch (Eds.). The social construction of technological systems", Cambridge, Mass: MIT

Press, 1987

[16] http://www.depts.ttu.edu/porkindustryinstitute/Honors%20A&P/SELYE%20by%20KrebK.htm

[17] http://www.amazon.com/exec/obidos/tg/detail/-/0131000691/102-3909148-1944114?v=glance

[18] http://www.csun.edu/~vcpsy00h/students/stress.htm

[19] Beehr, T.A.& Newman, J.E. (1978). "Job Stress, employ Health and Organisational Effectiveness-A fact analysis model and literature reviews." *Personal Psychology*, 31, pp.665-669.

[20] Caplan, R.D., & Jones, K.W. (1975). "Effects of work load, role ambiguity, and type A personality on anxiety, Depression, and heart rate." *Journal of Applied Psychology*, 60,713-719.

[21] Chermiss, C. (1980). "Staff burnout: "Job stress in human service." Beverly Hills: Sage.

[22] Dewe, P.J. (1989). "Examining the nature of work stress: Individual evaluations of stressful experiences and coping." *Journal of Human relations*, Vol.42, No.11, pp.993-1013.

[23] Ivancevich, J.M.& Matteson, M.T. (1980). "Stress and Work: A Managerial Perspective." Scottforesman & Co., Glen view Illinois.

[24] Ivancevich, J.M., Matteson, M.T. and Preston. (1982). "Occupational Stress: Type A behaviour and physical well being." A.M.J., 25,2, 373-391.

[25] Kahn et.al. (1964). "Organisational Stress: Studies in role conflict and ambiguity." Wiley, New York.

[26] Portello, J.Y. and Long, B.C. (2000). "Appraisals and Coping with work place interpersonal Stress: A model for women managers." *Journal of Counselling Psychology,* Vol.48, No.2, pp.144-56.

[27] Selye, H. (1974). "Stress without Distress." Harper and Row Publications, U.S.A.

[28] Selye, H. (1936). "A syndrome produced by diverse noxious agents." *Nature*, 138:32.

[29] Selye, Hans. (1978). "The general adaptation syndrome and the disease of adaptation." *Journal of clinical endocrinology*.

[30] Shailendra Singh. (1990). "Organisational Stress and Executive Behaviour." *Sreeram Centre for Industrial Relation and Human Resources*, New Delhi.

[31] Shailendra Singh, (1990). "Executive under stress- Exploration in the Structure and Dynamics." Classical Publishing Co., New Delhi.

[32] Vansell, M., Brief, A.P. and Schuler, R.S. (1981). "Role conflict and Role ambiguity: Integration of the literature and directions for future research." *Journal of Human relations*, Vol.34, No.1, pp.43-66.

[33] Ahmed, S. Nurala, B.S. (1985). "A Study of Stress among executives." *Journal of personality and clinical studies*, Vol.1, No (2), pp.47-50.

[34] Bajpai, B.L. (1992). "Stress management." *Financial Express*, Bombay, June.

[35] Halt, R.R. "Occupational Stress." (1982). In Handbook of Stress: Theoretical & Clinical Aspects. Leo Golberger & Shlome Breznats (Eds.), Free Press, London.

[36] Pestonjee D.M. (1992). "Stress and Coping the Indian Experience." Sage Publications, New Delhi.

[37] Sreelatha, P. (1991). "Stress: A Theoretical Perspective." Stress: Sources, Effects, and Resolution Strategies and Stress Research Indian Perspective in Organisational Stress. V.S.P.Rao Eda. Sage Publishing House, New-Delhi, pp6-163.

✡✡✡

11

STRESS MANAGEMENT (STRATEGY AND TECHNIQUES)

** Praveen K. Thakur*
*** Monika Gupta*
**** Dr. Pradeep Ahalawat*

* Sr. Lecturer, MMIM, MMU, Mullana.
** Lecturer, MMIM, MMU, Mullana.
*** Faculty, CDLU, Sirsa.

Introduction

Stress is a part of day-to-day living of every individual. The college students may experience stress in meeting the academic demands. People on the job, and business men may suffer stress to reach office in time and to complete the projects on time, Even the house hold ladies may experience stress in managing the home affairs. The reasons for stress differ from person to person. The stress, people experience, should not be necessarily treated as harmful. An optimum amount of stress can always act as an energizer or motivator, and propel people to apply the efforts and complete the work. But a high level of Stress can be a serious threat to the personality traits of an individual and can cause physiological and social problems.

What is Stress?

We generally believe that stress is caused by external events and the dynamics of the environment. But we need to emphasise the fact that stress is caused by our reaction to the external environment. The manner in which a person perceives and understands the changes, or a particular event can bring happiness or cause stress, depending upon how he/she reacts to it. When students are asked to prepare a presentation, some may take it to be an opportunity to reveal their talents and improve upon their weakness while others fear of revealing their weaknesses. So, stress is our reaction to external events and it can be positive or negative depending upon how we react.

We can define stress as "body's non-specific response to any demand made on it". Stress is not by definition synonymous with nervous tension or anxiety. On one side stress provides the means to express talents and energies and pursue happiness, on the other side it can also cause exhaustion and illness, physical or psychological.

Symptoms of Stress

As stated earlier stress is caused by our reaction to the external events and brings about changes in our response and our general behavior. The presence of stress can be estimated by the analysis of certain symptoms an individual shows. These symptoms can be divided into three different categories. They are feelings, behaviour and physiology. When an individual experiences stress, one or more of the following symptoms can be exhibited.

Feelings

- The individual becomes anxious about the outcomes and is scared. The person feels that he has got something to loose or something wrong will take place.
- In an anxious state the person does not want to be corrected or interrupted. He looks out for other areas where he can forget about the stress-causing event for a while. The person becomes irritable and moody.
- During high level of stress the individual develops a negative frame of mind and suffers from low self-esteem, The person looses faith in his capabilities, and is afraid of the failures. The individual does not have a focused approach and is not able to concentrate and is involved in his own plans and thoughts.

Physiological and Behavioural Changes

- Speech problems.
- Impulsive Behaviour.
- Crying for no apparent reason.
- Laughing at a high pitch and a nervous tone of voice.
- Grinding of teeth.
- Increase in smoking, use of drugs and alcohol.
- Trembling.
- Nervous ticks.
- Dryness of throat and mouth.
- Tires easily.
- Urinates frequently.
- Sleeping problems.
- Diarrhoea/indigestion/vomiting/nausea.
- Butterflies in stomach.
- Headaches.
- Premenstrual tension.
- Pain in the neck and or lower back.
- Susceptibility to illness.
- Loss of appetite or overeating.

Causes of Stress

Both positive and negative events in one's life can be stressful. However, major life changes are the greatest contributors to stress for most people.

1. If people have to travel a lot and have to move from place to place, it can cause stress.
2. Individuals can also be under stress if they are about to enter some new environment. They may be going to a new colony, a new college or they may be joining a new organization.
3. Some events, which are generally once in a lifetime can also cause stress. The social institutions of marriage or divorce can cause stress. Pregnancy can also generate Stress.
4. Some of the untoward incidents like, critical illness or death of a relative can also cause stress in individuals.

These are some of the major events in the life of the individual that cause stress. Environmental factors, that act as catalyst also cause increments in stress. They are:

- *Time pressure*
- *Competition*
- *Financial problems*
- *Noise*
- *Disappointments*

Stress Management

Stress can be managed if we understand the reasons that cause stress and the level of stress. We should also try to estimate if we could bring about any change in the environment that can reduce stress.

1. **Become aware of your stressors and your emotional and physical reactions.**

   Notice your distress. Don't ignore it. Don't gloss over your problems. Determine what events distress you. What you are telling yourself about meaning of these events. Determine how your body responds to stress. Do you become nervous or physically upset?

2. **Recognize what you can change.**

   Can you change your stressors by avoiding or eliminating them completely? Can you reduce their intensity (manage them over a period of time, instead of a daily or weekly basis)? Can you shorten your exposure to stress (take a break, leave the physical premises)?

   Can you devote the time and energy, necessary to making a change (goal setting, time management techniques, and delayed gratification strategies may be helpful here)?

3. **Reduce the intensity of your emotional reactions to stress.**

   The stress reaction is triggered by your perception of danger...physical danger and/or emotional danger. Are you viewing your stressors in exaggerated terms and/or taking a difficult situation and making it a disaster? Do you expect to please everyone?

   Are you overreacting and viewing things as absolutely critical and urgent? Do you feel you must always prevail in every situation?

   Work at adopting more moderate views; try to see stress as something you can cope with rather than something that overpowers you.

   Try to temper your excess emotions. Put the situation in perspective. Do not labor on the negative aspects and the "what ifs."

4. **Learn to moderate your physical reactions to stress.**

   Slow, deep breathing will bring your heart rate and respiration back to normal. Relaxation techniques can reduce muscle tension. Electronic bio feedback can help you gain voluntary control over such things as, muscle tension, heartbeat and blood pressure.

   Medications, when prescribed by a physician, can help in the short term, in moderating your physical reactions. However, they alone are not the answer. Learning to moderate these reactions on your own is a preferable, long-term solution.

5. **Build your physical reserves.**

   Exercise for cardio vascular fitness, three to four times a week (moderate, prolonged, rhythmic exercise is the best, such as, walking, swimming, cycling, or jogging). Eat well-balanced, nutritious meals. Maintain your ideal weight.

   Avoid nicotine, excessive caffeine, and other stimulants. Mix leisure with work. Take breaks, and get away when you can. Get enough sleep. Be as consistent with your sleep schedule as possible.

6. **Maintain your emotional reserves.**

   Develop some mutually supportive friendships/relationships. Pursue realistic goals that are meaningful to you, rather than goals others have for you that you do not share. Expect some frustrations, failures, and sorrows. Always be kind and gentle with yourself — be a friend to yourself.

Stress Management Techniques

A. Stress Diary - Finding Your Optimum Stress Levels

How to use tool: Keeping a stress diary is an effective way of finding out what causes you stress, the level of stress you prefer, and your effectiveness under pressure. In this diary keep track of your stress levels and your feelings, everyday. In particular, note down stressful events. Record the following information:

- At a regular interval, for example every hour, record routine stress. Note:
  - ✔ The time
  - ✔ The amount of stress that you feel (perhaps on a scale of 1 to 10)
  - ✔ How happy you feel
  - ✔ How efficiently you are working
- When stressful events occur, write down:
  - ✔ What the event was?
  - ✔ When and where it occurred?
  - ✔ What important factors made the event stressful?
  - ✔ How stressful the event was?
  - ✔ How you handled the event?
  - ✔ Did you tackle the cause or the symptom?
  - ✔ Did you deal with the stress correctly?

Analyzing the Diary: After a few weeks, you should analyze this information. It may be interesting, as you carry out the analysis, to note down the outcomes of the jobs you were doing, when you were under stress. This should give you two types of information:

1. You should be able to understand the level of stress you are happiest with, and the level of stress at which you work most effectively. You may find that your performance is good, even when you feel upset by stress.
2. You should know what the main sources of unpleasant stress in your life are. You should understand what circumstances make stresses particularly unpleasant, and whether your strategies for handling the stresses are effective or not.

B. Psyching Up - Raising Stress Levels to Improve Performance

How to use tools: When you are not feeling motivated towards a task, either because you are bored by it, or because you are tired, you may need to 'psych yourself up'. This will increase your arousal, so that you can perform effectively. You can try the following:

- Focus on the importance or urgency of the task
- Set yourself a challenge - e.g., to do the job in a particular time or to do it to a particularly high standard
- Break the job down into small parts, and take satisfaction from the successful completion of each element.
- Use suggestion: e.g., 'I can feel energy flowing into me'
- Get angry about something!

C. Anticipating Stress - Managing Stress by Preparing For It

How to use tools: By anticipating stress you can prepare for it and work out how to control it when it happens. You can do this in a number of ways:

Rehearsal:

By practicing for a stressful event such as, an interview or a speech, several times in advance, you can polish your performance and build confidence.

Planning:

By analyzing the likely causes of stress, you will be able to plan your responses to the likely forms of stress. These might be actions to alleviate the situation, or may be stress management techniques. It is important that you formally plan for your jobs - it is little use just worrying in an undisciplined way - this will be counterproductive. Formal planning of responses to stress is a technique used by top-level athletes to ensure that they respond effectively to the stresses of competition.

Avoidance:

Where a situation is likely to be unpleasant, and will not yield any benefit to you, it may be one you can just avoid. You should be certain in your own mind; however, that this is the case, and you are not running away from problems.

Reducing the Importance of an Event:

When an event is important to you, this can make it very stressful. This is particularly true where you are operating at a high level, where many people are watching, or where there is the prospect of a large financial reward, of promotion, or of personal advancement. The presence of family, friends or important people can also add to pressure. If stress is a problem under these circumstances, then think carefully about the event - take every opportunity to reduce its importance in your eyes:

- If the event seems big, put it in its place along the path to your goals. Compare it in your mind with bigger events you might know of or might have attended.
- If there is a financial reward, remind yourself that there may be other opportunities for reward later. This will not be the only chance you have. Focus on the quality of your performance. Focusing on the rewards will only damage your concentration and raise stress.
- If members of your family are watching, remind yourself that they love you anyway. If friends are real friends, they will continue to like you whether you win or lose.
- If people, who are important to your goals, are watching, then remind yourself that you may well have other chances to impress them.
- If you focus on the correct performance of your tasks, then the importance of the event will dwindle into the background.

Reducing Uncertainty: Uncertainty can cause high levels of stress. Causes of uncertainty can be:

- Not having a clear idea of what the future holds
- Not knowing where your organization will be heading
- Not having any career development plans
- Not knowing what will be expected from you in the future
- Not knowing what your boss or colleagues think of your abilities
- Receiving vague or inconsistent instructions

D. Get a hobby or two, relax and have fun: Talk with friends, or someone you can trust,about your worries/problems.

1. Learn to use your time wisely:

   Evaluate how you are budgeting your time.

   Plan ahead and avoid procrastination.

   Make a weekly schedule and try to follow it.

2. Set realistic goals and priorities
3. Practice relaxation techniques. For example, whenever you feel tense, slowly breathe in and out for several minutes.

E. Other Techniques:

1. **Meditation** can also be good to bring down the stress levels.
2. **Taking exercise**
3. **Effective Time Management**
4. **Good Food and Nutrition.**

Conclusion

When we discuss stress and its management, we should understand that this is not the exhaustive list of the stress factors and the various techniques. Stress can be confronted and reduced, if and only if we understand ourselves better, analyze the behavior, and identify the stressors. The stress management techniques will work if we are honest with ourselves, and adopt the techniques in their fullest spirit.

✫ ✫ ✫

12

ADAPTABILITY REDUCES THE STRESS

*Dr. Anil Dhawan

** Praveen Khurana

*** Amit Joshi

* Lecturer in Commerce, Mukand Lal National College, Yamuna Nagar.

** Lecturer in Commerce, Mukand Lal National College, Yamuna Nagar.

*** Lecturer in Commerce, Mukand Lal National College, Yamuna Nagar.

Introduction

Anything which is most inevitable in the social environment is 'Change'. For human beings, 'Stress' has very broad definition. As far as our body is concerned, stress is synonymous with change. Anything that causes change in your life causes stress. It does not matter whether change is a 'good change' or a 'bad change'. It means stress is that change for which a human being is either not ready to accept or not ready to adapt.

Objectives

Stress can be due to any type of change that causes physical, emotional or psychological strain. However, not all types of stress are harmful or even negative; rather some times a stressed person gives better performance. Like wise, many confusing and contradicting views are there in the minds of a common man. The paper proposes to dwell upon the following points:

1. What does stress mean?
2. What are the potential sources of stress?
3. How it affects a person in society and at work place?
4. How can one manage it?

Mr. X was transferred from a small city to a very large city, where his commuting time to work was nearly one hour. He disliked city noises, heavy traffic and crowds. The thoughts which were hanging upon his mind were, that he was wasting his time while commuting and his new job also had more responsibilities..Within a few months he developed intestinal problems. When a medical examination showed no medical causes for his ailments, he was sent to a counselor. He showed little improvement, and finally, his counselor in cooperation with his physician, recommended that he should be transferred to a smaller city. His firm arranged his transfer, and within a short time, his problems disappeared. Can you guess what the reason of his problems was? Of course, it was "stress." Stress has become a major concern of the modern times, as it can cause harm to employee's health and performance. Different psychologists and physiologists have defined stress differently.

Any change causing deviation in physical, psychological, or behavioral aspect of the personality of a person, from the usual state of affairs is stress. From this point of view, stress is more complex than anxiety, which operates solely in the emotional and psychological spheres. Thus, stress may be accompanied by anxiety, but it is more comprehensive than the latter. Stress, as per the medical explanation of the term, is the body's general response to environmental situations. Stress is anything that changes one's physical, emotional or mental state while encountering various stimuli in outside environment. 'Stress' is neutral word, It is not necessary that stress may always be dysfunctional. The term 'distress' has negative connotations indicating that the individual is exposed to noxious stimuli, and the term 'eustress' on the other hand has a positive meaning attached to it, indicating a sense of euphoria. The body responds to both, distress and eustress, since both are environmental factors to be reacted to, and handled by an individual. Eustress is 'positive' stress that accompanies achievement and exhilaration such as those found in managerial jobs in the form of meeting challenges, stress for creative work, entrepreneurial activities, keen competition etc., which stimulate better productivity. Distress occurs when we fell insecure, inadequate, helpless or desperate as a result of too much, or too little, pressure or tension.

Hans Selye, the father of stress research, points out that all noxious stimuli damage body tissues. The stressor, the antecedent stimuli that causes stress, affects several area of body. The body system acts immediately to build up its defense mechanisms (for example, fast heart beat, sweating etc.) to help the body deal with stressors or adapt to the changes, When stress becomes excessive, employees develop various symptoms of stress that can harm their job performance and health, and even threaten their ability to cope with the environment.In simple words, stress refers to pressure or tensions people feel in life. Stress can cause different problems, which in turn would affect the individual's performance.

Management of stress has become a challenging job for all those modern organizations which are proposing to improve the productivity by helping out their employees in overcoming stress. Generally, employees complain about stress while trying to balance work & family responsibilities.Stress is an increasing problem in organizations now a days, Majority of employees are stressed out from greater workloads and lack of job stability in today's world. Some other potential sources of stress in an organization have been jotted down in the following fig:

Potential Sources of Stress

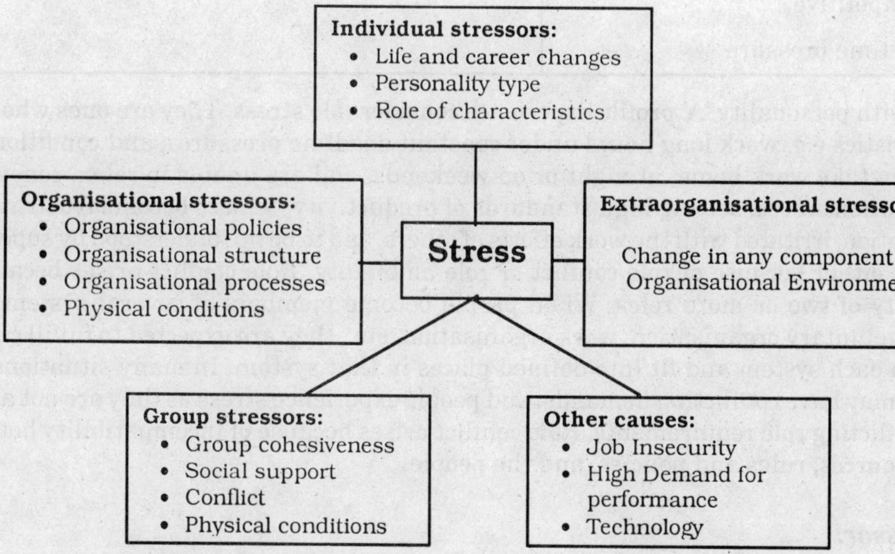

An Individual may have different types of stress in the context of organisational life or his personal life. Any change in life of an individual puts him in disequilibrium, and he is required to bring in a new equilibrium. In this process, he experiences stress. The impact of stress would depend upon the changes and the new equilibrium required as a consequence. Life's changes may be slow and gradual (getting older) or sudden (death of spouse). In both these cases,

Intensity of stress would be different. Like life changes, there may be changes in career, in the form of promotion, demotion, transfer, separation. With each change, some kind of stress is experienced. Young adults between 20 and 30 years of age have been reported to have experienced twice as many stressful events, compared to the older people.

Personality characteristics, such as authoritarianism, rigidity, masculinity, femininity, extroversion, supportiveness, spontaneity, emotionality, tolerance for ambiguity, locus of control, anxiety, and need for achievement are particularly relevant to individual stress. Recently, more attention has been paid to analyse type A and B personality profiles in the study of stress.

Table: Profiles of Type A and Type B personalities

Type 'A' Personality	*Type 'B' Personality*
Is always moving	Is never in hurry
Walks rapidly	Is patient
Eats rapidly	Does not brag
Talks rapidly	Plays for fun, not for win
Is impatient	Relaxes without guilt
Does two things at a time	Is mild mannered
Measures success by quantity	Has no pressing deadlines
Is aggressive	
Is competitive	
Feels time pressure	

People with personality 'A' profile experience considerable stress. They are ones who have the characteristics e.g. work long hours under constant deadline pressures, and conditions for overload, often take work home, at night or on weekends, and are unable to relax, constantly compete with themselves, setting high standards of productivity, tend to become frustrated by the work situation, irritated with the work efforts of others, and to be misunderstood by superiors. Role stress is either because of role conflict or role ambiguity. Role conflict arises because of incompatibility of two or more roles. When people become members of several systems like family, club, voluntary organisation, work organisation, etc., they are expected to fulfill certain obligations to each system and fit into defined places in that system. In many situations, the various roles may have conflicting demands, and people experience stress as they are not able to fulfill the conflicting role requirements. Role conflict arises because of incompatibility between job tasks, resources, rules and policies, and the people.

Group Stressor:

Group interaction affects human behaviour in society, as well as in an organisation. There may be some factors like, Lack of Group Cohesiveness, Lack of Social Support, and Conflict arising out of group interaction, which may become stressors for the individuals.

Organisational Stressor:

An organisation is composed of individuals and groups, and therefore, individual and group stressors may also exist in organisational context. The functioning of the individuals get adversely affected due to unfavorable and ambiguous policies. Thus, unfair and arbitrary performance evaluation, unrealistic job description, frequent reallocation of activities, rotating work shifts, ambiguous procedures, inflexibilities, inequality of incentives, etc. work as stressors. Defects in the organisational structure like, lack of opportunity for advancement, high degree of specialisation, excessive interdependence of various departments, line and staff conflict, do not let individual and groups to work effectively. Faulty organisational processes like, poor communication, poor and inadequate feedback of work performance, ambiguous and conflicting roles, unfair control systems, inadequate information flow, cause stress for people in an organisation. Lack of privacy, excessive noise, excessive heat or cold, pressure of toxic chemicals and radiation, air pollution, safety hazards, poor lighting, etc., are the physical conditions that produce stress in people.

Extraorganisational Stressor:

Since an organisation interacts continuously with its environment, events happening outside the organisation also work as stressors. Thus, social and technical changes, economic and financial conditions, social class conflicts, community conditions etc. work as stressors.

Other Stressors:

Some of the most visible causes of workplace which may generate stress among the employees are; job insecurity due to rationalization reforms at organizational or govt. level; high demands or unrealistic expectations for better performance; and those technical changes for which an individual is not ready to adapt. On the other hand, workers working with heavy machinery are under constant stress to remain alert. In this case, both the worker and their family members live under constant mental stress.

Stress and Job Performance

Stress can be either helpful or harmful to job performance, depending on its level. When there is no stress, job challenges are absent and performance tends to be low. As stress increases, performance tends to increase, because stress helps a person call up resources to meet job requirements. Constructive stress is a healthy stimulus that encourages an employee to respond to challenges. Eventually, stress reaches a plateau that corresponds approximately with a person's top day-to-day performance capability. At this point stress tends to produce no more improvement.

Finally, if stress becomes too great, it turns into a destructive force. Performance begins to decline at some point because excess stress interferes with performance. An employee loses the ability to cope; she or he becomes unable to make decisions, and exhibits erratic behaviour. If stress increases to a breaking point, performance becomes zero; the employee has a breakdown, becomes too ill to work, is fired, quits, or refuses to come to work to face the stress.

Too Much Work, Too Little Time	
A national sample of US employees finds that they:	
Feel overworked	54%
Are overwhelmed by workload	55%
Lack time for reflection	59%
Don't have time to complete tasks	56%
Multi-task too much	45%

Time when aversion starts & mind collapses:

When under severe stress, an individual fails to take clear-cut decisions, reevaluate and reassess the priorities and lifestyles, and ultimately, tends to fall into unproductive distractions. This can be described as a classic case of 'burnout'. The 'burnouts' often engage in reckless or risk-taking behaviours. Starting from glamour and sport celebrities, to common men, 'burnouts' are found everywhere. Chronic responsibility syndrome is a kind of burnout where people get mentally and physically exhausted from their workload. The symptom is often described as "there's simply too much work to do, and no one else can do it but me". Typically it will occur in hard working, hard driven people, who become emotionally, psychologically or physically exhausted. You are at risk of burnout where:

- You find it difficult to say 'no' to additional commitments or responsibilities.
- You have been under intense and sustained pressure for some time.
- Your high standards make it difficult to delegate to assistants.
- You have been trying to achieve too much for too long
- You have been giving too much emotional support for too long.

Often burnout will manifest itself in a reduction in motivation, volume and quality of performance, or in dissatisfaction with or departure from the activity altogether.

Different Individual Different Perception

Individual characteristics moderate the extent to which people experience stress in a given situation. Two people may be exposed to the same stressor, such as having too many deadlines, yet they experience different stress levels or exhibit different stress symptoms, reason being:

(a) Each of us perceives the same situation differently. People who are familiar with the situation and know how to protect themselves tend to experience less stress than those who are unfamiliar with in that situation. People with high self-efficacy or self sufficiency, are less likely to experience stress consequences in that situation, because the stressor is less threatening. Similarly, some people having optimistic traits are less prone, whereas others who have more pessimistic dispositions tend to develop more stress symptoms, probably because they interpret the situation in a negative light.

(b) The second reason may be that some people have more stress symptoms than others in the same situation, because both have different threshold levels of resistance to a stressor. Younger employees generally experience fewer and less stress symptoms than older employees, because they have a larger store of energy to cope with high stress levels. People who exercise regularly and have healthy lifestyle (e.g., diet, sleep) are less likely to experience negative stress outcomes.

(c) The other reason for different outcomes for the same level of stress is the approach which one uses different coping strategies. Some employees tend to ignore the stressor, hoping that it will go away. This is usually an ineffective approach, explains why they experience higher stress levels. There is some evidence (although still inconclusive) that women cope with stress better than their male counterparts.

It means, in the same situation, the effect of stress can be different on different individuals. It may lead to different types of disorders as far as physical and psychological problems of an individual are concerned. As far as behavior in an organization is concerned, people show dysfunctional behaviour because of high level of stress. Such behaviour may be in the form of alcoholism, drug addiction, increased smoking, sleeplessness, under/ overeating, etc. In extreme cases, when an individual is not able to bear stress, it may result in suicide. At the workplace, people may show behaviour like tardiness, absenteeism, and high turnover. In all these cases, it is the organization that suffers. So the search for finding out the remedies for the increasing level of stress among the employees becomes a priority for an organization.

Stress Management

Any high-level stress, affects an individual directly, and through him, his family and organization gets affected indirectly. Therefore, efforts at every end should be made to overcome its negative consequences. Such efforts can be made at two levels: individual level and organisational level.

Efforts at Individual Level

Individual coping strategies adopted by individuals, without reference to organization, tend to be more reactive in nature. Some individual strategies, such as physical exercise, relaxation, and planning the day long assignments (time management) can be both reactive and proactive, but most are geared towards helping the person who is already suffering from stress. Physical exercises of different types such as, walking, jogging, swimming, playing etc. are good methods of overcoming stress. The role of yoga, a scientific technique of physical exercise to keep the body fit, and to overcome stress, has been recognized in most parts of the world. Physical exercise helps people to cope with stress better, techniques, such as relaxation, enhanced self-esteem, and simply getting one's mind off work for a while can be realy helpful. The *relaxation* can be simple one or some specific techniques of relaxation such as biofeedback and meditation can be used. In biofeedback, an individual learns internal rhythms of a particular body process through electronic signals feedback, that is wired to the body area (for example, skin, brain, or heart). From this feedback, the person can learn to control body process in question. Mediation, on the other hand, involves quite concentrated inner thoughts, in order to rest the body physically and emotionally. Transcendental mediation is a more popular practice of meditation. Meditation has been recognised as a powerful technique for reducing stress. Whether a person takes easy one, or specific relaxation technique, the intention is to overcome stressful situation or manage a prolonged stressful situation more effectively. *Work-home Transition* is also like a relaxation technique. In this technique, a person may take pressure reducing type exercise in the last 30 or 60 minutes of the work time. For instance, during the last hour of work, the person can review the day's activities; list the priorities of the activities that need to be attended to the next day. Thus, he can finish his day's work and come back in a relaxed manner.

Because of increasing stress, special *cognitive therapy* techniques have been developed by psychologists. In these techniques, lectures and interactive discussion sessions are arranged to help participants in recognizing events at work, cognitions he may elicit and the effects of such cognition on their physiological and emotional responses to help them out to over come the stress. One more way out to cool down oneself is Networking (Social Support Network), it is the formation of close associations with trusted, empathetic co-workers and colleagues, who are good listeners and confidence builders. Such persons provide mental support to get the person through stressful situations.

Initiative by the Organization

Organisational coping strategies are more proactive in nature, that is, they attempt at removing existing or potential stressors, and prevent the onset of stress in individual jobholders. To a very great extent, these can be controlled by creating supportive organisational climate, which depends upon managerial leadership, rather than the use of power and money to control organisational behaviour. A major source of stress is the monotonous and disinteresting jobs being performed by employees in the organisation. Through more rational designing of jobs, jobs can be enriched leading to role clarity, This simple phenomenon can help in reducing stress. Some times, an individual may have generated stress, because he is not able to fulfill his self-actualization needs. Career Planning and counseling helps the employees to obtain professional advice regarding career paths, that would help them to achieve personal goals. It also makes them aware of what additional qualifications, training and skills, they should acquire for career advancement. The organisation can also hold periodical workshops for control and reduction of stress. Such workshops may help individuals to learn the dynamics of stress and methods of overcoming their ill effects. Similarly, the organisation can make arrangement for assisting individuals in overcoming their personal and family problems. This arrangement may include, managing personal finance, dealing with family problems, dealing with health problems, and dealing with other kinds of personal and family stresses.

Conclusion

There are thousands of reasons for generating stress. This stress may affect adversely the physique, psyche, social status, family environment, and above all, congenial environment at work place. The effected person can not control all the components of environment. But one thing, which can be controlled only by him is – Perception. Perception reflects the attitude; one may be having, 'positive' as well as 'negative' attitude. The behaviour is the outcome of attitude, which is also no exception to the one of effected components of personality of an individual. It means, the person who is suffering from stress should put in maximum efforts to improve his personality, so that he is able to overcome the various shortcomings as well as the complexes about himself. After this exercise he will be capable to compete and achieve the set targets. The other important aspect which one must take care of is to maintain the emotional balance i.e., he should be capable enough of setting priorities among various home, social and workplace assignments. Organizations should also help out the effected person to overcome the stress through more rational designing of jobs, and through training and skills for their career advancement. In this way an individual will readily adapt to the changes instead of generating 'Stress'.

"It is not the strongest of the species that survive, nor the most intelligent, but the one most responsive to change." - Charles Darwin.

☆☆☆

13

STRESS! WHAT IS THAT?

* Dr. P. K. Mehta
** Dr. P. K. Sharma

* Director, Saraswati Institute of Management & Technology, Teek, Kaithal (Haryana).

** Director, School of Management, Vardhman Mahaveer Open University, Kota (Rajasthan).

Why worry? A Message

In life, there are two things to worry about; either you are well or you are ill. If you are well, then there is nothing to worry about. But if you are ill, there are only two things to worry about; either you will get well you die. If you get well, there is nothing to worry about; but if you die; there are only two things to worry about; either you go to heaven or you go to hell. If you go to heaven there is nothing to worry about; and if you go to hell, you will be so busy shaking hands with your old friends; you won't have any time to worry. So why worry at all?

A True Picture

Let us take a glimpse of the work place of out times. Managers, tearing in to their work, day in and day out, with ulcers quietly forming in churning stomachs. Always on move or flying over time-zones, chasing ever elusive revenue targets upsetting the delicate balance of sleeping and waking. Too busy to join the family at dinner time. High-Pressure-automated-work-environment, unrealistic deadlines, executives in conflict with subordinates for instructions, not-obeyed, with peers for non-cooperation and seniors over maze of instructions issued at any point of time. At the top of it, not daring to show at the meetings that can not be postponed. The rules of the game are very simple and straight forward. Work and just work, and go on working in order to survive, stay and grow. Nothing less, nothing more. Intimidating, isn't it? This is a sample of the picture of job environment of our times, which is true cent percent.

A word about Stress

In 21st century first ten (10) diseases that kill millions every year are life style (read stress) related. 75 % of sick days are caused by work place related illness. Work place illness can be extremely fatal to your health. Action is the solution to conquer work place related stress. If you are snapping at boss, co-workers or clients, or seething inside; know that you are under stress and you got to kill it at the earliest possible.

Stress is a term that medical researchers took from engineering, which means inherent capacity to withstand strain. **Strain** is pressure on something too much to handle or manage. We need certain level of stress **(eustress)** but not too much and for too long **(distress)**. While eustress helps to keep us alert, motivates us to face challenges, and drives us to solve problems; distress on the other hand results when body over-reacts to events. It leads to physical, psychological and social problems. In this age of 24-hours Banking/ATMs, round the clock flight / transport schedules, 7-11 restaurants cut , throat competition and 24*7 work environment, it is neither possible nor always possible both for employer and employee to offer or chose mutually workable work schedules. We may know it or not ,like it or dislike it ; every situation has an inbuilt element of stress in it. Anything and everything can cause stress both on and off the job. This is a rule and not an exception. It is neither desirable nor practicable to avoid or eliminate stress at work. Stress has come to stay as a part-n-parcel of work and workplace of today. Let us accept this fact. Once we start appreciating importance of work in our lives then we can better appreciate that work and stress can not exist without each other.

This means work is the main source of stress in our life, while some amount of stress is equally necessary to make work happen; an element of utmost import to conduct the business of life. The relationship is very simple. **Stress and Work are Bhai- Bhai.** Stress can visit a human being; if he works. Also ,one experiences stress since one do not wish to work. Work is basis of our livelihood. It is in the best interest of both the executive and the organization for which he or she works that reasonable steps be taken to live and work sensibly.

In the light of the compulsions of business world of today we must re-look at stress in a non-conventional manner. The article discusses ways to deal effectively with built up of anxiety, tension, and irritation caused due to work. We do not have to look beyond work / working hours for solutions to counter its ill effects.The article also suggests some time tested and type tested repackaged sustainable hints for executives to take note of ; to keep the built up of stress level in check. One need not necessarily take a corrective therapy; invest in extra time money and energy to unwind and smoothen rough edges of the mind/matter. Just enjoy doing work.

Positive Aspects of Stress

Enhance personal growth and development. Stimulate creative thinking. Raise productivity. Help to introduce innovative procedures to enhance the job performance of sub-ordinates. Foster team work.

Anatomy of Work

Work is a trouble in itself. In a way ,those who chose to work invite trouble(s). Stress can visit a human being; if he works. Those who work get troubled from those who do not work. Those who work more get troubled more. Simple!. Since work likes to get done and finished; it prefers to land up on the desk of those who do and finish it up . Those who finish their work attract more Work. Those who finish their work regularly find more work waiting to be done. As a result, those who work remain busy. Though work is a trouble maker causing stress to those who often work longer, harder and live their lives out of their brief-case. **It's heartening to observe that Work has healing effect too on its doer.** This is very vital for a practitioner manager to understand. While stress is the norm in organizations of today, work has become the biggest differentiator for performance appraisal of employees at all levels.

Work is worship , they say ; the strongest tool in the hands of human kind to deliver 'Karma'. Scholars, since times immemorial, have equated work with karma i.e. duty. Religious scriptures refer to and use (work, karma and duty) three words, interchangeably. Perhaps the most important lesson we learn from Sri Bhagwat Geeta is the' Philosophy of Karma. Let us repackage this time tested and type tested mantra in simple words. **Vyast Raho Mast Raho (VRMR) i.e., Remain Busy Be happy.**

Logically speaking, if I work more I am expected to get more in life. **Getting more and out of it is the sole basis for commercial mindset and modern movement for consumerism sweeping the country.** Work is the basis of our livelihood. Work helps to run business of our life. Just look around , all successful people have one thing in common .They work day-in and day-out. always on the move, doing something or the other. Fortunately , for us, and unfortunately for them, we seek their time and attention. We invite them to deliver lectures, to inaugurate establishments and solicit them to grace public functions. We remain ever-ready to listen to them or just to be seen with them in any and every possible manner. This further makes them busier. They are busier-bodies. The secret of their energy is the work, they remain busy doing.

The crux of the matter is that in context of the modern day work place, those who work-n-work-hard, are too tired already to take time off. They do not find any time to do yoga, walk on tread mill, do breathing exercises or, take time off to go on an extended vacation.

Major causes of stress on the job and away from it:

On job: The most stress producing factors are work and time pressure, disparity between what I have to do on the job and what I would like to accomplish. The general political climate of the organization. Stagnation Lastly, lack of feed back on work performance.

Away from job: Three major reasons are identified i.e., financial worries, problems with children, physical injury, illness or discomfort.

Personality traits: Attitude, belief system, habits and emotional distortions

Environmental: Pollution, seasonal changes and psychological fears etc etc.

Some useful practicable hints to reduce stress:

(At Individual Level)

Be Simple, Be Obedient Be Positive: Live a simple, important and meaningful life; meaningful to the self and others. Be respectful to them. Be obedient to your parents, teachers and elders. Be overt in exhibiting your obedience towards your boss. Work for it. Obedience has become the scariest virtue today, a causalty in this world of internet and information explosion. Try to forget and forgive. Learn to respect others and their view-point. Laugh a little as laughter is the best medicine. To unwind effortlessly, share your moments of joy and sorrow with family and friends. Maintain positive outlook.

Be Happy: Try to remain happy. Or just wear an inch of smile on your face. This will improve your face value, for sure..

Be a Family Man: Give full attention to your family . Treat your spouse as a partner- in-progress in the business of life. Attend family functions as far as possible. Once home, avoid sitting on couch, munching wafers or watching TV. Instead, take your family for post-dinner stroll, up to the nearest Park / Mall. Shower your children with the same love, affection and care, you shower on the children of your boss. Be good. Be good to others. Do not expect others to be good to you. You are good because you chose to be one. You are good because you yourself feel good about it.

Hobby: Engage yourself in some worthwhile hobby. Develop interest in one. Indulge in it during your free time, or listen to music. It helps to soothe nerves.

Health: Take care of your health. Health is wealth. Eat well Sleep well. Avoid intoxicants. Only a healthy person can take rigor of work. Take health insurance of the self and your spouse.

Have faith in God: Have faith in God. Faith can heal and repair body as well as soul. Thank God for showering pleasures of life on us.

Respect Life: We have been blessed with only one life. This is crucial. Let us take a leaf from the teachings of Sri Swami Gitanand Ji Maharaj; **Jeeven se hi sabb mil sakta hai sub kuchh de kar bhi jeevan nahi mil sakta. Iss liye samay ka sadupyog karo.** (We can achieve everything in this life, we can not earn life even if we give everything. So, we should make the best use of it).

(At work place)

Quiet Time: Spend some time, quietly. Talk you yourself . Keep taking stock of the situation as a routine, to steer your actions clear of hurdles. Engage yourself in an activity or follow trail of your heart in free hours. Try to separate work from home life ; though difficult but nor impractical to achieve, work hard-n-smarter

Communicate: Communicate effectively with peers and your boss. Develop soft skills especially communication skills. Try to listen (managers are generally poor listeners for some good reasons)

Get organized: Manage the self. Learn to develop Time Management Skills; Prioritize your work. Make list of jobs to be done a day in advance. Select five most important jobs-to-do from the list on the basis- What is expected? What gives the greatest reward? What gives the highest return? Be flexible in execution towards goals accomplishment Close the day. Carry forward unfinished jobs to the next day. Add fresh ones to the list. Work on it and continue.

Relax: Take mini breaks from work. Withdraw from the issues you are handling and the situation you are in , temporarily. Just take a break. Let off some steam by talking to people.

Delegate: Delegate responsibility with commensurate authority to work instead of carrying entire load on yourself.

Procrastination: Stay clear from it. Avoid it. A stitch in time saves nine. Once delayed, work gets piled up and becomes fire which needs fighting at a war footing, there by consuming more energy, money and time than required at the first place.

Become Tech. Savvy: We live in the age of Information Technology (IT) and Communication . Become friendly with computers, machinery, gadgets , tools and processes and techniques. There is a tip for managers——train-retrain.

Think Welfare: As a manager if you take care of the welfare of your employees, you do not have to bid farewell to them. Save the trouble and cost of replenishment, and ensuing moral boosting.

Reward-n-Appreciate Work: Appreciate performance. Practice culling black sheep in the flock. Give preferential treatment to those who perform. Reward such workers profusely. Improve your accessibility to your juniors and peers.

Strategize: If you can not withstand the rigor of of your job , don't worry ; make alternate arrangements. Find out the job you love. If possible, develop your hobby in to a profession. Work towards it. If you make your job your hobby; you do not have to work for the rest of your life.

(Social)

Maintain Hygiene: Be neat-clean -n- presentable.

Commute safely: Obey rules of the road. Reach office safe, on time, fit-n-fine. Vigorously take on the rigor of the day.

Respect Law of the Land: Respect rule- of- the- land. Have faith in the policies of the government. Place your fullest confidence in, and seamless support to the objectives, policies and programs of the establishment you work with. Try making improvement in the system you are part of Pay your tax on time and buy peace of.

Earn By Honest Means: Earn by honest means. Give your hundred percent to the job you are in. Work hard for it. Keep proper record of your earnings and expenses. Prepare home budget. Save some for the rainy day.

Serve Your Customers: As a business person, work toward betterment of the self , your establishment and the state. Manufacture and offer quality products and services at affordable price to your customers. Make perceptible positive improvement in the quality of their life through your products and services.

Take Pride in Your Work: Chose the profession you fancy. Make it your passion. Practice work ethics. The biggest ethical practice is to earn by doing the work, we are paid for. Practice basic ethics, Therefore, Just work.

Stress, Work and Personality

Personality is the outgrowth of early experiences that either can lead to an accurate perception of reality and instill a sense of mastery over the environment, or can lead to distorted perception of reality and instill doubts, fears and other limitations that individuals impose upon themselves. Predispositions and attitudes, acquired in childhood, become part of our emotional make-up, and they are very difficult to influence or change.

This is a relevant piece of information for employer and employees to understand. An Employer must seek to identify suitable traits in the applicant during the selection process while prospective interviewee must pose equally relevant question to himself/herself; Is he/she cut for the job he/she is interested in.? Or does he have in him the flair that is crucial to successfully carry out the job he seeks to take up. Ask yourself "Am I cut out for the Job?". Your answer shall lay down the foundation stone for a meaningful, satisfying and stress free innings in your career for mutual benefit. A good beginning for the good of every stake-holder.

References

[1] Executive Stress. An American Management Survey Report.1979.

[2] Sri Gita Manthan. Sri Swami Gitanand Ji Maharaj.

[3] Atmanand. Annual Magazine , SA Jain College, Ambala City. 2005-06.

[4] Executive Skills. Symbiosis Centre for Distance Learning. 2002.

[5] Thought for Today, Prajapita Brahama Kumaris Ishwariya Vishwa Vidyalaya.

[6] Excel Self Development Digest, Madras Academy for Excellence, 2001.

✡✡✡

14

ORGANISATIONAL ROLE STRESS AMONG TEACHERS

(A COMPARATIVE STUDY OF TECHNICAL AND NON-TECHNICAL TEACHERS)

** Sandhya Mehta (Ph. D Scholar)*

*** Sandeep Kaur*

* Assistant Professor, Guru Nanak Institute of Mgt & Tech, Ludhiana.

** Sr. Lecturer, Guru Nanak Institute of Mgt & Tech, Ludhiana.

Educational researchers have long been concerned with role stress among teachers. The concept of role and its two related aspects, role space and role set, have a built-in potential for conflict and stress .The present study was carried out to compare and analyze the organizational role stress among the technical and non-technical teachers in the Ludhiana district. The organizational role stress scale by Udai Pareek was administered (1971).

The findings indicated that. Inter -Role Distance, Role Stagnation, Role Expectation Conflict, Role Erosion, Role-Overload, Role Isolation, Personal Inadequacy, Self Role Distance, Role Ambiguity are acceptable at 5% level of significance and 1% level of significance. It means that the hypothesis that "There is no significant difference in the mean scores of the teachers in technical and non-technical institutes" is acceptable. Resource Inadequacy is not acceptable at both the levels, which means that there is difference in resource inadequacy of technical and non-technical teachers .So the hypothesis is rejected at this dimension. The study also brought the facts into light that there is no difference in the mean scores of technical and non-technical teachers in terms of Inter -Role Distance, Role Stagnation, Role Expectation Conflict, Role Erosion, Role-Overload, Role Isolation, Personal Inadequacy, Self Role Distance, Role Ambiguity but there is difference in the mean scores of teachers of technical and non-technical in terms of Resource Inadequacy when the age is taken to be less than 30 years. The technical teachers do differ from non-technical teachers in terms of scores of Personal Inadequacy and Role Ambiguity when the age is taken to be more than thirty.

Modern day occupational settings are characterized by heavy stress which influences individual efficiency and work performance leading to decreased job satisfaction. Education sector is no exception to this phenomenon. The occupation role stress is faced specially by technical teachers owing to long working hours, the pressure to keep oneself updated according to latest developments in the field, challanges posed by nuclear family system and hectic lifestyles. This study was conducted with the aim of investigating the effect of role stress in a sample of 200 lecturers of technical and non-technical teachers

An instrument designed by Udai Pareek (1981) known as Organisational Role Stress Scale was administered on the selected sample size. Various studies have been conducted in the educational settings to absorb the organizational role stress (Pestonjee D M and Azeem Syed Mohd, 2001; A.-S. Antoniou, F. Polychroni, A.-N. Vlachakis, 2006; A.-S. Antoniou, F. Polychroni, A.-N. Vlachakis, 2006; Woosley, 2000; Saul Neves de Jesus, Joseph Conboy, 2001; Athanasios Koustelios, Nicholas Theodorakis, Dimitris Goulimaris, 2004) Mohan V; Chauhan D (1999).

Objectives of the Study

1. To study the organizational stress among the teachers of technical and non-technical institutes in Ludhiana district.
2. To study the organizational stress among the teachers of technical and non-technical institutes having age less than 30 and more than 30.
3. To suggest measures to overcome stress

Hypothesis

1. There is no significant difference in the mean scores of the teachers in technical and non-technical institutes having age less than 30 for different parameters of ORS scale.

2. There is no significant difference in the mean scores of the teachers in technical and non-technical institutes having age more than 30 for different parasmeters of ORS scale.

Research Methodology

The primary data was collected using selective sampling technique on a sample size of 200 comprising of 100 from technical and 100 from non-technical teaching institutes. ORS scale was administered to find out the organizational stress on various parameters.

The sample of the present study was 200 teachers of technical and non-technical teachers in areas of Ludhiana district.

Design of Sample

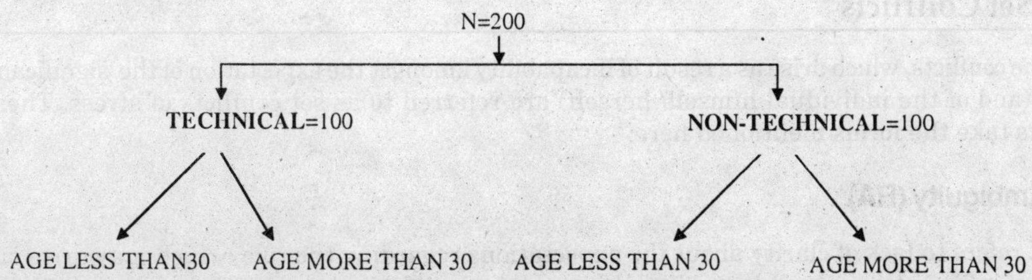

ORS Scale (Organizational Role Stress scale)

It is a point scale indicating how true a particular statement is for the role the respondent is asked to assign '0'to a statement if he never or scarcely feels this way;'1' to a statement if he occasionally feels this way;'4' if he very frequently feels this way. Hence the score of each role stress may range between 0 to 20 and total ors score may vary between 0 to 200. The ratings of the respondents may be added row wise to give scores on the 10 role stress dimensions

Role Space

The role space generally deals with the individual, the role he performs at a particular point of time and the other roles that the individual occupies. Any conflict among the above mentioned variables leads to role space.

These stresses may take the forms

Inter – Role Distance (IRD)

It is experienced when there is a conflict between organizational and non- organizational roles. For Example, the role of executive vs. the role of a husband/ wife.

Role Stagnation (RS)

It's the feeling of being stuck in the same role. Such a type of stress results in perception that there is no opportunity for the future progress of one's career.

Self - Role Distance (SED):

When the role a person occupies goes against his / her self-concept, then he / she feels self - role distance type of stress. This is essentially a conflict arising out of a mismatch between the person and his/ her job mentioned next.

Role Set

Role set is characterized by organizational system which defines the various roles assigned to various individuals or role occupants. These kinds of conflicts may result in different kinds of organizational role stress, namely, Role Ambiguity, Role Overload, Role Erosion, Resource Inadequacy, and Role Isolation

Role Set Conflicts

The conflicts, which arise as a result of incapability amongst the expectation of the 'significant' others (and of the individual himself/ herself) are referred to as set conflicts of stress. These conflicts take the forms mentioned here:

Role Ambiguity (RA)

It refers to lack of clarity about the expectations regarding the role, which may arise out of lack of information or understanding. It may exist in relation to activities, responsibilities, personal styles and norms and may operate at three stages:

- When the role sender holds his/her expectations about the role,
- When he/she sends it, and
- When the occupant receives those expectations.

Role Expectation Conflict (REC)

This "type of stress is generated by different expectations by different significant persons, i.e., superiors, subordinates and peers, about the same role; and the role occupant's ambivalence, as to whom to please.

Role overload (RO)

When the occupant feels unable to meet the expectations of the role allotted to him, he experiences role overload.There are two Aspects of this stress: quantitative and qualitative. The former refers to having too much to do, while the latter refers to things being too difficult and the accountability in the role.

Role Erosion (RE)

This type of role stress is the function of the role occupant's feeling, that some functions 'which should properly belong to his/ her' role are transferred to / or performed by some other person. This can also happen when the role occupant performs the functions but the credit for them goes to someone else.

Resource Inadequacy (RIN)

This type of stress is evident when the role occupant feels that he / she is not provided with adequate resources for performing the functions expected from his / her role.

Personal Inadequacy (PI)

It arises when the role occupant feels that he / she docs not have the necessary skills and training for effectively performing the functions expected from his / her role. This is bound to happen when the organization does not impart periodic training to enable the employees to cope with the fast changes both within and outside the organization.

Role Isolation (RI)

This type of role stress refers to the psychological distance between the occupant's role and other roles in the same role set. While IRD(Inter Role Distance) refers to the distance among various roles occupied by the same individual, role isolation (RJ) is characterized by the feelings that others do not reach out easily, indicative of the absence of strong linkages of one's role with other roles.

Delimitations of the Study

1. The sample was delimited to only 200 teachers teaching in district Ludhiana (Punjab).
2. The study was equally balanced among technical and non-technical teachers.
3. The study was equally balanced among technical and non-technical teachers having age less than 30 years and more than 30 years

Analysis and Interpretation

Mean, Median, Standard Deviation, of the scores on ORS scale was calculated to verify the normality of the data. Later Z-values were calculated to the significance of difference in the mean scores of various groups and subgroups.

Sr. No.	*Dimensions of ORS*	*Mean*	*Standard Deviation*
1	Inter -Role Distance	6.62	3.566907
2	Role Stagnation	6.68	3.051345
3	Role Expectation Conflict	6.25	3.242318
4	Role Erosion	7.61	3.419773
5	Role-Overload	6.73	3.378049
6	Role Isolation	6.78	3.230474
7	Personal Inadequacy	6.04	4.102032
8	Self Role Distance	6.71	4.05591
9	Role Ambiguity	5.72	3.360736
10	Resource Inadequacy	6.73	3.653848

Sr. No.	Dimensions of ORS	TYPE	Mean	S.D	Z-value
1	Inter -Role Distance	Technical	7.140	3.753	1.111
		Non -Technical	6.044	3.202	
2	Role Stagnation	Technical	7.160	2.787	1.230
		Non -Technical	6.126	3.144	
3	Role Expectation Conflict	Technical	6.360	3.231	0.205
		Non -Technical	6.174	3.186	
4	Role Erosion	Technical	7.460	3.406	-0.143
		Non -Technical	7.598	3.387	
5	Role-Overload	Technical	7.020	3.695	0.585
		Non -Technical	6.468	2.942	
6	Role Isolation	Technical	6.660	2.782	-0.165
		Non -Technical	6.808	3.527	
7	Personal Inadequacy	Technical	6.860	4.504	1.328
		Non.-Technical	5.352	3.456	
8	Self Role Distance	Technical	7.360	4.355	1.241
		Non -Technical	5.968	3.535	
9	Role Ambiguity	Technical	6.260	3.433	1.087
		Non -Technical	5.249	3.135	
10	Resource Inadequacy	Technical	7.900	3.418	2.314
		Non -Technical	5.660	3.426	

Sr. No.	Dimensions of ORS	TYPE	Mean	S.D	Z-value
1	Inter -Role Distance	Technical	6.720	3.234	1.387
		Non -Technical	5.520	2.874	
2	Role Stagnation	Technical	7.280	2.792	1.037
		Non -Technical	6.320	3.694	
3	Role Expectation Conflict	Technical	5.920	3.378	-0.368
		Non -Technical	6.280	3.530	
4	Role Erosion	Technical	7.920	3.936	0.105
		Non -Technical	7.800	4.123	
5	Role-Overload	Technical	5.800	3.082	-0.641
		Non -Technical	6.360	3.094	
6	Role Isolation	Technical	7.360	2.564	0.885
		Non -Technical	6.560	3.721	

7	Personal Inadequacy	Technical	7.080	4.949	0.681
		Non -Technical	6.240	3.677	
8	Self Role Distance	Technical	7.120	4.343	0.869
		Non -Technical	6.080	4.112	
9	Role Ambiguity	Technical	6.120	3.032	0.082
		Non -Technical	6.040	3.824	
10	Resource Inadequacy	Technical	7.520	2.502	3.484
		Non -Technical	4.920	2.768	

It is clear that there is no significant difference in the mean scores of the teachers in technical and non-technical institutes having age less than 30 for different parameters of ORS SCALE except role inadequacy of technical and non-technical teachers having age less than 30 years.

Sr. No.	*Dimensions of ORS*	*TYPE*	*Mean*	*S.D*	*Z-value*
1	Inter -Role Distance	Technical	7.560	4.234	0.783
		Non -Technical	6.680	3.694	
2	Role Stagnation	Technical	7.040	2.835	1.081
		Non -Technical	6.080	3.415	
3	Role Expectation Conflict	Technical	6.800	3.082	0.918
		Non -Technical	6.000	3.082	
4	Role Erosion	Technical	7.000	2.784	-0.923
		Non -Technical	7.720	2.731	
5	Role-Overload	Technical	8.240	3.908	1.736
		Non -Technical	6.520	3.043	
6	Role Isolation	Technical	5.960	2.865	-1.389
		Non -Technical	7.240	3.609	
7	Personal Inadequacy	Technical	6.640	4.102	2.378
		Non -Technical	4.200	3.082	
8	Self Role Distance	Technical	7.600	4.444	1.419
		Non -Technical	6.040	3.234	
9	Role Ambiguity	Technical	6.400	3.851	2.327
		Non -Technical	4.320	2.268	
10	Resource Inadequacy	Technical	8.280	4.159	1.776
		Non -Technical	6.200	4.123	

It is evident that there is no significant difference in the mean scores of the teachers in technical and non-technical institutes having age more than 30 for different parameters of ORS SCALE" except for Personal Inadequacy and Role Ambiguity of technical and non-technical teachers having age more than 30 years.

To conclude, the present study, threw up following facts:

- The technical teachers do not differ from non-technical teachers in terms of their Inter -Role Distance, Role Stagnation, Role Expectation Conflict, Role Erosion, Role-Overload, Role Isolation, Personal Inadequacy, Self Role Distance, Role Ambiguity as a whole, but there is difference in resource inadequacy of technical and non-technical teachers.
- The study also brought the facts into light that than there is no difference in the mean scores of technical and non-technical teachers in terms of Inter -Role Distance, Role Stagnation, Role Expectation Conflict, Role Erosion, Role-Overload, Role Isolation, Personal Inadequacy, Self Role Distance, Role Ambiguity, but there is difference in the mean scores of teachers of technical and non-technical in terms of Resource Inadequacy when the age is taken to be less than 30 years.
- The technical teachers having age, more than 30 years do not differ from non-technical teachers in terms of mean scores in Inter -Role Distance, Role Stagnation, Role Expectation Conflict, Role Erosion, Role-Overload, Role Isolation, Personal Inadequacy, Self Role Distance, Resource Inadequacy, but they are different in the mean scores of Personal Inadequacy& Role Ambiguity.

Suggestions

The overall scores indicate that the technical teachers experience resource inadequacy .In case of technical education the resources like computer lab, internet facility, LCD projector interactive board etc may be essential hence the authorities should ensure that proper resources in terms of infrastructure and various facilities are provided. In case of teachers with less than thirty years of experience, more resource inadequacy may be due to uneven distribution of resources therefore the authorities should pay attention to this area.

Since there is a difference in the personal inadequacy in case of technical and non-technical teachers, short term training programmes (STTP) should be a regular part so that the teachers are equipped with the latest knowledge in that area. It is more important in case of technical education where changes take place at a rapid pace.

Technical teachers with more than thirty years were found to be more role ambiguous which could be due to the reason that as a teacher matures in her role they may be involved in developmental and administrative activities hence in addition to the teaching workload, their workload in various other activities needs to be judiciously distributed and incorporated into their job descriptions. It is suggested that every teacher should know about his/her job description

References

[1] Pestonjee DM, Azeem SM(2001): A study of Organizational Role Stress in relation to Job Burnout among university teachers. IIMA Working papers (Indian institute of management Ahmedabad, Research and Publication Department).

[2] Lease HS(1999): Occupational role stressors, coping, support, and hardiness as predictors of strain in academic faculty: an emphasis on new and female faculty. Research in Higher Education, 40:285-307.

[3] Maslach C, Schaufeli WB, Leiter MP(2001): Job Burnout. Annual Review of Psychology, 52:397-422.

[4] Thorsen EJ(1996): Stress in academe: What bothers professors? Higher Education, 31:471-489.

[5] Dua JK(1994): Job stressors and their effects on physical health, emotional health, and job satisfaction in a university. Journal of Educational Administration, 32:59-78.

[6] Richard VG, Krieshok ST(1989): Occupational stress, strain, and coping in university faculty. Journal of Vocational Behavior, 34:117-132.

[7] Narayanan L, Menon S, Spector PE (1999): Stress in the workplace: A comparison of gender and occupation. Journal of Organizational Behavior, 20:63-73.

[8] Pestonjee DM, Kumar PM(2000): Role stress and job satisfaction amongst doctors. IIMA Working papers (Indian institute of management Ahmedabad, Research Publication Department) Harden MR, Crosby JR: The good teacher is more than a lecturer – the twelve roles of the teacher. AMEE Medical Education Guide No 2 .Medical Teacher, 22:334-345.

[9] Pareek U (2005): The Role. In Training instruments in Human Resource development and Organizational Development. Edited by: Pareek U. New Delhi: Tata McGraw-Hill;:475-567.

✲ ✲ ✲

15

Stress at Work Place: A Review Article

** Dr. Pawan Kumar*

*** Rajinder Singh*

* Lecturers, Dronacharya Institute of Management and Technology, Kurukshetra.

Introduction

Workplace stress has a negative impact on business as well as on the individual employee. Increase in job stress creates emotional, financial, and safety concerns for employers and managers. Stress in the workplace is a greater threat to employee health and well-being than ever before. While technology has made aspects of many jobs easier, it has also added to the anxieties of office life through information overload, heightened pressure for productivity, and a threatening sense of impermanence in the workplace. In 1996, the World Health Organization labeled stress a "worldwide epidemic." Today, workplace stress is estimated to cost American companies more than $300 billion a year in poor performance, absenteeism and health costs.

What is workplace stress?

Stress—the responses our bodies and minds have to the demands placed on them—is a normal part of life and a normal part of any job. Without stress, we wouldn't meet deadlines, strive to hit sales or production targets, or line up new clients. Meeting the demands and challenges of a job is part of what makes work interesting and satisfying, and it's often what allows people to develop new skills and advance in their careers. In the workplace, we regularly experience stress-causing situations, react to them with heightened tension, and then return to a more relaxed state when the crisis, big or small, is resolved.

However, problems occur when stress is so overwhelming or constant that the tension never abates and we never get to relax.

What we think of as "**job stress**" is what happens when:

- The challenges and demands of work become excessive.
- The pressures of the workplace surpass workers' abilities to handle them.
- Satisfaction gives way to frustration and exhaustion.

When stress crosses the line from normal to excessive, it can trigger physical and emotional responses that are harmful to employees and businesses alike. And unfortunately, for many people "stress" has become synonymous with "work."

Recent changes in technology and management have forced organizations and management scientists to change their outlook towards work and workforce. Various researcher and scholars have conducted many studies in this area. Some studies have been reviewed to point out the causes of stress at work as well as the measures to reduce the same. Among the general causes, some causes specific to the call centre industry have been highlighted in this paper.

Objectives of the Paper

1. To highlight the causes for stress among employees.
2. To identify the strategies to remove the stress.

Research Methodology

The secondary information has been used for the study. Data is collected from magazines, journals, textbooks and various websites. By using secondary data efforts have been made to highlight the causes for stress and finding out some suggestions to coping with the stress.

Causes of in workplace stress

Workplace stress is usually the result of high demands on the job, real or perceived,lack of control concerning those demands, poor day-to-day organization and communication, and an unsupportive work environment.

The following table lays out many of the factors that lead to job stress:

Types of Job Stressors	*Examples*
Specific work factors	Excessive workload. Tedious or meaningless tasks. Long hours and low pay. Infrequent rest breaks. Unreasonable performance demands.
Physical environment	Noise and overcrowding. Poor air quality. Ergonomic problems. Health and safety risks (heavy equipment, toxic chemicals).
Organizational practices	Unclear responsibilities or expectations. Conflicting job demands. Multiple supervisors. Lack of autonomy or participation in decision-making. Inefficient communication patterns. Lack of family-friendly policies.
Workplace change	Fear of layoff. Frequent personnel turnover. Lack of preparation for technological changes. Poor chances for advancement or promotion. Tensions brought about by greater workplace diversity.
Interpersonal relationships	Distant, uncommunicative supervisors. Poor performance from subordinates. Office politics, competition, and other conflicts among staff. Bullying or harassment. Problems caused by excessive time away from family.

Source: http://www.helpguide.org/mental/work_stress_management.htmJob Stress Management:

Causes of Stress in Call Centers

Timing of Work

It's the greatest cause for stress and unique to the Indian call center industry. The industry works largely during the night to coincide with the UK and US daylight hours. Certainly, there are daytime shifts but the night remains the peak load period.

Newcomers have the toughest time. No call center industry in the world faces this problem as India does. (b) Its impact is large and is a major cause of high attrition. (c)There are no easy answers to this problem. These work timings are in the very nature of the job in India.

Repetitive of Same Work

The second biggest cause for stress is doing the same thing 8 hours a day, every day. Internationally, there has been a lot of debate on what to do on this count and some suggestions have included job-rotation with other functions for a few days every quarter. Example – if a call floor person can spend three days a quarter in HR or procurement or administration, it might help to relieve some of the stress. Another oft-repeated suggestion: remove the tyranny of the scripted conversation, hire carefully, train people well, and let them handle each call at their natural best.

Excessive Workload

Though the number of hours a day ,a call center employee works, may be the same—in some cases actually less—than others, it is the intensity and relentless pace at which work tends to happen that makes work load an issue. Though IT and IT services employees for instance may work much longer hours, these are interspersed with either chats with colleagues, smoke and coffee breaks taken at will and visits to other departments or customers. Call floor employees on the other hand have no such luck. In addition the team leader and above managers daylight hours. Certainly, there are daytime shifts but the night remains the peak load period.

Newcomers have the toughest time. No call center industry in the world faces this problem as India does. (b) Its impact is large and is a major cause of high attrition. (c) There are no easy answers to this problem. These work timings are in the very nature of the job in India.

Repetitive of Same Work

The second biggest cause for stress is doing the same thing 8 hours a day, every day. Internationally, there has been a lot of debate on what to do on this count and some suggestions have included job-rotation with other functions for a few days every quarter. Example – if a call floor person can spend three days a quarter in HR or procurement or administration, it might help to relieve some of the stress. Another oft-repeated suggestion: remove the tyranny of the scripted conversation, hire carefully, train people well, and let them handle each call at their natural best.

Excessive Workload

Though the number of hours a day, a call center employee works, may be the same—in some cases actually less—than others, it is the intensity and relentless pace at which work tends to happen that makes work load an issue. Though IT and IT services employees for instance may work much longer hours, these are interspersed with either chats with colleagues, smoke and coffee breaks taken at will and visits to other departments or customers. Call floor employees on the other hand have no such luck. In addition the team leader and above managers have higher load because they often stay beyond a shift for meetings with managers. Those with less than a year's experience have fewer problems as some amount of time is spent in training and for the first few months on a job, the metrics are easier.

Irritation due to Callers

This is a tough one. Irate customers cause a lot of stress. It is a fact that team leaders and their seniors don't directly interact with customers and very few of them actually get the brunt. Again, this is a stress factor that is inherent in the nature of the job – most often customers call when they have a problem. Often, they are further irritated by long call queues and the inability of call center executives to offer a quick solution to their problems.

Worse, some are put off by scripted conversations and the rather stilted manner in which the whole dialogue sometimes tends to occur. For call floor executives, this is a tough one, because most neither have the freedom to change the script, nor are they allowed to put the phone down on any customer, no matter how abusive he or she may get. Phone-cuts can get you fired instantly. In extreme cases of customer abuse, the standard practice is to get a team leader to listen in on the conversation—then either take it over, or politely but firmly, cut it off.

Stress due to Travelling Time

Most of the bigger centers in India are thousands of people strong; as a result these call centers require a lot of real estate; and are often situated on the outskirts of town. So the travel time from residence to the workplace also cause stress for everyone, irrespective of experience or job role.

Large Number of Calls

In larger centers with lots of customers, there is often not even a second's difference between one call being closed and the other coming up—which can be very disconcerting. Not surprisingly, first timers and those with less than one year in the business feel the pressure a lot more, though it remains a big issue with all call floor employees irrespective of experience.

Long Working Hours

Is a combination of work load, call volume and travel time that adds to a long day. Most call center employees in Mumbai, Gurgaon and Bangalore for instance, budget at least two hours for travel up and down to work. With a nine hour designated work day, that is a minimum of 11 hours spent on work or getting to work every day. Some call centers that encourage overtime might have employees working longer, 13-14 hour days on a routine basis. Operational heads who work the shift and stay back for customer conference calls from the US, tend to put in 16-18 hours on a regular basis.

Insufficient Breaks

Is one of the key reasons for call center stress all over the world. In an industry that is very quantitative measures driven, and where measures are counted in seconds, too many breaks are not allowed. The better ones in India would have designated break periods of about 15 minutes in every 2.5 hours plus half hour for lunch.

A quick look at comparative figures for countries like Australia however suggests that the Indian industry may have fewer problems on this count than most others do.

Pressure To Perform On Metrics

First timers find the entire exceedingly quantified model of measuring performance a lot more stressful than those who have learnt to live with the system. Those with more than five years of experience feel it the least.

Measures to Reduce Stress at Work

What can managers or employers do to reduce stress at work?

Stress on the job, creates high costs for businesses and institutions, reducing morale, productivity, and earnings. Clearly, it is in every employer's best interests—fiscal and otherwise—to reduce workplace stress as much as possible. Businesses can lower and prevent job stress through two methods:

- **Stress management** programs and training for employees.
- **Organizational changes** that improve working conditions.

Stress Management

Nearly half of large American corporations provide their employees with stress management training and Employee Assistance Programs (EAPs). EAPs are designed to help workers with personal problems that may be adversely affecting their on-the-job performance. The confidential services include counseling, mental health assessment and referrals, workshops on topics such as time management and relaxation, and legal and financial assistance.

Organizational Change

While EAPs can be very beneficial to workers, the relief they provide may be superficial and short-lived if important root causes of stress in the work environment are not addressed. **Lasting stress reduction is brought about by institutional change.** Managers are the key holders of corporate culture. No meaningful job or workplace is, or should be expected to be, stress-free. However, less stress occurs when a business or institution encourages employee participation from the bottom up, implements policies that take employee needs into account, and empowers employees to do their best.

Given below are some ways in which an organization can foster low levels of job stress and high levels of productivity:

Improve communication

- Share information with employees to reduce uncertainty about their jobs and futures.
- Clearly define employees' roles and responsibilities.
- Make communication friendly and efficient, not mean-spirited or petty.

Consult your employees

- Give workers opportunities to participate in decisions that affect their jobs.
- Consult employees about scheduling and work rules.
- Be sure the workload is suitable to employees' abilities and resources;
- Avoid unrealistic deadlines.
- Show that individual workers are valued.

Offer Rewards And Incentives

- Praise good work performance verbally and institutionally.
- Provide opportunities for career development.
- Promote an "entrepreneurial" work climate that gives employees more control over their work.

Cultivate A Friendly Social Climate

- Provide opportunities for social interaction among employees.
- Establish a zero-tolerance policy for harassment.
- Make management actions consistent with organizational values.

What can employees do to reduce job stress?

While organizational change comes from management, there are still many things employees—individually or collectively—can do to reduce workplace stress.

Stand Up for Yourself

- **Get a job description.** If your employer hasn't provided a specific, written description of your job, ask for one, or, better, ask to negotiate one. The act of negotiating a job description "does more to dispel a sense of powerlessness than anything else we know. You can object to what and insist on what you do want. If there is a compromise, it's because you agreed to it. With a clear job description, your expectations are spelled out, as are your boss's."

< **Change your job.** If you like where you're working but your job is too stressful, ask if the company can tailor the job to your skills or move you to a less pressured slot.

- **Get support**. Use the local, state, and federal agencies created to support workers' interests — and your union, if you belong to one — to back you up in situations that expose you to unnecessary danger, unsafe or unhealthful conditions, or undue harassment. While some locations and agencies are more sympathetic to employees' rights than others, sometimes simply mentioning that you know where to turn for help is enough to start an employer thinking about improvement.
- **Get a new job**. If the level of stress at your job is harming your health and your relationships, and you don't see any prospect of real change, it may be time to move on.

Eliminate Self-Defeating Behaviours

Many of us make job stress worse with patterns of thought or behavior that keep us from relieving pressure on ourselves. If you can turn around these self-defeating habits, you'll find employer-imposed stress easier to handle.

- **Resist perfectionism.** No project, situation, or decision is ever perfect, and you put undue stress on yourself by trying to do everything perfectly. When you set unrealistic goals for yourself or try to do too much, you're setting yourself up to fall short. Do your best, and you'll do fine.
- **Clean up your act.** If you're always running late, set your clocks and watches fast and give yourself extra time. If your desk is a mess, file and throw away the clutter; just knowing where everything is saves time and cuts stress. Make to-do lists and cross off items as you accomplish them. Plan your day and stick to the schedule — you'll feel less overwhelmed.
- **Flip your negative thinking.** If you see the downside of every situation and interaction, you'll find yourself drained of energy and motivation. Try to think positively about your work, avoid negative-thinking co-workers, and pat yourself on the back about small accomplishments, even if no one else does.

References

[1] Shrivastav, Avinash Kumar (2005), Roll stress across management levels in an organization, The ICFAI journal of Organizational Behaviour, Vol. IV, No. 4.

[2] Chiryath, Suran (2006), Stress and coping mechanism of female cashew workers: A study, The ICFAI journal of Organizational Behaviour, Vol. V, No. 4.

[3] Bhattacharya, Mandira and S. S. Jha (2006), Stress in Organizational Context, The ICFAI journal of Organizational Behaviour, Vol. V, No. 1.

[4] Robbins, P. Stephen, Organizational Behaviour, Pearson Education.

[5] Luthans, Fred, Organizational Behaviour, McGraw Hill.

[6] Greenberg, Jerald and Robert A. Baron, Behaviour in Organization, Prentice Hall India.

[7] http://www.helpguide.org/mental/work_stress_management.htmJob Stress Management

[8] http://management.about.com/od/yourself/ht/ReduceStress05.htm

[9] http://www.jobseekersadvice.com/employment_issues/articles/how_to_reduce_stress_at_work. htm

[10] http://www.careerjournal.com/myc/survive/19980813-earley.htm

16

TECHNOSTRESS OF LIBRARY PROFESSIONALS — THE PATH FOR RECOVERY

** Anju Khurana*

* Librarian, AIMT, Ambala City.

Introduction

Rapid technological change has become a fact of life in the libraries of the 21st Century. While this change touches all parts of the library organization, nowhere is it more visible, or its effects more keenly felt, than in reference departments. Consider these "snapshots"—fictional, but real enough:

- A librarian begins a mediated online search session by apologizing to the user: "I hardly ever do this any more. Most people just search on the CD-ROMs." During the search, he/she mistakenly downloads too large a file, resulting in a "disk full" error.
- A user comes to the reference desk with a question that could be answered in five minutes with a "ready reference" database search. As the librarian hesitates, trying to decide whether to go online for this user, he/she sees three others waiting for help: one whose CD-ROM printer has evidently jammed, one who is waving from an online catalog terminal, and another who is carrying a volume of L'Annee Philologique.

Free time will not be taken over by these commitments can be difficult, especially for someone dedicated to their profession. The solution is to learn how to say NO when you already have a full plate. Finally, remember to use some of your free time to exercise and relax. By dedicating time to rejuvenating your body and mind, recovery from the rigors of work is possible. If you do nothing else but follow these simple tips, you will attain the mastery of library stress.

Stress-A "Modern Disease"

Each of these scenarios portrays a mixed blessing: the dramatic and liberating benefits of information technology, coupled with new time demands, knowledge/skill deficiencies, and the resulting psychological pressure.

One name for this kind of pressure is technostress. Craig Brod, who may have coined the term and certainly brought it into the popular consciousness, defines technostress as:

"... a modern disease of adaptation caused by an inability to cope with the new computer technologies in a healthy manner. It manifests itself in two distinct and related ways: in the struggle to accept computer technology, and in the more specialized form of over identification with computer technology."

The most commonly studied aspects of technostress are machine-based stress (physical and psychological, caused by poor ergonomics, badly designed software, etc.); computer anxiety; and computer obsession. The populations most often studied in the mainstream psychological literature are clerical and office workers, professionals, executives, home computer users, hackers, students, and adolescents.

The effects of technostress on librarians have been studied by Bichteler, Champion, Dobb, and Sievert et al. Among the many discussions of the related problem of resistance to technological change in libraries, those by Fine, Malinconico, Luguire, and Giesbrecht and McCarthy are especially relevant.

While reference librarians are as prone as anyone to suffer from poor ergonomics or badly-designed software, and while some certainly become obsessively involved in over identification with the computer, the technostress phenomenon of greatest interest here is "computer anxiety."

Brod's elaboration on this term seems to ring true for many librarians:

"The primary symptom of those who are ambivalent, reluctant, or fearful of computers is anxiety. This anxiety is expressed in many ways: irritability, headaches, nightmares, resistance to learning about the computer or outright rejection of the technology. Techno anxiety most commonly afflicts those who feel pressured—by employer, peers, or the general culture—to accept and use computers."

While it is fortunately rare for a reference librarian to be truly computerphobic to the extent that he/she "locks up" or panics, milder symptoms of technostress are fairly common.

These include:

- feelings of isolation and frustration.
- negative attitudes toward new computer-based sources and systems.
- indifference to users' computer-related needs (as in "It's not my job to fix that printer").
- self-deprecating thoughts or statements about one'sability to cope.
- an apologetic attitude toward users.
- a definition of self as "someone who doesn't search."

Case Study-Technostress and its Components

This page presents the results of an online survey on technostress (computer-related stress) among library staff members, taken in August 2003. This survey was posted on the web for 10 days and collected 92 responses, most coming from people who work in academic libraries.

Highlights:

- 59% of survey participants said their level of computer-related stress has increased in the past 5 years, 34% felt it has not changed much, and only 4% believed it has decreased.
- 65% of participants reported that this type of stress is a somewhat serious problem for them, 8% said it is very serious, while 27% felt it is not at all serious.
- Leading causes chosen from a list of possibilities were information overload, networking problems, security issues, computer hardware and ergonomics, and vendor-produced databases. Security issues may have drawn special attention because of the "Blaster" and "SoBig" attacks going on at the time. Interestingly, library catalogs and web sites ranked low on the list of causes; Participants also listed several other causes.
- The survey also collected numerous strategies for managing and coping with technostress. Prominent themes in these responses include the need for individuals to cultivate flexibility and continuous learning, and for organizations to provide training and support.

This was an informal poll, not a scientific sample. Respondents were self-selected .The survey questions elicited subjective perceptions of stress levels, not objective measures of symptoms or behavior. Thus, we can't conclude from these results that X percentage of library staff suffer from any given level of computer-related stress. Nonetheless, since 92 people took the time to respond in the ways described below, I do think it's reasonable to conclude that substantial numbers of library staff are experiencing this type of stress. That in itself should be of concern to those who manage and study libraries. This survey was conducted by John Kupersmith (1999-2003).

Survey Results-

1. Do you work in:	*responses*	*Percent*
an academic library?	53	58 %
a public library?	18	20 %
another type of library?	13	14 %
A library-related business or organization?	5	5 %
(none of the above)	3	3 %
Total	92	100 %
Increased	54	59%

2 In the past 5 years, has your level of technostress:	*Responses*	*Percent*
Don't know	2	2%
Decreased	4	4 %
Total	91	100%
Not changed much	31	34 %

3 For you personally, is the problem of technostress:	*Responses*	*Percent*
Not at all serious	25	27 %
Somewhat serious	60	65 %
Very serious	7	8 %
Don't know	0	0 %
Total	92	100 %

4. What are the main causes of technostress for you? Check the 3 most important causes below. (Arranged in order as ranked by participants)	*responses*	*percent*
Information overload	54	59 %
Networking problems	40	43 %
Security issues (viruses, authentication, etc.)	38	41 %
Computer hardware and ergonomics	38	41 %
Vendor-produced databases	28	30%
Application software (word processors, etc.)	21	23 %

Library catalogs	9	10 %
Library web sites	9	10 %
Other web sites	6	7 %

Successful Coping- The Path For Recovery

Coping involves reconfiguring your life landscape. Take the time to downsize. Rearrange your priorities, tasks and activities. Use any combination of the strategies described below to create more balance and less stress in your life.

(a) Mentoring

Making use of mentors is a giant step towards becoming a happy, stress-free librarian. Mentoring in the library field can come in many forms. Finding a mentor is easiest when your library already has a mentoring system in place. Having a colleague as a mentor will help you find answers in a very low-key, informal manner. Look to your local, state, and national library associations as well; many of these organizations have mentoring programmes. Everyone can feel his/her stress dissipate when he/she finds solutions to the work-related problems.

(b) Asking For Advice

If you work as a librarian long enough, chances are you will run across unfamiliar situations that you are not sure how to handle. Try posting your question on library-related listservs. You can receive responses from people of varying backgrounds and environments, which can give you more opinions and options. The sharing of information and stories among colleagues is a great way to make a stressed librarian feel like he or she is not alone.

(c) Creating A Network

Learn when and how to delegate. It's important to recognize what you have to do yourself and what you can allow others to do. Don't be afraid to ask for help when you need it. Perhaps, you can partner with someone or form a team to accomplish some tasks. Through sharing, your workload and stress load can be lightened.

(d) Prioritizing And Being Selective

Being stressed will affect your job performance and your quality of life. Learn the power of prioritizing and being selective in your commitments. Learn to say NO and you will be one step ahead of the pack. No matter how much we love our work, or want to stay on top of the growing paper piles on our desk, it is not healthy to spend all of our free time doing work, thinking about work, or worrying about work.

(e) Making Healthy Lifestyle Choices

Engaging in healthy habits such as eating well, getting enough sleep, and exercising helps to form a solid base upon which we can build stress-busting habits. Stress is dissipated when you do something that stimulates the mind or the body in an activity that is completely separate from work. By taking your mind off of work, you will be able to relax, your body will be less tense, and come the next workday, you will find yourself renewed, rested and ready once more to face the daily challenges of your profession.

Remedies: * Let it flow over you.

- Deep breathing.
- Roll with the flow
- Realise that the technology changes are going to continue and that I have a choice: move with it or get stressed (and left behind). I choose to move with the technology!
- Keep reading and learning always
- Vacations
- I'm younger and a new librarian so honestly I'm not having terrible stress. One things that helps is that I almost never use computers outside of work and keep technology low in my home (ie no games, no cell phone, no dvd player,...).
- Take physical stretching/exercise breaks
- Have written to-do lists
- Try to keep information organized at some level
- Hum a little tune
- Laugh a lot
- Take a deep breath and remind yourself that things really are better than they were — we can now access so much information quickly and (usually) more easily than in the past. There *is* too much, too quickly, but I can choose the most important....
- Just keep trying
- Time management, to-do lists, and a willingness to delete or ignore the unimportant
- Keeping up-to-date on specific areas of interest
- Keep learning, attend workshops and share knowledge with colleagues.
- Accept that occasionally a source will be missed in responding to a research request
- Use the help tools as often as possible for the different software applications
- For some of the issues—learn more about it and practice. For information overload—prioritize, know when to say "enough"
- Try to learn as much as you can
- Go home & leave work at work; yoga/meditaion/prayer.
- Stay up to date and stay calm
- The best way for me to cope has been to learn more about the technologies so I can feel more empowered to troubleshoot or otherwise try to solve those inevitable technology glitches that occur when I have multiple systems talking to each other
- Gardening. Deep breaths. Going for walks
- Complete change of pace for time outside of work is essential
- The ability to focus on one issue at a time helps; making a list can help this
- Through Training

- Focus on task goals, rather than the particular software tools/interfaces that may actually impede progress
- When possible, minimize time spent on line. Unsubscribe to e-letters and try to avoid new ones
- Calm attitude
- Relaxing breaks
- Separate work from home life—leave stress at the office
- Just cope, then go home and garden
- Focus on the software needed for the job and keep current. Sharing solutions with others helps. Network with the techies. Laugh often; laugh hard
- Exercise, 'proper' diet, plenty of sleep, sailing on the lake, realize that the fast pace of tech innovation will take this moment away without a tear for the latest new thing...
- I haven't found a "best" way yet other than chilling out. There will always be another problem tomorrow
- Learn more, and make lots of friends in the IT department
- Completely remove self from the environment — Vacation
- Communication rather than complaining

Summary And Conclusion

All stress is not bad; the outcomes depend upon how you handle it. Stress is the pressure that chisels away at our feeling of well-being and, if left unchecked, at our health. The key to successful stress-busting is learning how to control our response to stressful situations, and how to handle our jobs without letting the pressure escalate and overwhelm us. Information sharing and mentoring is a great avenue for seeking help, when we come across a stumbling block, big or small. Limiting ones association and committee work to make sure that both our work time and free time will not be taken over by these commitments, can be difficult, especially for those dedicated to their profession. The solution is to learn how to say NO when you already have a full plate. Finally, remember to use some of your free time to exercise and relax. By dedicating time to rejuvenating your body and mind, recovery from the rigours of work are possible. If you do nothing else but follow these simple tips, you will attain the mastery of library stress.

References

[1] Caputo, Janette S. *Stress and Burnout in Library Service*. Phoenix, AZ: Oryz Press, 1991.

[2] Harrison, Lucy. "Stress Relief: Help for the Technophobic Patron from the Reference Desk". *The Reference Librarian*, No. 69/70, 2000: 31-47.

[3] Nawe, Julita. "Work-related stress among the library and information workforce". *Library Review*, Vol. 4 44, Issue 6, 1995: 30-37.

[4] Reinhold, Barbara. *Toxic Work: Overcoming Stress, Overload, and Burnout and Revitalizing Your Career* NY: Dutton, 1996.

[5] http://www.jkup.net/tstress.html

17

Stress in Software Industry and Its Remedies

* *Shivani Nagpal*
* *Kamaljeeet Kaur*

* Lecturers-MCA Deptt., AIMT, Ambala City.

IT Careers are generally more stressful than other careers. They are often characterized by hard work, long hours, tight deadlines.

Introduction

What is stress - "Stress is tension from extraordinary demands, constraints, or opportunities". There are many factors in our daily lives that cause stress, but how does technology affect stress?Does it affect it positively or negatively? Is there anything unethical about the technology and the way it is utilized? Through an exploration of Company X, one will see both the positive and negative impacts of technology on workplace stress, and discover some of the underlying ethical issues involved.

Company X utilizes various types of technology, from pagers and cell phones to personal computers and numerous types of technical software. In the article, "Workplace Depression Blamed on IT Stress", David Wiliamson states, "Technology designed to help people work efficiently is now forcing employees into a state of 'digital depression'."

Within Company X, employees and subcontractors utilize cell phones, pagers, radios, and e-mail. As such, employees are rarely unavailable and it is not uncommon to be interrupted during one's lunch hour. While this inability to "escape" may cause stress, these same types of technology can assist in relieving stress. For those who travel, cell phones can provide a feeling of safety since help can be a phone call away when one's car breaks down.

E-mail and cell phones can both assist in keeping one in touch with the office. For working parents, there is comfort in knowing that one's children or family will always be able to have contact in case of emergency. Each of these uses can assist in the reduction of stress.

Anne Mulcahy, Chairman and CEO of Xerox Corporation, identifies another factor regarding technology that may increase stress. In an article published by Business Wire, Mulcahy is quoted as saying, "Technology has overwhelmed us with documents...they are a hidden and often misunderstood aspect of business cost, productivity and infrastructure" .Within Company X, the production of documents is an ongoing process. There are contracts, change orders, billings, pay requests, letters, memos, reports and various other documents that need to be created. Once created, originals, copies and computer files must be properly filed and stored, which makes for more work that can create stress.

Another technological factor that can cause stress is computers and computer software. Within the last year, several upgrades to the computer network and software systems have been implemented at Company X. While upgrades to the accounting software have reduced stress caused by software errors, technological upgrades have been needed at some of the workstations, which have increased stress caused by slow computer response time.

With employees at Company X relying more and more on the technology offered by computers, coordination of computer support has become another factor increasing stress among some employees.

Using Internet for personal reasons like, personal e-mail, planning vacations or gaining knowledge on world events may be unethical but it does help in reducing stress.

While technological advances can be seen as detrimental to the work environment by creating stress in the work place, it can also be seen as having created greater and more efficient ways of doing business. Through a review of the technology utilized by Company X and the ethics involved, it can be seen that there have been both positive and negative impacts to the stress levels of employees. As employees "surf the net" on the job, management has found the need to limit access to certain sites for moral and ethical reasons, but realizes that access to information regarding world events aids in reducing stress. As David Williamson again quotes Euryn Williams, "It's about seeing the technology as an opportunity rather than a threat".

Case Studies

Six software professionals under the age of 33 have died and 2 top executives from renowned software companies have become paralyzed because of stress-related heart ailments in the last six months in Chennai, says a study by Mitran Foundation, a Bangalore-based voluntary association of practicing doctors.The study, conducted at a cost of Rs 45 lakhs, covered more than 4,000 software professionals from 80 companies who were In service for a minimum of three years. The email responses were scientifically tabulated and the findings were ready in 2002.

"The study confirmed that the number of suicides, divorces, heart ailments, BP and diabetes patients and mental depression are the highest in the software industry. The fancy salaries of software professionals are no longer something to rejoice about ," said Dr Dwarakanath (The director of the Mitran Foundation)."We found that the software industry has simply no routine. Deadlines hang before them and every day they chase new problems. There is no physical exercise and new food habits favored by pizza culture fuel the problem. Cervical spondilitis and wrist problems due to uncomfortable handling of the computer mouse, eye problems and discomfort in bowel movements are common".

Factors affecting Stress in IT Industry- Call Centers

Work Timing (Table-1)

It's the greatest cause for stress and unique to the Indian IT industry. Not surprising, considering that the industry works largely during the night to coincide with the UK and US daylight hours. Certainly, there are daytime shifts but the night remains the peak load period. As a result, 38.4% of all respondents interviewed said their work shifts caused serious stress. This average however covers the fact that some of those interviewed would be day-timers either call floor employees who work the day shift or senior non-call floor people.

Table-1

Least Affected	
e-serve	6.1
EXL Services	15.2
WNS Global Services	23.3
Most Affected	
Hinduja TMT	83.3
Daksh	63.6
MSourceE	60.0

Repetitive Nature of Work (Table-2)

The second biggest cause for stress with 31% of all respondents saying that doing the same thing 8 hours a day, every day, can be very stressful. Internationally, there has been a lot of debate on what to do on this count and some suggestions have included job-rotation with other functions for a few days every quarter. Example – if a call floor person can spend three days a quarter in HR or procurement or administration, it might help to relieve some of the stress. Another oft-repeated suggestion: remove the tyranny of the scripted conversation, hire carefully, train people well, and let them handle each call as their natures best allow them to.

Either way, there is no easy solution to this one though data seemed to suggest that there was an element of acclimatization to this problem. Those on their first job felt it a lot more (36%) than those who had worked earlier, usually in another call center.

Table-2

Least Affected	
EXL Services	12.1
MSourceE	22.9
WNS Global Services	23.3
Most Affected	
ICICI OneSource	47.7
Convergys	41.4
Daksh	39.4

Workload (Table-3)

Though the number of hours a day a call center employee works may be the same—in some cases actually less—than others, it is the intensity and relentless pace at which work tends to happen that makes work load an issue. Though IT and IT services employees for instance may work much longer hours, these are interspersed with either chats with colleagues, smoke and coffee breaks taken at will and visits to other departments or customers. Call floor employees on the other hand have no such luck. In addition the team leader and above managers have higher load because they often stay beyond a shift for meetings with managers. Those with less than a year's experience have fewer problems as some amount of time is spent in training and for the first few months on a job, the metrics are easier.

Table-3

Least Affected	
EXL Services	9.1
Sutherland Tech	15.2
24/7 Customer	17

Most Affected	
WNS Global Services	43.3
Hinduja TMT	43.3
HP Global	41.4

Irate customers (Table-4)

This is a tough one. About 30% of all those interviewed said irate customers caused a lot of stress. This data hides the fact that team leaders and their seniors don't directly interact with customers and very few of them actually get the brunt. Again, this is a stress factor that is inherent in the nature of the job – most often customers call when they have a problem. Often, they are further irritated by long call queues and the inability of call center executives to offer a quick solution to their problems.

Table-4

Least Affected	
WNS Global Services	0
EXL Services	3
24/7 Customer	8.7
Most Affected	
Convergys	55.2
GE Capital	41.9
Daksh	39.4

Long Working Hours (Table-5)

Is a combination of work load, call volume and travel time that adds to a long day. Most call center employees in Mumbai, Gurgaon and Bangalore for instance budget at least two hours for travel up and down to work. With a nine hour designated work day, that is a minimum of 11 hours spent on work or getting to work every day. Some call centers that encourage overtime might have employees working longer 13-14 hour days on a routine basis. Operational heads who work the shift and stay back for customer conference call from the US tend to put in 16-18 hours on a regular basis.

Table-5

Least Affected	
HCL Tech-BPO	8.8
EXL Services	9.1
GE Capital	9.7

Most Affected	
Sutherland Tech	72.7
ICICI OneSource	47.7
Daksh	39.4

Insufficient Breaks (Table-6)

Is one of the key reasons for IT stress all over the world. In an industry that is very quantitative measures driven, and where measures are counted in seconds, too many breaks are not allowed. The better ones in India would have designated break periods of about 15 minutes in every 2.5 hours plus half hour for lunch.

Table-6

Least Affected	
24/7 Customer	0
HP Global	3.4
Wipro Spectramind	3.5
Most Affected	
Sutherland Tech	42.4
ICICI OneSource	31.8
convergys	20.7

Health Issues (Table-7)

23% of all employees say health issues are a cause of stress. In a single company 56% say health issues are causing pressure at work. For more on call center related illnesses see following tables. By and large, first timers seemed less effected and health issues as stress-contributors seemed to increase with time. Only exception was people with more than five years in the industry who are more likely to be keeping saner hours and lifestyles. More men have a harder time of it surprisingly than women do.

Table-7

Least Affected	
WNS Global Services	6.7
eFunds	10.9
e-Serve	15.2
Most Affected	
HCL Tech-BPO	55.9
EXL Services	45.5
ICICI OneSource	40.9

(Source Tables 1-7 DataQuest)

Summary of Common Short Term or Early Stress Symptoms

Physical Symptoms

- Headaches (tension and migraines)
- Stomach problems
- Over and under eating
- Sleep disturbances
- Chronic mild fatigue
- Muscle aches and pains
- Skin rashes
- Teeth grinding
- Muscle tics
- Chronic mild illnesses
- Sexual disfunction
- Diarrhoea
- Constipation

Psychological Symptoms

- Forgetfulness
- Anger
- Frustration
- Anxiety
- More irritability with family members
- More use of alcohol, or cigarettes
- More use of drugs or sleeping pills
- Depression
- Feeling powerless
- More irritability with or isolation from co-workers
- More problems at work

Summary of Common Long Term Symptoms of Stress

Physical Conditions

- Hypertension
- Heart disease
- Strokes
- Diabetes
- Ulcers
- Infectious diseases
- Spastic colon

Psychological Problems

- Serious depression
- Accidents
- Domestic violence
- Suicidal behavior
- Alcoholism
- Serious substance abuse
- Other debilitating psychological disorders

Occupational Stressors

Physical Stressors

- Chemical agents
- Physical agents (noise, heat, radiation, cold)
- Hazards which cause fear
- Uncomfortable work area

Social Stressors

- High job demands
- Low job control
- Low social support
- Lack of input into decisions
- Conflicting demands
- Repetitive tasks or machine paced work

- Shift work; especially rotating shifts
- Poor supervision
- Poor relations with co-workers
- Lack of promotions
- Job insecurity
- Excessive overtime

Coping Strategies

(1) Healthy use of Computers

More and more of our working time is spent in front of computers. While they can be a tremendous help in our work, they can also increase stress levels if the computer work is poorly designed. Cumulative trauma disorders can be a particular physical hazard of increased computer use.

Good ergonomics is a key to healthy computer use. State health departments usually have someone who is an expert in this area. They can help you with proper equipment, lighting and pace of work issues. They can also help you reduce the risk of repetitive strain injuries among your staff.

(2) Staff Involvement in Choosing New Equipment

This is a common sense strategy that is often overlooked. Allowing the end users to be able to make informed choices about the type of equipment to be purchased. This can have payoffs for both job satisfaction and productivity.

(3) Talk to HR Department

Large companies tend to have an HR (Human Resources) Department with someone designated to be the "go to" person for any employee issues. You can speak with them on a personal level as you need to help resolve your issue. It helps to get your stress out in the open because many times, you are not the only one experiencing stress. HR may decide to step in and hire outside consultants who are experts in work related stress.

(4) Share Your Workload

Unless you are the only one working in your department you can usually find someone who can help share your workload. Don't wait until you are about to explode before you let your boss know that you have too much on your plate. It's better to speak up right away, otherwise when deadlines are missed, others will turn to you and ask why you didn't seek help sooner.

Strategies to Improve Personal Coping Mechanisms

Individual strategies are easier to initiate, but should never be seen as an equivalent substitute for organizational change. These strategies can, however, be very useful companions to structural change efforts.

One good distinction for person change strategies is the difference between functional and dysfunctional coping mechanisms. All human beings have coping mechanisms. Unfortunately, these mechanisms are not always the most effective or functional. The goal is to replace dysfunctional coping mechanisms with functional ones. Some healthy choices:

(1) Improving the Diet of Employees

Possible work place strategies: bring in a nutritionist for a day of training, encourage employees to keep diet diaries for a week, offer nutritional foods at the worksite, form a healthy snacks club.

(2) Encouraging the Employees to Exercise

Start a walking club at lunch time, bring in a fitness trainer for an in-service day, provide exercise equipment or facilities.

(3) Training in Deep Muscle Relaxation Techniques

Psychologists have known for some time that anxiety and deep muscle relaxation are mutually exclusive. That is, you can't be anxious and relaxed at the same time.This can be a useful strategy for dealing with stress. The goal is to train your employees to be able to become relaxed on demand, thereby cutting the stress cycle short. One widely used relaxation technique was developed by Edmund Jacobsen. It is an effective method for training individuals how to relax their major muscle groups. There are other useful techniques available for employees working on computers.

Possible workplace strategies: Many stress management consultants are able to train your employees in these techniques. A good use of an in-service training day would be to bring in a consultant and either have them train all your employees, or intensively train a small group who would then become your in-house trainers. You want to be sure that you learn some "quick" relaxation techniques. These can be performed in just a few minutes on the job.

(4) Training in Effective Cognitive Strategies

Remember that something is not stressful unless it is perceived or appraised as stressful. Cognitive psychologists have developed techniques that replace negative cognitions (that is Ñ negative thoughts like "I will never be able to figure this out", with more positive, empowering thoughts like, "I can get this done if I just take it one step at a time"). Another useful strategy is called thought stopping. Since we know that negative thoughts can increase anxiety and therefore stress symptoms, psychologists have learned to train individuals to literally "stop" these thoughts before they become too repetitive. These techniques have been found to be extremely useful for people who have serious problems with anxiety or depression. However, they can also be effective tools in the workplace.

Some possible workplace strategies: These techniques require a trained professional. You should find a competent cognitive psychologist in your area and ask him/her to come in for an in-service day or work through an Employee Assistance Program.

(5) Training in Substance Abuse Awareness

Individuals who are under a great deal of stress begin to self-medicate themselves in order to feel better. They may drink more, take more prescription medication, or take illegal drugs.

Every organization has individuals who may already have serious problems in this regard. These individuals probably need professional help. Substance abuse awareness is best used as a preventative measure.

Possible work place strategies: there are many resources available in the community for substance abuse awareness training. Many human service agencies are willing to do this kind of outreach for free, and many schools are now hiring well qualified counselors who could be an important resource to your employees, or you can establish your own employee assistance program.

(6) Organize Discussion Groups on Healthy Stress Reducers

The idea is to get employees to share effective strategies with each other. This strategy does not need external resources. You can simply pull together a meeting where people share the stress reducers that work for them. You may want to prepare a handout ahead of time that reviews examples of healthy coping mechanisms. This approach is that it also provides a mechanism for giving social support to employees.

(7) Transition Time

Many employees leave their jobs only to return to stressful conditions at home. They may have families to take care of, meals to cook, or older parents to visit. Remember that it can take a good 20 to 30 minutes for the body to return to baseline after experiencing a stressor. If the employee is "stressed out" and then has to deal with a difficult situation at home, chances of having long-term health consequences increase. Transition time can be a useful technique in short circuiting the stress response at home. The basic idea is to train employees to find a way to relax for 20-30 minutes before assuming family responsibilities. This allows the body's autonomic responses (heart rate, blood pressure, etc.) to return to baseline.

(8) Leaving Stress at the Front Door - Training on Family Dynamics and Parenting Skills

There's been a good deal of research showing that, as stress increases, so do family problems. It is very easy for angry, frustrated employees to take stress out on their families. Even healthy, supportive families can go through some rough times. Improving your employees' abilities to handle pressures at home can have major payoffs for your organization.

Possible workplace strategies: Many human service agencies can provide your staff with training on family dynamics, dealing with aging parents and parenting skills. You could also consider forming a short term discussion group for employees who are interested in these topics.

Organization Response to Reduce Stress Among its Employees

Sensing the high stress levels among employees that lead to lower productivity and higher attrition rates, Information Technology and business process outsourcing firms are resorting to unconventional methods, including teaching dancing and music, to tackle and beat the stress India's largest IT services firm **Tata Consultancy Services**, for instance, creates fun at work which is facilitated through different clubs like Theatre Club, Bibliophile Club, Adventure & Trekking Club, Fitness Club, Sanctuary Club, Music Club and Community Services Club, among others. Maitree, an initiative by TCSers and their spouses, organises several activities like treks, classes and workshops on creative arts besides picnics and other community initiatives.

Infosys, on its part, has a custom-designed instrument, which assists in increasing self-awareness. Guidance is provided to identify ways of effectively coping with the stress.

Summary

Even though IT jobs are stressful, IT workers are happier now than they were a year ago. According to the March 2005 Hudson Employment Index, compiled by independent research firm Rasmussen Reports, 77 percent of IT workers say they are happy with their jobs. In May 2004, only 66 percent of IT workers said they were happy at work.

Kevin Knaul, executive vice president of IT and telecommunications practice for Hudson North America, says increasing optimism about hiring and the related prospect of a return to normal workloads has contributed to the increased job satisfaction scores. More than one-third of IT workers surveyed said that their companies were hiring. "There's a return to normalcy," says Knaul. "IT workers aren't just happy to have a job anymore."

In fact, the data shows that IT workers may be the happiest of all workers. Compared with employees in other industries surveyed by Hudson (a division of the staffing and executive search company Hudson Highland Group), IT workers generated the highest positive response rate to the job satisfaction question. Health-care workers were a close second at 76 percent.

Knaul cautions, however, that CIOs should continue to monitor staff morale because, now that the job market is picking up, some workers could be tempted to leave. "Turnover kills the productivity of an IT department," Knaul notes.

A recent survey by CIO shows that IT executives are indeed concerned about morale. Among the top staffing challenges for this group surveyed by CIO in January: preventing burnout (83 percent) and low morale (60 percent). The survey also cited stress as a major contributor to low morale. A whopping 76 percent of IT executives said that stress among IT staff was high or very high.

Conclusion

Employers are waking up to the fact that job stress that creates reduced productivity, resignations and psychological problems for their employees is bad for business. To combat stress many employers are introducing programs and procedures such as offering flexible schedules, telecommuting, job sharing, mentoring, and open door communications. A culture shift needs to take place at many companies to combat stress related problems. Employees need to feel they have input regarding project deadlines, scheduling and staffing. Bosses need to become team leaders and coaches as opposed to autocratic despots who operate and decompress. The good news is that stress, while not being totally eliminated, should be decreasing in the future at numerous companies, Nevertheless, this isn't to say you won't end up in a stressful situation from time to time.

References

[1] Rives , Karin and Vicki Lee Parker. "War News Distracts Workers." Knight Ridder /Tribune Business News. ITEM03082009. (2003).Infotrac. University of Phoenix Online Collection. 9 April 2003. Keywords: Workplace Technology Stress.

[2] University of Phoenix, ed. Organizational Behavior. 7th ed. University of Phoenix custom edition e-text. New York: John Wiley & Sons, Inc., 2002. MGT331 – Organizational Behavior. Resource. University of Phoenix. 7 April 2003 https://mycampus.phoenix.edu/secure/resource/resource.asp

[3] Williamson, David. "Workplace Depression Blamed on IT Stress." Western Mail. 452.80 (2003): 9. Proquest. University of Phoenix Online Collection. 9 April 2003. Keywords: Workplace Technology Stress.

[4] "Xerox CEO Anne Mulcahy Tells High-Tech Leaders the New World Order Requires a New Work Order." Business Wire. (2003): 5066. Infotrac. Univeristy of Phoenix Online Collection. 9 April 2003. Keywords: Workplace Technology Stress.

✡✡✡

18

TEACHER STRESS IN THE FIELD OF EDUCATION AND WELLNESS PROGRAMME

** Priyanka Panwar*
** Arti Rana*

* Lecturers, Department of Computer Science, Shri Atmanand Jain Institute of Management and Technology, Ambala city.

Introduction

A certain amount of stress in teaching is inevitable, even beneficial. Hinton and Rotheiler (1998) point out that the excitement and challenge of teaching naturally causes the raised adrenaline levels associated with stress, while Dunham (1992) illustrates that teachers work at peak efficiency when the demands placed on them are in balance with their own perceived coping ability, and that too little challenge and too much can be equally detrimental. Teacher stress becomes problematic, and potentially harmful, when the challenges teachers face outpace their perceived ability to cope, or when they perceive that important needs are not being met.

This paper begins by exploring the nature of stress in teachers, and suggests its common causes and effects. It then proposes ways to reduce teacher stress, and prevent it from reaching unhealthy levels, by creating a caring working environment: first, by administrators (Institutions caring for teachers); then, by faculty members as a community (teachers caring for each other); and finally, by individual teachers (teachers caring for themselves).

Causes of teacher stress

Stress in teachers can be more insidious than in other professions by its "fuzzy" nature: it arises from a vague system of rules and returns; it is often self-inflicted; and unlike the business or medical professions, the debilitating effects are not often counterbalanced by moments of exhilaration and satisfaction (Claxton, 1989, p. 49). While all the possible permutations of the causes and effects of stress have yet to be thoroughly investigated, it is probable that other things being equal, stress tends to affect younger, less experienced teachers over older, more experienced ones; those of given lower academic rank over higher; single teachers over married; and women over men, although men are at greater risk of self-destructive reactions to stress (Griffith et al., 1999).

Teacher stress can be caused by a number of factors, both external and internal. External causes may include institutional conditions such as large, mixed-ability classes, lack of student discipline and motivation, lack of resources, overwork or uneven distribution of workloads, poor communication, unclear expectations, and inadequate rewards and recognition (Brown & Ralph, 1998; Gmelch, 1993; Travers & Cooper, 1998).

Problematic relationships with colleagues can generate other stressors, such as personality conflicts, lack of community spirit, feelings of isolation, lack of support, and limited academic and social interaction with other teachers (ibid.).

Internal causes may include an aggressive, impatient, competitive "Type A" personality; workaholism; negative attitude toward students; and in particular, unrealistic self-expectations (ibid.). Some of the causes of teacher stress mentioned above are beyond the control of individual teachers, arising from external circumstances that require cooperation from administrators and colleagues to change, while others are within the teacher's control and can be managed with the help of appropriate coping strategies. There are numerous reports in the literature on teacher stress and burnout. A nation wide survey done in the United States indicates that there has been a considerable rise in the stress levels of teachers over the years. Burnout in teachers (described by Maslarch, 1982, as a three dimensional phenomenon characterized by feelings of exhaustion, depersonalization, and a lack of personal accomplishment) can not only manifest itself as various physical ailments and emotional problems, but can result in teachers actually leaving their chosen career. Administrators in the National Education Association worry that thousands of sensitive, thoughtful and dedicated teachers are abandoning the teaching profession. Canadian teachers are affected too. In a national study done by the Canadian Teachers' Federation 55% of teachers responding to a stress scale questionnaire indicated that they were almost always exhausted at the end of a regular day. All of this research has resulted in some positive changes in the operation of the education system, however, it appears that the emphasis for change often relates directly to: a) the physical environment the teacher works in, b) a shift in task overload, c) training in the area of conflict resolution and d) training in communication skills. What is missing in the data is the importance of the personal health and well-being levels of the teachers themselves, and how this important aspect can play a role in managing stress.

Effects of teacher stress

Behaviors symptomatic of teacher stress include poor time management; inability to concentrate; job dissatisfaction; irritation and aggression; introversion and withdrawal from supportive relationships; inappropriate, cynical humor; abuse of alcohol, caffeine or tobacco; and if left untreated, absenteeism, resignation, and withdrawal from the profession. Emotional consequences include feelings of anxiety, dissatisfaction and resentment; depression; inability to relax and unwind; feelings of inadequacy and low self-esteem; and ultimately burnout. Long-term physical effects include fatigue and low energy; frequent colds; irregular sleeping patterns, insomnia and bad dreams; appetite disorders; and potentially, psychosomatic illness and heart disease (Brown and Ralph, 1998; Hinton and Rotheiler, 1998; Travers and Cooper, 1998).

The next sections will explore ways in which teacher stress can be treated at each of these three levels: administrative, collegial, and individual.

Three ways in which the administrations can help create a more positive working environment for faculty are:

1. ***Treat faculty as an investment:*** An important first step in improving the overall quality of education is for administrations to view faculty members as valuable investments rather than expendable assets. Many universities neglect an important resource by assuming faculty to be self-sufficient with no further need for training or support (Gmelch, 1993, p. 35). This situation can be remedied, in part, by administrative faculty staying current in the field, and encouraging, supporting and rewarding teaching faculty who do the same. Providing support for research, in-service training and other professional development activities, at all levels, is also important. As Brown (2002) memorably observed, "Treat [teachers] like professionals and they will be professionals; treat them like part- time scum and they will be part-time scum!" Furthermore, institutions that invest their resources in helping faculty do the best possible job are more likely to feel inclined to protect their investments, resulting in greater job security for faculty.

2. ***Provide clear expectations, feedback, and rewards:*** A clear statement of expectations and rewards in all areas of responsibility (teaching, research, and service) helps faculty perform at their best (Gmelch, 1993, p. 26). Regular feedback in each of these areas is also essential. In many institutions, feedback on teaching comes only in the form of a series of yes/nos or multiple-choice questions on surveys administered to students at the end of the semester. Whether such instruments are capable of including all the subtleties of good teaching is highly questionable (Palmer, 1998, p. 143; Simmons, 1996,

pp. 12-16). In addition, administrators may not even see the results at all (Naoumi & Fujimaki, 2002); or if they do, the results can easily be ignored or selectively invoked (Palmer, op. cit.). While the number of students and volume of questionnaires may make it logistically difficult at larger institutions, administrators could profitably pay attention to qualitative as well as quantitative feedback from students. In addition, while classroom observations tend to inspire a sense of dread in many teachers, who equate them with judgment rather than support (Claxton, 1989, p. 34), they can be a source of constructive feedback if used well, and when a trusting relationship exists between the observer and teacher (Woodward, 2001). One American university obtained good results by training education majors to be participant-observers in classes, giving feedback to the teacher from the perspective of an informed student. Feedback from faculty indicated that they found the system so valuable that they often actively sought the participant- observers' advice: "What do you think happened yesterday when we had that conflict in class?" or "Any suggestions about how I can make the transition to the next topic without losing the students who still don't understand the last one?" (Palmer, 1998, p. 160)

3. ***Establish support systems for teachers:*** A simple and important first step in supporting teachers is, keeping two-way lines of communication open between teaching and administrative faculty. Teachers need to know that they can safely consult a respected senior colleague when they have questions or concerns; one way of providing this has been to establish a "consulting teacher" among the senior faculty, who teaches a reduced load and is available for consultation with newer teachers (Palmer, 1998, p. 159).

Also, as an alternative to support groups in which teachers who teach similar courses can meet on a regular basis to share concerns and ideas (possibly including senior colleagues as guiding members) are also helpful (Claxton, 1989; Daniels *et. al.*, op. cit.).

Managing Stress

(a) Teachers caring for each other

Supportive relationships with co-workers are a teacher's best protection against the sense of isolation that is a major cause of teacher stress (Griffith *et al.*, 1999). A harmonious atmosphere among the staff, characterized by interdependence and togetherness, helps create an optimal working environment (ibid.). Development of such an environment is hindered, however, by an academic culture that builds barriers between colleagues and discourages professional interaction and shared knowledge (Palmer, 1998; Daniels *et al.*, 1998).

Every teacher can benefit from an informal support network of trusted colleagues who can discuss concerns and share failure stories without fear (Kyriacou, 1998, p. 10). A particularly valuable skill in members of such a network is the ability to listen. Asking colleagues for help is a risk and an admission of vulnerability (Troman, 2000), and teachers who overcome their anxieties and lay bare their concerns often find themselves surrounded by colleagues who ply them with advice, thereby (consciously or unconsciously) casting themselves in the role of sempai (senior) passing down knowledge to their kouhai (juniors) and thus increasing the latter's feelings of inadequacy and reinforcing fears of lowering defenses (Claxton, 1989, p. 81).

As an alternative, Palmer (1998, pp. 151ff) describes a "clearness committee" as practiced in Quaker communities since the 17th century, in which one "focus person" describes the problem and the other members respond only in the form of an honest, open question, offering no advice either during or after the session, but rather helping the focus person to discover his or her own solution. Even without convening a formal "committee", individual teachers can resist the temptation to play the sempai-kohai game when a colleague shares a problem, and instead help that person find clearness. Palmer (op. cit.) describes how the process of seeking clearness can bring revelations not only to the focus person, but to other participants as well.

Pairs or small groups of teachers can provide valuable support for each other, including helping each other keep "new semester's resolutions", giving "wake-up calls" to partners who seem to be succumbing to stress (Claxton, 1989, p. 83), and practicing what Claxton (op. cit., p. 78) calls "creative ranting and raving", in which one partner complains as much as possible (preferably in a self-consciously exaggerated and irrational way) for ten minutes strictly measured by the other, after which the two turn their attention to seeking constructive solutions.

Finally, small gestures such as words of appreciation, sweets, and back pat can help foster a sense of camaraderie among faculty. And in times of stress, as Claxton (1989, p. 75) notes: "Cuddles and hugs, preferably accompanied by deep sighs, are highly recommended – although they can be risky in staffrooms."

(b) Teacher caring for themselves

Many of the internal causes of teacher stress can be reduced by appropriate coping strategies (the definition of which, of course, depends on what each individual finds most effective). One important step is to recognize and avoid counterproductive coping strategies; these include disengagement (giving up, withdrawal, pretended or real indifference); suppression of conflicting activities (putting hobbies, personal commitments or rest on hold when there is work to be done); alcohol, tobacco and drugs; and defensiveness (Griffith et al., 1999; Claxton, 1989). Good organization and time management, including concentrating on one task at a time, are keys to reducing stress, as is a sense of humor and perspective, as well as realistic self-expectations, which may mean aiming for excellence in one area of faculty responsibility and competence in others, rather than excellence in all (Gmelch, 1993).

Other effective strategies for reducing stress include physical activity (working out, individual or team sports); entertainment (movies, dining out, TV, concerts, reading for pleasure); and personal interests (hobbies, musical instruments, or cultural activities). While drawing a clear line of demarcation between work and personal time is difficult for teachers, setting aside some personal time off limits to work (which may consist simply of idleness or unstructured leisure) is recommended (Gmelch, 1993). There are also many who find meditation, progressive relaxation, and deep breathing helpful. Finally, perhaps the most effective strategy for reducing stress is knowing one's own stress points and practicing the coping techniques that work best.

Teacher Wellness Programme

Health and wellness experts such as Ardell (1986), Travis (1981), and Pelltier (1996), suggest that attention to personal lifestyle can improve well-being; that making healthy lifestyle choices can increase our levels of joy, satisfaction and zest for living. Healthy and well employees are also more productive employees. Teacher wellness might be the missing link in the strategic planning process of education reform, and could assist in the transformation and revitalization of both the institution system and individual teachers.

There are many definitions of wellness: an integration of body, mind and spirit; a way of life which we design to enjoy the highest level of health and well-being; or a link between our physical, social, spiritual, intellectual, occupational and emotional selves. What we have discovered as we attempt to balance our roles of teacher, student, consultant, wife and mom, is that it doesn't really matter what definition we choose to work with - what does matter is how we choose to put our 'teacher wellness plan into action'.

There are many different wellness models teachers can follow. A model developed by Dr. Donald Ardell - a guru of sorts in the wellness field,it is simple, easy for us to follow, and is the only wellness model we have found that reminds us that "We" are ultimately in charge of our own well-being.

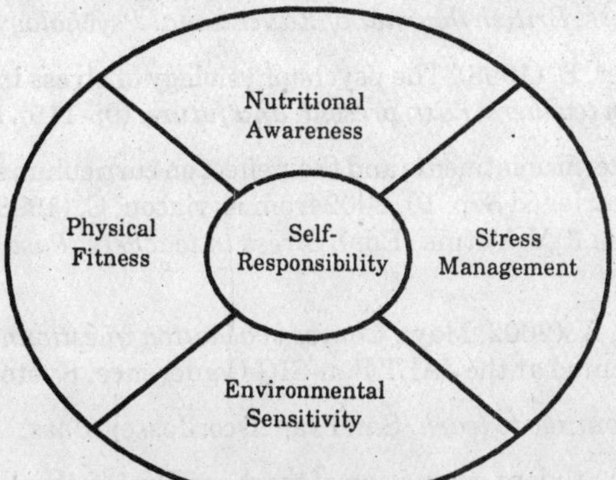

Source: Dimensions of Wellness Dr. Donald Ardell (1977)

Conclusion

Excessive teacher stress, left undiagnosed and untreated, can have long-term negative consequences not only for individual teachers, but ultimately for the entire institution. A caring work environment, however, is highly effective in reducing teacher stress and making it easier to treat. This paper has presented ways in which administrations can work to create caring work environments, and also ways for teachers to care for themselves and each other while waiting for institutions to undergo the slow process of change. When put into practice, these ideas can not only make teachers' lives more bearable, but at the same time, help them to work more efficiently, and thereby improve the quality of education as a whole.

References

[1] Arudou (Aldwinckle), D. (2002, February). Education and employment status: why JALT should take interest in the issues. *The Language Teacher* 26 (2), 27-28. Retreived on Sep. 10, 2002 from Brown, J. D. (2002, May). *Problems and suggestions for language teaching in Asia.* Plenary address, JALT Pan-SIG conference, Kyoto Institute of Technology.

[2] Brown, M. & Ralph, S. (1998). The identification of stress in teachers. In J. Dunham & V. Varma (Eds.), *Stress in teachers: Past, present, and future.* (37-56). London: Whurr.

[3] Claxton, G. (1989). *Being a teacher: A positive approach to change and stress.* London: Cassell.

[4] Daniels, H., Creese, A., & Norwich, B. (1998). Teacher support teams. In J. Dunham & V. Varma (Eds). *Stress in teachers: Past, present, and future.* (120-138). London: Whurr

[5] Dunham, J. (1992). *Stress in teaching.* London: Routledge.

[6] Eliot, T.S. (1950). The aims of education: the conflict between aims. In Eliot, T.S. (1965). *To criticize the critic and other writings.* London: Faber & Faber.

[7] Fox, M.H., Shiozawa, T. & Aldwinckle. D. (1999, August). A new system of university tenure: remedy or disease? *The Language Teacher 23* (8), 13-18. Retrieved Sep. 10,2002 from

[8] Gmelch, W.H. (1993). *Coping with faculty stress.* Newbury Park, CA: Sage.

[9] Griffith, J., Steptoe, A. & Cropley, M. (1999). An investigation of coping strategies associated with job stress in teachers. *British Journal of Educational Psychology, 69,* 517-531.

[10] Hinton, J. W. & Rotheiler, E. (1998). The psychophysiology of stress in teachers. In J. Dunham & V. Varma (Eds), *Stress in teachers: Past, present, and future.* (95-119). London: Whurr.

[11] Kirk, D. (2001). Limited-term aointments and their effect on curriculum development. *The Language Teacher* 25 (2), 31-33. Retrieved Sep. 10, 2002 from Kyriacou, C. (1998). Teacher stress: past and present. In In J. Dunham & V. Varma (Eds). *Stress in teachers: Past, present, and future* (1-13). London: Whurr.

[12] Naoumi, E. & Fujimaki, K. (2002, May). *Course evaluation questionnaires: Student and teacher perceptions.* Paper presented at the JALT Pan-SIG Conference, Kyoto Institute of Technology.

[13] Palmer, P. (1998). *The courage to teach.* San Francisco: Jossey-Bass.

[14] Simmons, T. (1996, Oct.) Student evaluation of teachers: Professional practice or punitive policy? *SHIKEN* 1. (1), 12-16. Retrieved Sep. 10, 2002 from

[15] Swindoll, C. (1982). *Strengthening your grip.* Dallas: Word, Inc.

[16] Travers, C. & Cooper, L. (1998). Increasing costs of occupational stress for teachers. In J. Dunham, & V. Varma (Eds). *Stress in teachers: Past, present, and future* (57-75). London: Whurr.

[17] Troman, G. (2000). Teacher stress in the low-trust society. *British Journal of Sociology of Education, 21,* 331-353. van der Linde, C. H. (2000). The teacher's stress and its implications for the school as an organization: How can TQM help? *Education, 121* (2), 375-382.

[18] Woodward, T. (2001, November). *Planning lessons and courses.* Plenary address at PAC3 at JALT 2001, Kitakyushu.

✲✲✲

19

STRESS AVOIDANCE STRATEGIES FROM SHRIMAD BHAGVAD GITA

** Giridhar Gopal*

*** Rimpi Walia*

* Lecturer, M. M. Institute of Management, Mullana.

** Assistant Professor, M. M. Institute of Management, Mullana.

Introduction

There is a general tendency in every human being to get happiness. We are always in search of the happiness. No one likes sorrow or sadness in his or her life. Call them necessities, comforts or luxuries; all these are synonymous with happiness. When we get these things, we feel happy and sometimes proud as well. On the other hand, when we loose them, we feel pain and discomfort in our life. No one wants discomforts but still everyone gets these. The various factors or situations, such as death of a relative, termination from job, failure to cope with job assignments etc. cause stress in our mind. The same thing which seems to be the cause of happiness, becomes the cause of sorrow, the next day or the next moment. For example, the home in which we are living happily, if, due to an earthquake,it falls, then it becomes the cause of sorrow or sadness. No one wants tension, stress and sorrow in life but still every one feels it at one time or the other.

We are not able to live our lives free from stress.. Once faced with stress, we try to find out the solutions or the strategies to overcome it. Most of the strategies which are available, or well known, are basically the remedial ones. It is well said that prevention is better than cure, hence it is better to go for those strategies which, lead to avoidance of stress or are preventive in nature. In this context the Bhagvad Gita, expounded thousands of years ago by the Super Management Guru, Bhagwan Sri Krishna, enlightens us on various stress management techniques, leading to a harmonious and blissful state of affairs as against conflicts, tensions, low efficiency and productivity, absence of motivation and lack of work culture etc.

Stress Avoidance Strategies from Shrimad Bhagwad Gita

1. Utilization of Available Resources

Many times,we get stress because we are not able to make use of our available resources properly, or we under estimate those. In this context, we would like to discuss a small story which we all might have studied in our school time. Once a poor person goes to a Sadhu and says that I am very poor, please help me. The Sadhu asks him to give his one eye for Rs. 1 lakh but he refuses. Then the Sadhu asks him to give his other parts of the body each one for lakhs of rupees, but still he says 'how can I give my parts of body for money'. The Sadhu says 'You can see how wealthy you are, as you have a human body costing crores of rupees. Do not say that you are poor, rather make use of your body and do efforts.' In the management science too the first lesson is: choose wisely and utilise optimally the scarce resources, if you want to succed in yours venture. During the curtain raiser before the Mahabharata War, Duryodhana chose Sri Krishna's large army for his help, while Arjuna selected Sri Krishna's wisdom for his support and succeeded. This episode gives us a clue that, just by selecting our resources wisely and utilizing them, even if these are limited in quantity, we can live a stressfree life.

2. Attitude Towards Work

The 38th Shaloka from second chapter of Shrimad Bhagvad Gita tells us what should be our attitude towards work. It says that we get stressed when we feel sorrow, sadness or unhappiness in work. For example, if in one month, a sales manager has been able to achieve the targets, he gets appreciation from the head office, but if in some other month, he is not able to reach the targets the head office is not happy. The manager starts giving excuses and blaming his sales force. This is not the right approach as, if you want to take the appreciation for your good work, then you should also take responsiblity for underperformance. This shaloka says that by taking all the situations equally, that is happy from your success and by not feeling sad from your failures, you can live a stress free life. Bhagvad Gita advises us to work without attachment.

3. **Work Commitment**

The popular verse 2.47 of the Gita advises non-attachment to the fruits or results of actions performed in the course of one's duty. Dedicated work has to mean 'work for the sake of work'. If we are always calculating the date of promotion for putting in our efforts, then such work cannot be commitment-oriented bringing excellence in the results, but it will be promotion-oriented resulting in inevitable disappointments. By tilting the performance towards the anticipated benefits, the quality of performance of the present duty suffers on account of the mental agitations caused by the anxieties for the future. Some people argue that being unattached to the consequences of one's action would make one un-accountable as accountability is a much touted word these days with the vigilance department sitting on our shoulders. But they do not know the proper meaning of detachment. Detachment does not mean that we should not perform our duties, or should do our duties with disinterest, but it means that we should work sincerely only for the sake of work. Take the example of a bank cashier. Suppose that on some day, in his bank, he receives 20 crore of rupees and on some other day, he receives only 50 thousand rupees. Does he feel happy on the day he receives 20 crores or does he feel sad on the day he receives only 50 thousand ? The answer is 'no', because he knows that this money is not his personal one. Hence, he is not attached with the money; he is simply performing his duty. Bhagvad Gita advises us to work without attachment in the same manner .

4. **Avoid Selfishness**

This vision was presented to us in the very first mantra of lsopanishad which says that whatever exists in the Universe is enveloped by God. How shall we enjoy this life then, if all are one? The answer it provides is enjoy and strengthen life by sacrificing your selfishness and not coveting other's wealth. The same motivation is given by Sri Krishna in the Third Chapter of Gita when He says, 'He who shares the wealth generated only after serving the people, through work done as a sacrifice for them, is freed from all the sins. On the contrary those who earn wealth only for themselves, eat sins that lead to frustration and failure.'

5. **Work Results**

The Gita further explains the theory of non- attachment to the results of work in Ch.18 Verses 13-15 the import of which is as under:

If the result of sincere effort is success, the entire credit should not be appropriated by the doer alone. If the result of sincere efforts is a failure, then too the entire blame does not accrue to the doer. The former attitude mollifies arrogance and conceit, while the latter prevents excessive despondency, de-motivation and self-pity. Thus both these dispositions safeguard the doer against psychological vulnerability, which is the cause for the Modem Managers' companions like Diabetes, High B.P. Ulcers etc.

Assimilation of the ideas behind 2.47 and 18.13-15 of the Gita leads us to the wider spectrum of lokasamgraha or general welfare, which automatically helps us to live a stressfree life. This is also another dimension in the work ethics.

Conclusion

To conclude, we would like to say that stress which is termed to be a new age killer, causes various mental and physical problems. One way out is, that when you get stressed, start taking remedial actions to overcome it, and the other way is to follow the guidelines and strategies suggested by Bhagwan Shri Krishna and live life accordingly. Someone may say that these strategies are comparatively difficult to follow practically as we may not be easily able to remain detached towards the work. Its solution is also given by Shri Krishna in 35th shaloka of chapter 6——— No doubt, our mind tries not to follow the directions given by us, but still through practice, we can bring it under our control and hence can easily avoid stress and live a peaceful life. In brief Gita prescribes us the following capsules:

- Cultivate sound philosophy of life.
- Identify with inner core of self-sufficiency.
- Strive for excellence through work is worship.
- Build up an internal integrated reference point to face contrary impulses, and emotions.

✫✫✫

20

Occupational Stress and Its Management Strategies

*Sapna Bhandari
*Anju Bala
*Rajiv Kheterpal

* Lecturers-MBA Deptt., AIMT, Ambala City.

Stress

We can define Stress as "body's non-specific response to any demand made on it". Stress is not by definition synonymous with nervous tension or anxiety. On one side, Stress provides the means to express talents and energies, and pursue happiness on the other side, it can also cause exhaustion and illness, either physical or psychological.

Hans Selye (one of the founding fathers of stress research) identified another part of this problem, when he saw that different types of definition operate in different areas of knowledge. To a lawyer or a linguist, words have very precise, definite and fixed meanings. In other fields, ideas and definitions continue evolving, as research and knowledge expands.

Selye's view in 1956 was that "stress is not necessarily something bad – it all depends on how you take it. The stress of exhilarating, creative successful work is beneficial, while that of failure, humiliation or infection is detrimental." Selye believed that the biochemical effects of stress would be experienced, irrespective of whether the situation was positive or negative.

Workplace Stress

Stress—the responses our bodies and minds have to the demands placed on them—is a normal part of life and a normal part of any job. Without stress, we wouldn't meet deadlines, strive to hit sales or production targets, or line up new clients. Meeting the demands and challenges of a job is part of what makes work interesting and satisfying, and often allows people to develop new skills and advance in their careers. In the workplace, we regularly experience stress-causing situations; react to them with heightened tension, and then return to a more relaxed state, when the crisis, big or small, is resolved.However, problems occur when stress is so overwhelming or constant, that the tension never abates and we never get to relax.

Job Stress

Job stress comes in many different forms and affects your body in various ways.

- Minor sources of stress may include equipment that won't work or phones that won't quit ringing. Major stress comes from having too much work, not having enough work, doing work that is unfulfilling, fearing a job layoff, or not getting along with your boss.
- Usually it is the major source of stress that leads to burnout, causing people to become unhappy and less productive in their work. Job stress can affect your health and home life as well. Low levels of stress may not be noticeable; slightly higher levels can be positive and challenge you to act in creative and resourceful ways; and high levels can be harmful, contributing to a chronic disease.
- Job stress can be defined as the harmful physical and emotional responses that occur when the requirements of the job do not match the capabilities, resources, or needs of the worker. Job stress can lead to poor health, and even injury.

The concept of job stress is often confused with challenge, but these concepts are not the same. Challenge energizes us psychologically and physically, and it motivates us to learn new skills and master our jobs. When a challenge is met, we feel relaxed and satisfied. Thus, challenge is an important ingredient for healthy and productive work. The importance of challenge in our work lives is probably what people are referring to, when they say "a little bit of stress is good for you.

But for David and Theresa, the situation is different the challenge has turned into job demands that cannot be met, relaxation has turned to exhaustion, and a sense of satisfaction has turned into feelings of stress. In short, the stage is set for illness, injury, and job failure

We think of "job stress" when:

- The challenges and demands of work become excessive.
- The pressures of the workplace surpass workers' abilities to handle them.
- Satisfaction becomes frustration and exhaustion.

When stress crosses the line from normal to excessive, it can trigger physical and emotional responses that are harmful to employees and businesses alike. And unfortunately, for many people "stress" has become synonymous with "work."

NIOSH Model of Job Stress

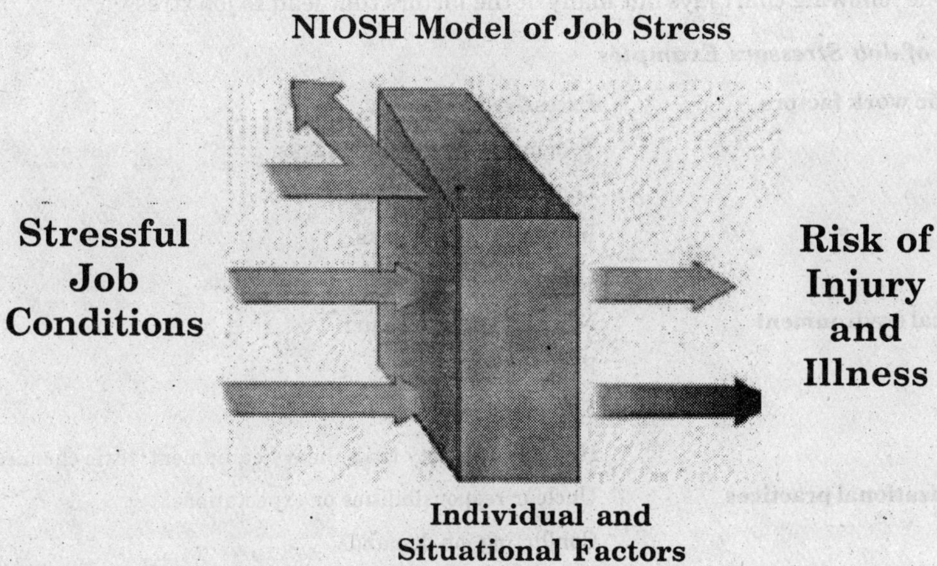

NIOSH Publication No. 99-101: STRESS...*At Work*

Symptoms of stress:

- Rapid heartbeat
- Headache
- Stiff neck and/or tight shoulders
- Backache
- Rapid breathing
- Sweating and sweaty palms
- Upset stomach, nausea, or diarrheoa

Others:

- Anger
- Frustration
- Depression
- Sleep disturbance

Causes of Stress in the Workplace

Some jobs are stressful by definition because they're physically dangerous (such as firefighting or criminal justice), involve matters of life and death (emergency functions), or are psychologically demanding (social work, teaching). But people who stamp metal or crunch numbers, can also be subject to stress on the job. Workplace stress is usually the result of high demands on the job, real or perceived, lack of control concerning those demands, poor day-to-day organization and communication, and an unsupportive work environment.

The following chart lays out many of the factors that lead to job stress:

Types of Job Stressors Examples	
Specific work factors	Excessive workload.
	Tedious or meaningless tasks.
	Long hours and low pay.
	Infrequent rest breaks.
	Unreasonable performance demands.
Physical environment	Noise and overcrowding.
	Poor air quality.
	Ergonomic problems.
	Health and safety risks (heavy equipment, toxic chemicals).
Organizational practices	Unclear responsibilities or expectations.
	Conflicting job demands.
	Multiple supervisors.
	Lack of autonomy or participation in decision-making.
	Inefficient communication patterns.
	Lack of family-friendly policies.
Workplace change	Fear of layoff.
	Frequent personnel turnover.
	Lack of preparation for technological changes.
	Poor chances for advancement or promotion.
	Tensions brought about by greater workplace diversity.

Interpersonal relationships	Distant, uncommunicative supervisors.
	Poor performance from subordinates.
	Office politics, competition, and other conflicts.
	Bullying or harassment.
	Problems caused by excessive time away from family.

Causes of Job Stress:

- Last minute deadline changes
- Dealing with customers issues/problems
- Payment and financial problems
- Conflicts with staff
- Being fired

Other:

- Attending meetings and presentations
- Starting a new job

Reactions of job stress:

- Feels irritated
- Short tempered
- Less productive
- Feels fatigued

Others:

- Non punctuality
- Absenteeism
- Avoidance of work

Stress Management

Stress management is thought to be the ability to experience stress without the accompanying mental or physical stress response/ symptoms. Stress management encompasses techniques intended to equip a person with effective coping mechanisms for dealing with psychological stress, with stress defined as a person's physiological response to an internal or external stimulus that triggers the fight-or-flight response.

Strategies to Cope with Job Stress

- Take a walk
- Call family members/friends

- Medicine
- Deep breathing
- Smoke cigarettes
- Vacation
- Listen to music
- A nap
- Yoga
- Meditation

Research Methodology:

Objective of the Study

- To find out the appropriate symptoms of job stress
- To find out the situation that is stressful
- To know the reaction of respondent towards job stress
- To find out best strategy to cope with job stress during work

Research design: ***Descriptive research***

Descriptive research is used to obtain information concerning the current status of the phenomena to describe "what exists" ,with respect to variables or conditions in a situation. The methods involved range from the survey which describes the status quo, the correlation study, which investigates the relationship between variables, to developmental studies which seek to determine changes over time.

Data collection:

Primary data and secondary data

Source of primary data:

Primary data was collected with the help of questionnaire.

Source of secondary data:

Secondary data was collected with the help of books, journals and internet

Sample design:

Sample size: 251 respondents

Sample area: Ambala Distt.

Analysis and Interpretation

Number of respondents
According to Sex

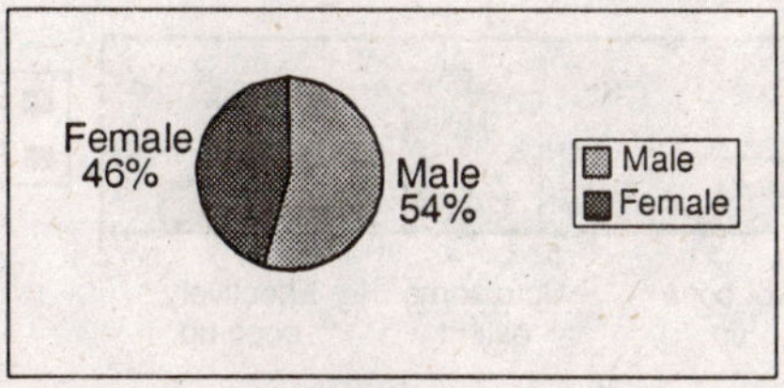

Stressful work situation:-

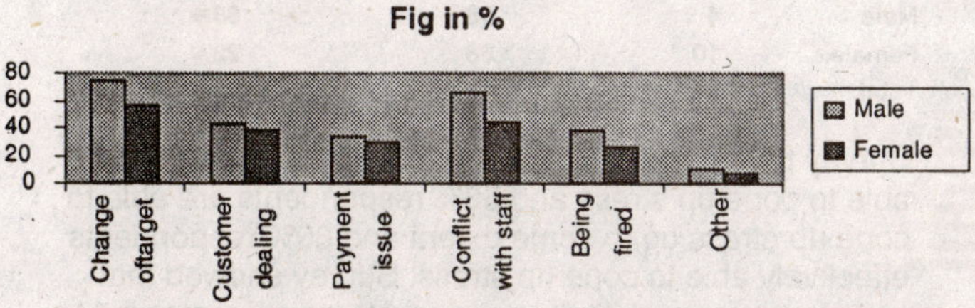

	Change of target	Customer dealing	Payment issue	Conflict with staff	Being fired	Other
Male	74	43	34	65	38	10
Female	56	39	30	45	26	8
Total	65	41	32	55	32	9

Survey indicated that last minute change of target and conflict with staff are the most stressful situations. At work place male experience more stress as compared to female

Reaction towards stress at work

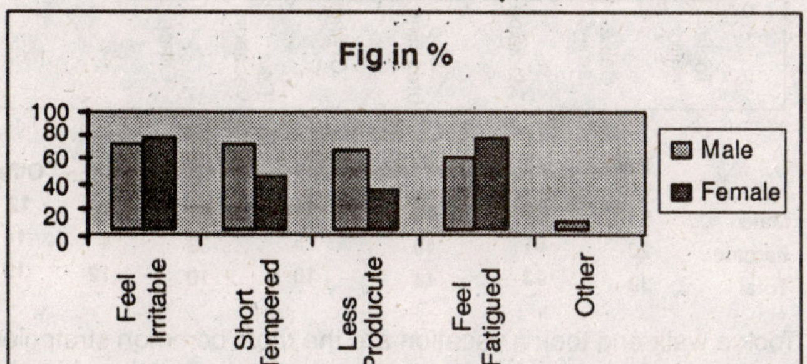

	Feel Irritable	Short tempered	Less Producute	Feel Fatigued	Other
Male	74	78	68	62	8
Female	78	48	38	78	2
Total	78	61	62	70	6

Survey showed that most of the respondents feel irritable and fatigued followed by short tempered stress at work place. Female feel more irritable and fatigued as compared to male but male got short tempered more quickly as compared to female.

Ability to cope up stress:-

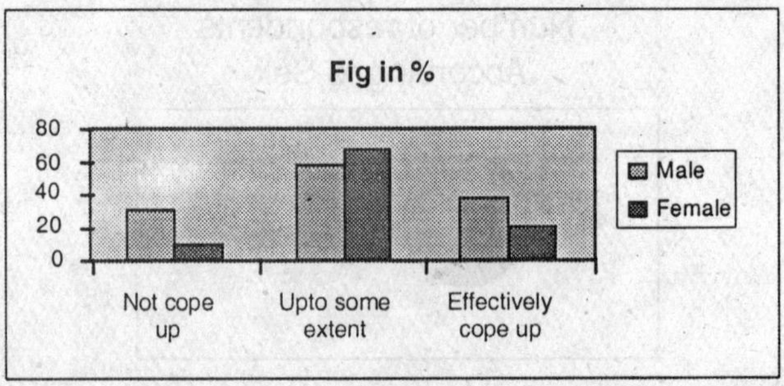

	Not cope up	Upto some extent	Effectively cope up
Male	4	68	88
Female	10	68	22
Total	7	68	80

Survey revealed that 7% of the total respondents are not able to cope up stress and 63% respondents are able to cope up stress up to some extent and 30% respondents effectively able to cope up stress. Survey showed that male have more ability to cope up stress as compared to female.

Strategies help to cope up stress during work

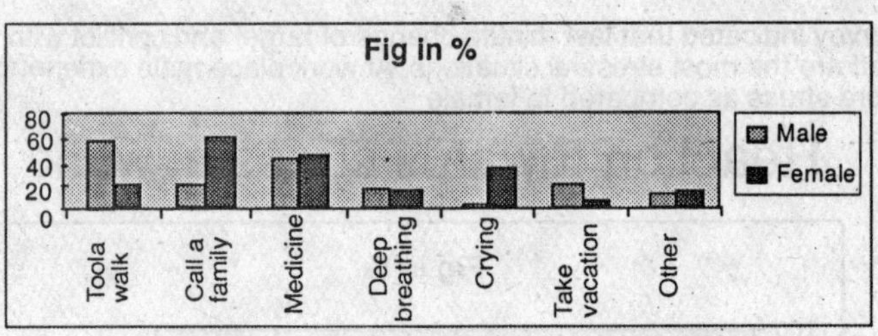

	Take a walk	Call a family	Medicine	Deep breathing	Crying	Take a vacation	Other
Male	63	23	43	11	8	20	12
Female	20	61	43	15	33	4	14
Total	33	43	44	16	10	12	10

Took a walk and took a vacation are the most common strategies used by male during work whereas call a family membersfriend and crying are the mostly used by female as compared to male. Medicine and deep breathing are mostly used by both male and female.

Strategies help to cope stress after work:

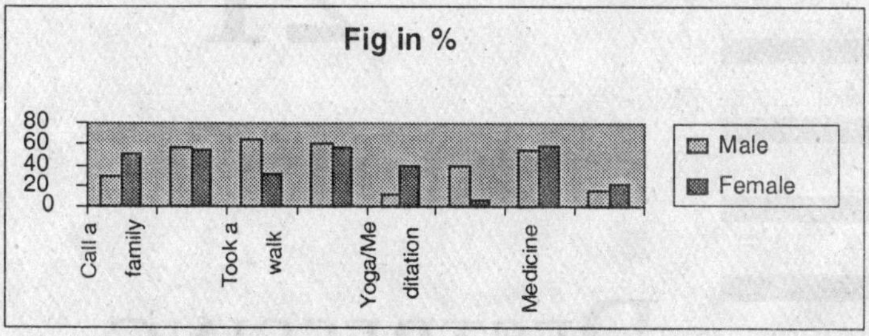

	Call a family	Listen to music	Took a walk	Took a nap	Yoga/Meditation	Smoke/Drink	Medicine	Others
Male	30	57	65	60	12	40	54	15
Female	50	55	31	56	40	6	58	21
Total	40	56	48	58	26	23	56	18

Listen to music, took a nap and medicine are the most common strategies used by both the group to cope up stress after work. Took a walk and smoke/drink are the most common strategies used by male more as compared to the female and call a family member/friend, yoga/meditation and crying are mostly used by female as compared to male.

Findings

It has been found that 79% of the respondents felt stress in their daily life, and female dominates the male. It has been observed that work life is more affected by stress followed by family and leisure activities. Family life of female is more affected by stress as compared by male. Study revealed that headache is the most common symptom of stress followed by upset stomach. Female showed more symptoms as compared to male.

Survey depicted that most of the respondents felt irritable and subsequent lag fatigued, followed short tempered due to stress at workplace. Female felt more irritable and fatigued as compared to male, and male got short tempered as compared to female. It has also been found that medicine and deep breathing are the most common strategies to cope up stress during work in both the groups and a nap followed by Music and medicine are the most common strategies after work.

Limitation

- Shortage of time
- Less awareness about the topic among the common masses
- Sample size is small

Reference

[1] www.altavista.co.in

[2] www.google.co.in

[3] NIOSH Publication No. 99-101: STRESS..*At Work*

[4] Rao V.S.P. HRM Text and cases Excel Books, New Delhi

21

DESTRESSING THROUGH MUSIC THERAPY

* Sarika Jain

The word Federation of Music Therapy defines it as "the use of music and/or its musical elements in a process designed,to facilitate and promote communication, relationship, leadering mobilisation, expression and organisation in order to develop potentials and develop or restore functions of the individuals".

Does music really heal? OR does it just soothe? It might sound incredible but the body's plumbing system (blood hormones, glands nerves cells, muscells, organs, bones, brains) and the divine life – energy system are continuously affected by sound waves from the environment. In his book Cymatics, Hans Jenny describe hows how every healthy atom of the human body has its own vibrational and resonant frequency. Dr. Dhingra Cities an example "Anxiety is a result of high adrenaline or cortisol (stress hormons) levels. The moment one listens to shooting music,.the levels reduce and the patient feels calmer.

The Mind-Body Balance is Restored Thereafter

According, to recent research, music counters all kinds of blockages, retention of bodyly fluids diabetes, arthritis, menstrual, cramps and inflammations. It aids the development of communication and motor skills in children with learning or physical disablilities. It helps release vital healing hormones and combats stress and depressions. It also shows impressive results in schizophrenia. The basic premises of the therapy is to reprogramme the body and establish an equilibrium.

Music as a Stress Buster

However, music therapy is not just for those who suffer from an illness. Even health people can use music to reduce everbody stress through active music making like drumming of through passive listening. Like media professional Kanupriya Kumar does. After those unending deadlines at work and driving in Delhi's Maddening traffic, it is music that keeps me sane. Every evening, I listen to Ghalib and forget the woes of the world and the freaky boss! she calls music her soul's Laudromat – it makes her soul squeaky clean! she is not the only one Unnikrishnan PP, an undergraduate student and a trained classical singer, hums his favourite raga whenever he is in the pits and needs to bust his stress or boost his spirit.

But when music can range from the deafening peak of percussion to the lowest note on a strainged instrument, what does one choose? Says cardiologist Dr. Neelam Verma, who has been "prescribing" music for nearly a decade, It depends on individual need. I generally, combine percussion with the flute or the sitar, making sure the tempo matches the pace of the heart.

Pick a Raga

The foundation of all healing music is its under tones (drones). Most drones are prolonged, continuous and undisturbe; the magic comes from the tones intervals. Most instruments like the jaw harp, bagpipe, sitar chinning bowl, mountain horn, various single or multiple stringed instruments can be tuned to certain undertones. According, to cardiologist, Dr. Neelam Verma, music works best when used with yoga or meditation. For example a person suffering from arthritis should combine music with regular exercise and meditation, while those with the cardiac problems should opt pranayam with music. Some drugs are also more effective during a certain part of the day. Bharavi and Lalit in the morning hours, Megh and Malhar in the day, Yaman and Bhopali in the evening. Take your Pick!

22

Occupational Stress in the Present Social Environment and Its Management Techniques

*Anjali Sharma
**Monika Mehta

* Lecturers, MBA Deptt., AIMT, Ambala City.

- "Job stress can be defined as the harmful physical and emotional responses that occur when the requirements of the job do not match the capabilities, resources, or needs of the worker. Job stress can lead to poor health and even injury."

  [Stress at work, United States National Institute of Occupational Safety and Health, Cincinnati, 1999.]

- "The emotional, cognitive, behavioural and physiological reaction to aversive and noxious aspects of work, work environments and work organizations. It is a state characterized by high levels of arousal and distress and often by feelings of not coping."

  [Guidance on work-related stress: Spice of life - or kiss of death,European Commission, Directorate-General for Employment and Social Affairs]

- "Stress is the reaction people have to excessive pressures or other types of demand placed on them."

[Managing stress at work: Discussion document, United Kingdom Health and Safety Commission, London, 1999.]

Introduction

STRESS is a word that can be used to describe both the cause and the results of pressure building up in the body and mind. Commonly, bullying, job insecurity, relationship difficulties, and many other situations associated with the home or work place generate stress internally and externally. At its root, stress is caused by the difference between expectation and reality. The health and safety executive's definition is that stress occurs "When the demands placed upon a person exceed the capacity to cope with them". If the factors causing stress build up for too long, we can experience 'symptoms'- usually at physical and emotional level.

Although, these signs are called symptoms, stress is not an illness: stress is a psychological condition which has unpleasant physical side effects- but it is a condition which can be addressed by learning about it and changing behaviour associated with pressure to work hard, it can also arise from boredom, procrastination, perfectionism.

Stress, Health, and Productivity

Some employers assume that stressful working conditions are a necessary evil that companies must turn up the pressure on workers and set aside health concerns to remain productive and profitable in today's economy. But research findings challenge this belief. Studies show that stressful working conditions are actually associated with increased absenteeism, tardiness, and intentions by workers to quit their jobs — all of which have negative effects on the bottom line.

Recent studies of so-called healthy organizations suggest that policies benefiting worker health also benefit the bottom line. A healthy organization is defined as one that has low rates of illness, injury, and disability in its workforce, and is also competitive in the marketplace.

Stress at Work or Job Stress

Job stress can be defined as the harmful physical and emotional responses that occur when the requirements of a job do not match the capabilities, resources, or needs of the worker. Job stress can lead to poor health and even injury.

The concept of job stress is often confused with challenge, but these concepts are not the same. Challenge energizes us psychologically and physically and motivates us to learn new skills and master our jobs. When a challenge is met, we feel relaxed and satisfied. Thus **"a little bit of stress is good for you"**.

NIOSH Approach to Job Stress

On the basis of experience and research, NIOSH (National Institute for Occupational Safety and Health) favours the view that working conditions play a primary role in causing job stress. However, the role of individual factors is not ignored. According to the NIOSH view, exposure to stressful working conditions (called job stressors) can have a direct influence on worker safety and health. But as shown below, individual and other situational factors can intervene to strengthen or weaken this influence.

Examples of individual and situational factors that can help to reduce the effects of stressful working conditions include the following:

- Balance between work and family or personal life
- A support network of friends and co-workers
- A relaxed and positive outlook.

NIOSH Model of Job Stress

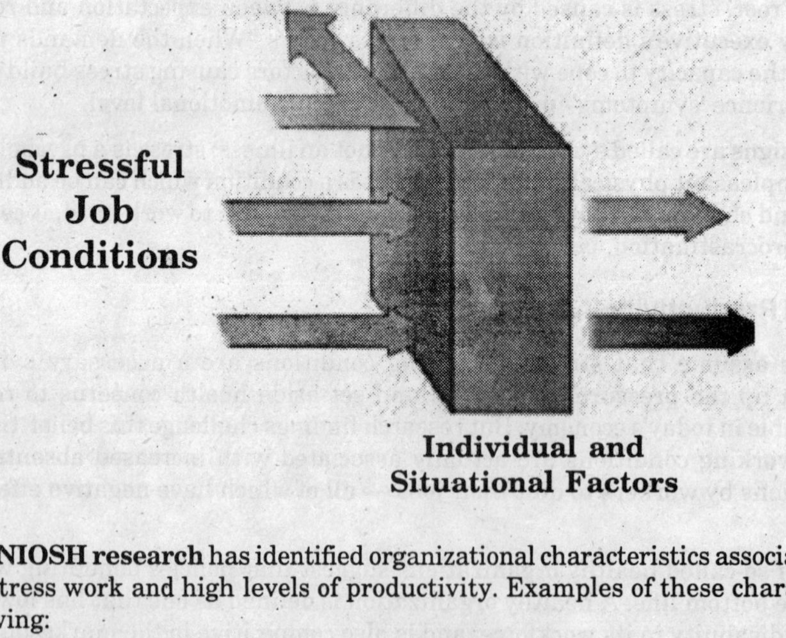

NIOSH research has identified organizational characteristics associated with both healthy, low-stress work and high levels of productivity. Examples of these characteristics include the following:

- Recognition of employees for good work performance
- Opportunities for career development
- An organizational culture that values the individual worker
- Management actions that are consistent with organizational values

Known causes of stress

Nearly everyone agrees that job stress results from the interaction of the worker and the conditions of work. Views differ, however, on the importance of ***worker characteristics*** versus ***working conditions*** as the primary cause of job stress. These differing viewpoints are important because they suggest different ways to prevent stress at work.

According to one school of thought, differences in individual characteristics such as personality and coping style are most important in predicting whether certain job conditions will result in stress—in other words,.what is stressful for one person may not be a problem for someone else. This viewpoint leads to prevention strategies that focus on workers and ways to help them cope with demanding job conditions.

Although, the importance of individual differences cannot be ignored, scientific evidence suggests that certain working conditions are stressful to most people. The excessive workload demands and conflicting expectations describe good examples of stress. Such evidence argues for a greater emphasis on working conditions as the key source of job stress, and for job redesign as a primary prevention strategy.

Apart from extreme mental or physical hardships, it is difficult to categorize about what will cause stress. We have attempted to list those sources of stress that we most frequently hear about:

Job Conditions That May Lead to Individual Stress

- **Unfair Treatment...**

None of us likes to work in situations where we, or others, are aggrieved by a sense of Unfairness. Not being able to remedy situations where people are taken advantage of, manipulated or discriminated against, can be a prime source of stress building up...

- **Exhaustion...**

Feeling pushed to perform, to be perfect, to take on more responsibility, to please everyone, to compete, to attract more money, to stay ahead of others, to work all hours – all are conditions which can be brought on by others, or by our own demands of ourselves.

I wish I could get out of this but...

Trapped in a job that pays the mortgage but no longer satisfies; fearful of tackling a bullying boss because of the consequences; holding secrets on behalf of others – or yourself; getting so specialized you can't see any career options; holding on until retirement; difficult relationships in the team – most of us try to find ways out of these situations but if our efforts prove fruitless, it might be time to talk to someone who can help make changes...

- **My body is complaining...**

Working conditions that are too hot, too cold, have bad seating or bad lighting can make you feel tense, even when the work itself is easy. Similarly, tasks that are too repetitive, for too long hours, cause eye, wrist or back strain, take all the joy out of the working day. We can all endure bad working conditions for a short time, but the body starts to tell you when it has had enough...

What Workers Say About Stress on the Job

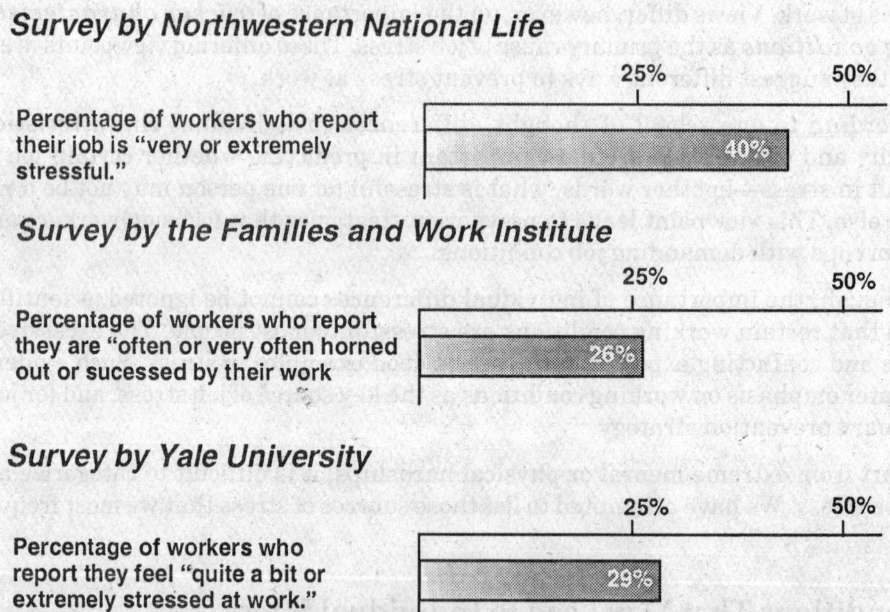

(*Source:* Employee burnout: causes and cures, Part :Employee stress levels, Northwestern national life insurance,Minneapolis,1992,as reported in work in America,Vol.17,No.6,June 1992)

Job Conditions That May Lead to Organizational Stress

- **The Design of Tasks**. Heavy workload, infrequent rest breaks, long works hours and shift work; hectic and routine tasks that have little inherent meaning, do not utilize workers' skills, and provide little sense of control.
- **Management Style**. Lack of participation by workers in decision making, poor communication in the organization, lack of family friendly policies, company's insensitivity to employees' family needs.
- **Interpersonal Relationships**. Poor social environment and lack of support or help from co-workers and supervisors e.g. Employees physical isolation reduces her opportunities to interact with other workers or receive help from them.
- **Work Roles**. Conflicting or uncertain job expectations, too much responsibility, **too many "hats to wear."**
- **Career Concerns**. Job insecurity and lack of opportunity for growth, advancement, or promotion; rapid changes for which workers are unprepared.
- **Environmental Conditions**. Unpleasant or dangerous physical conditions such as crowding, noise, air pollution, or ergonomic problems.

Victims of Stress

All of us are affected at one time or another by work-related stress. Although occupational stress is by no means a new phenomenon, it is becoming increasingly globalized and affects all countries, all professions and all categories of workers, including both blue and white-collar workers, as well as families and society in general. While stress at work is most frequently considered in the context of the industrialized countries, workers in developing countries are also undoubtedly affected.

The evidence also indicates that a broad and growing range of occupations are prone to work-related stress. The following table lists those occupations which equal or exceed the rate of 6 on a stress rating scale of 0 to 10 elaborated by the **University of Manchester Institute of Science and Technology, (U.K.)**

Occupations with high stress levels	
Occupation	***Rating scale***
Miner	8.3
Police officer	7.7
Prison officer	7.5
Construction worker	7.5
Airline pilot	7.5
Journalist	7.5
Advertising executive	7.3
Dentist	7.3
Actor	7.2
Doctor	6.8
Broadcasting personnel	6.8
Nurse	6.5
Film production crew	6.5
Ambulance personnel	6.3
Musician	6.3
Firefighter	6.3
Teacher	6.2
Social worker	6.0
Personnel manager	6.0

(*Source:* Conditions of work digest: Preventing stress at work)

Gender Responses to Stress

One of the most basic behavioral differences between men and women is how they respond to stress. Researchers found that men often react to stress with a **"fight-or-flight"** response, but women are more likely to manage their stress with a **"tend-and-befriend" response.**

Psychology professor and lead researcher Shelley E. Taylor points out that this stress response is seen in many species. Females respond to stressful conditions by protecting and nurturing their young (the **"tend"** response), and by seeking social contact and support from others – especially other females (the **"befriend"** response).

Gender, Work and Stress

The relationship between gender, work and stress is complex. Several factors appear to magnify the impact of stress on women, chief among them being the preponderant role that women still play in the provision of family care. It is well-established that the total workload of women who are employed full-time is higher than that of full-time male workers, particularly where they have family responsibilities.

Research carried out in Sweden found that the total workload of women employed full time is much higher than that of men employed full time, and that the total workload for women employed part time is as much as that of men employed full time. Sweden is a country in which 86 per cent of women are in the workforce, but the division of labour between spouses at home has remained much the same.

Total workload of women and men as related to the number of children living at home

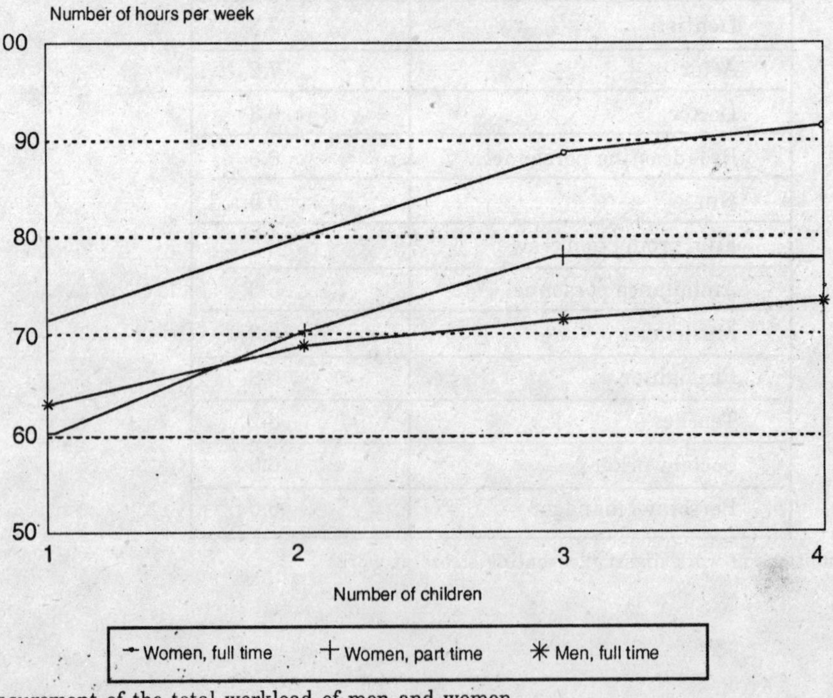

Source: The measurement of the total workload of men and women
M. Frankensteiner, Stochholm, 1991

In addition to their family responsibilities, other factors also tend to make women more vulnerable to work-related stress. These include:

- Lower levels of control in their jobs, since the great majority of women still tend to occupy less senior jobs than men.
- The higher proportion of women who work in *precarious* forms of employment;
- The proliferation of women in high-stress occupations, such as nursing, teaching and work with visual display units (VDUs); and the prejudice and discrimination suffered by many women who are in more senior positions, such as managerial jobs, both as a result of organizational and corporate policy and from their colleagues at work.

The sex divide: how men and women react under pressure

India has had a woman prime minister, a woman as head of the Police service and a woman in space. We may believe we are all equal now. But when it comes to stress – think again.

Most studies show equal numbers of men and women complain of stress. But that's where equality ends. Experts in the science of stress say that men and women are stressed by different things and they react in different ways.

It's not just that traditional roles persist – so that most working women have more responsibility for the family and home while men are more likely to be focussed on breadwinning. We also think differently too.

Reaction of Men and Women Under Pressure

- **women and stress**

Do women really suffer more from stress? Experts in stress-related illness believe that modern life does place more strains on women than men. However, as women often cope better with stress, this tends to even out the stress toll.

Why Women Get Stressed?

Most women today work. In fact, over the last few decades, the British work force has become increasingly female. Women, therefore, face all the stresses which the modern workplace brings. Yet at the same time, many working women also do the lion's share of childcare, housework and caring for older relatives. This means women are coping with strains from several fronts at once.

There are several **other reasons** women specifically face stress.

- **Pregnancy**

Pregnancy can be stressful as women face a barrage of tests, financial worries and uncertainties about what childbirth and motherhood will bring. Research has shown that babies of very anxious mothers tend to be smaller or born earlier and may even suffer development delays. A recent study at one London hospital found the stress hormone cortisol passes from anxious mothers to their unborn babies and may cause these babies to be more prone to stress themselves in later life.

■ **Having a new baby**

Looking after a new baby is stressful for anyone, but more so if you are alone, or have relationship problems with your partner, or are short of money. These pressures can lead to postnatal depression, which one in five mothers suffer.

■ **Looking after children**

Being a full-time mum is no opt-out. Indeed, one recent survey, cited in a parenting magazine, found that 51% of full-time mothers felt regularly stressed, compared to 29% of women working full-time.

■ **Caring for relatives**

Caring for elderly or sick relatives – a job which frequently falls to women – can be very stressful. There are 6.8 million people in Britain caring for disabled or frail elderly friends and relatives and most of them are women.

■ **Bereavement**

Any loss can lead to stress, and losing a loved one is especially stressful. Women are more likely to suffer bereavement as they generally live longer than men. A recent US study also found that widows suffer more stress and depression after bereavement than widowers. These symptoms were likely to lead to medical problems such as cancer or heart attack and thoughts of suicide.

Women Coping with Stress

Yet while women may face multiple pressures, they are often better than men at seeking help when it all gets too much. Women are happy to talk over their feelings with friends or partners, and are more likely to see their GP (General Practioner) when they feel anxious or stressed, rather than waiting for a physical problem to develop.

Men and Stress

One battle for a seat on the early morning train, you are up against deadlines all day, you leave the office late and get home too tired to talk to your partner or the kids. Or maybe you are out of work and spend the day worrying over how the next bill will get paid.

Whether you are in work or out, it is often the traditional role of breadwinner which is the source of stress for most men. And over the last few decades –as society has changed – men seem to have become increasingly vulnerable to stress and other mental health problems.

In most families men are still the main providers. But recent years have brought dramatic changes to the workplace which pile on the pressure.

■ **Unemployment**

Although lots of jobs are stressful, studies have found that being without a job is the most stressful role of all. Men are more likely than women to experience long-term unemployment.

One in seven men who lose their job develops depression within six months, according to mental health charity Mind. Being unemployed for long periods has also been shown to harm your physical health.

■ **Changing roles**

Since the 1980's there has been a steady rise in women at work. For some families this has meant a reversal in the role of breadwinner – bringing tensions and feelings of confusion for many men.

'Stress is not just about having a hyperactive lifestyle,' says Peter Baker, editor of the men's health website, malehealth.co.uk. 'Having no role and being hard-up is very stressful too.'

■ **Men at work**

The new trend of 'hire and fire' in the companies has created widespread insecurity at work, both for those directly affected and those who fear they may be next in line. This is even true in Indian context.

■ **Working longer**

Meanwhile, work itself has become more stressful, experts in stress management believe, with the constant attack of technology in the form of e-mails, mobile phone calls and faxes, and the growth of a culture of long hours.

In Europe, specifically in Britain, Men in full-time employment work an average 42 hours compared to 38 for women – although obviously many people work far beyond these averages. *Taking the Strain (2000),* a survey published by the Chartered Management Institute, revealed that 91% of managers regularly exceeded their contracted hours.

Men Coping with Stress

Men also react under stress very differently from women. They are less likely to talk about how they feel, and less likely to seek help from a doctor or anyone else. Most men only visit their GP when medical symptoms of stress emerge, such as chest pains, headaches and stomach upsets, but some don't even bother to go then.

It all goes back to the way boys are conditioned not to show emotion, says Peter Baker. 'Men have difficulties admitting stress even to themselves.'

■ **Escape routes**

Rather than try to resolve their stress, he says, they are more likely than women to try to escape by drinking to excess, smoking too much, driving aggressively or resorting to violence.

Although the latest research suggests that men are as likely to suffer from depression as women, they are less likely to be diagnosed by a doctor. And over the last two decades, men have also turned increasingly to suicide. Three-quarters of suicides in the UK are by men, according to Mind.

■ **Express yourself**

The solution is not easy, says Peter Baker. But it will mean men becoming more willing to acknowledge their stress, to talk about it with friends and family, to express their emotions generally and – importantly – to seek help from a doctor or other professional.

The Effects of stress

Because stress is so widespread, it has a very high *cost for individuals, companies and organizations, and for society.*

For the *individual,* in addition to the devastating impact of the serious health impairments referred to above, the loss of capacity to cope with working and social situations can lead to less success at work, including loss of career opportunities and even employment. It can give rise to greater strain in family relationships and with friends. It may even ultimately result in depression, death or suicide.

For the *company or organization*, the costs of stress take many forms. These include absenteeism, higher medical costs and staff turnover, with the associated cost of recruiting and training new workers. It has also been shown in recent years that stress takes a heavy toll in terms of reduced productivity and efficiency.

What Can Be Done About Job Stress?

The ***two different approaches*** for dealing with stress at work are explained as:

- **Stress Management.**

The companies can provide stress management training and an employee assistance program (EAP) to improve the ability of workers to cope with difficult work situations. Nearly one-half of large companies in the United States provide some type of stress management training for their workforces. Stress management programs teach workers about the nature and sources of stress, the effects of stress on health, and personal skills to reduce stress-for example, *time management or relaxation exercises*. EAPs provide individual counseling for employees with both work and personal problems. Stress management training may rapidly reduce stress symptoms such as anxiety and sleep disturbances; it also has the advantage of being inexpensive and easy to implement. However, stress management programmes have two major disadvantages:

- The beneficial effects on stress symptoms are often short-lived.
- They often ignore important root causes of stress because they focus on the worker and not the environment.

- **Organizational Change.**

In contrast to stress management training and EAP programs, the companies can try to reduce job stress by bringing in a consultant to recommend ways to improve working conditions. This approach is the most direct way to reduce stress at work. It involves the identification of stressful aspects of work (e.g., excessive workload, conflicting expectations) and the design of strategies to reduce or eliminate the identified stressors. The advantage of this approach is that it deals directly with the root causes of stress at work. However, managers are sometimes uncomfortable with this approach because it can involve changes in work routines or production schedules, or changes in the organizational structure.

As a general rule, actions to reduce job stress should give top priority to organizational change to improve working conditions. But even the most conscientious efforts to improve working conditions are unlikely to eliminate stress completely for all workers. For this reason, a combination of organizational change and stress management is often the most useful approach for preventing stress at work.

Effects of Stress on the Body

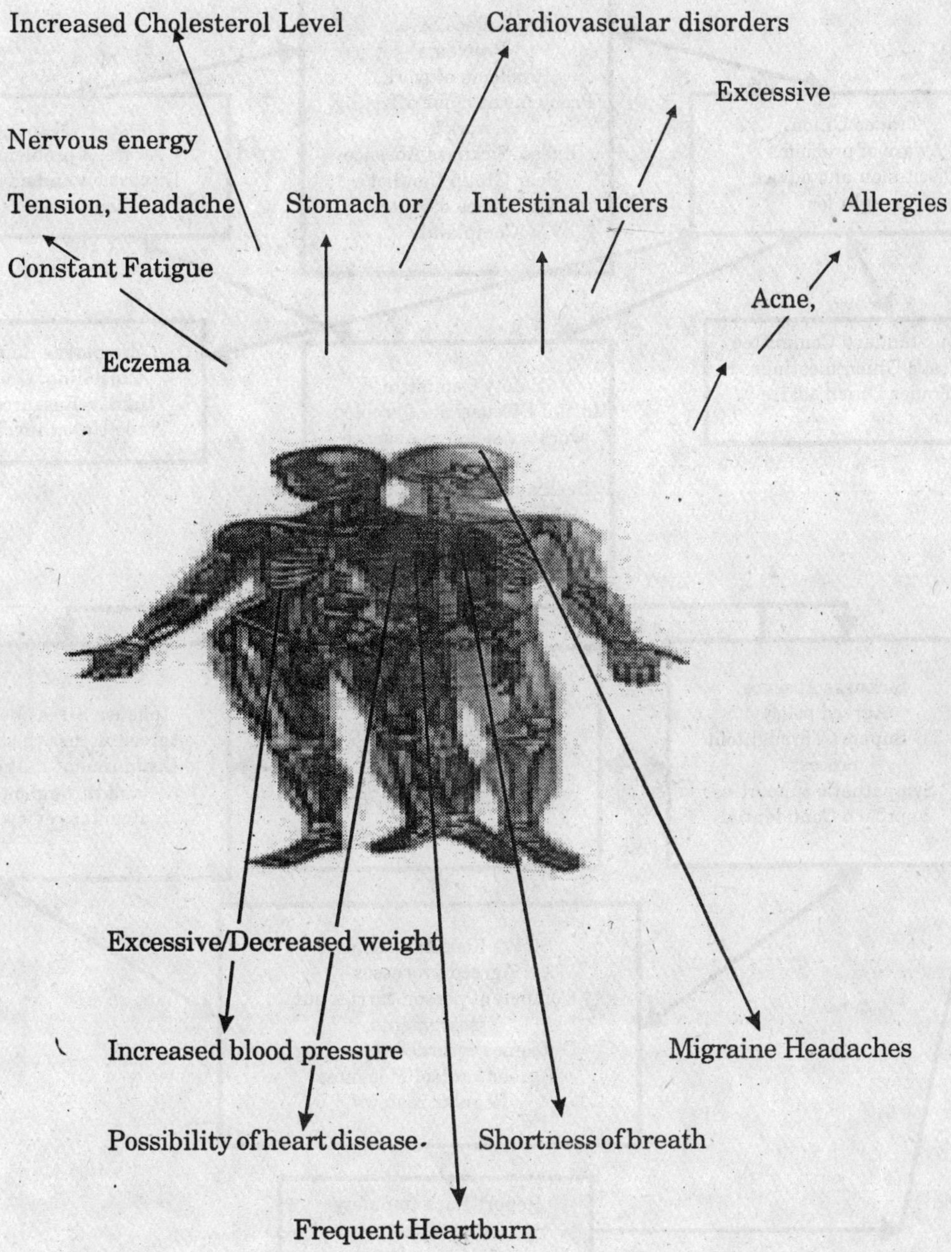

Handling Workplace Stress Problems

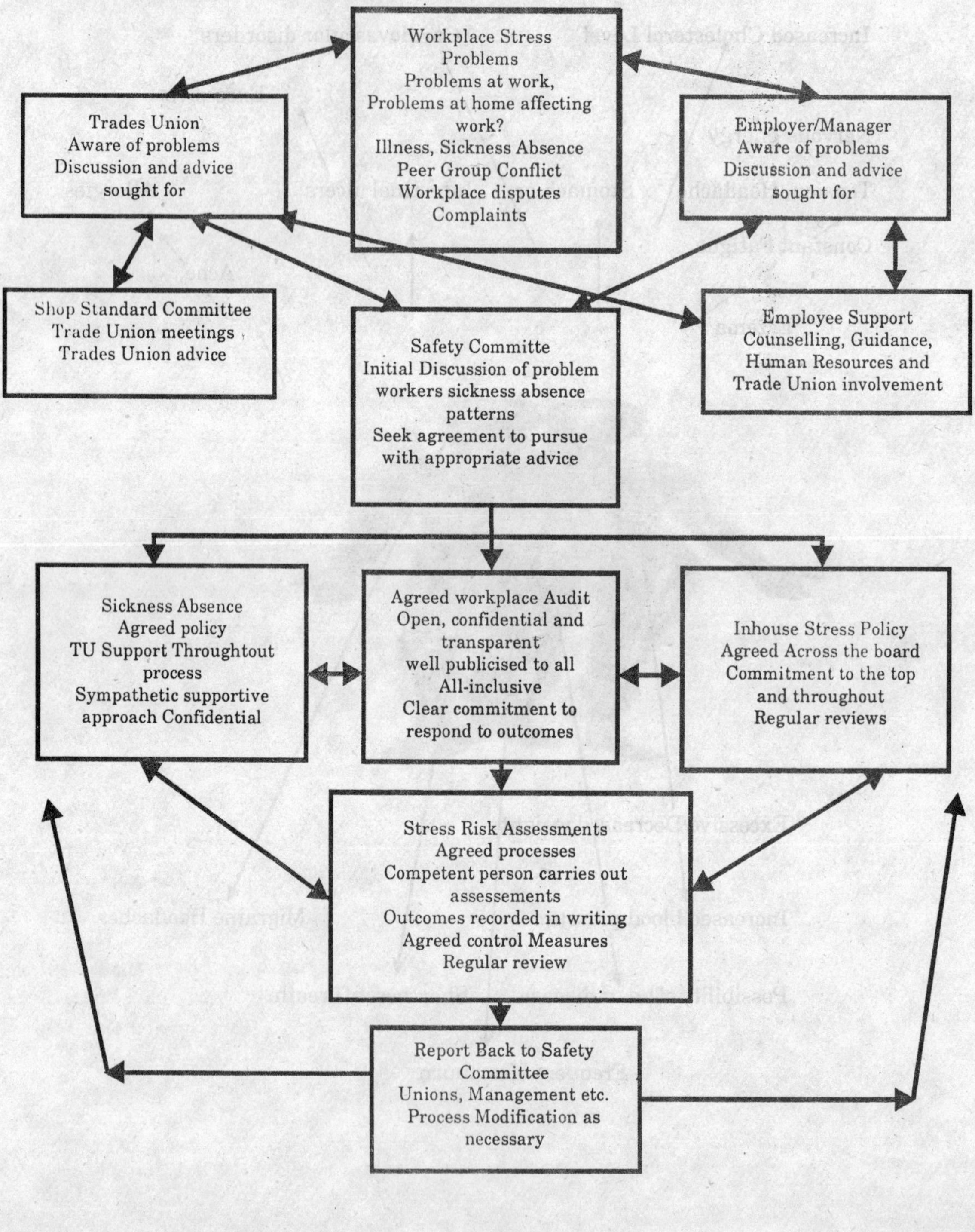

Stress Management

To avoid the problems associated with stress, people need to manage their stress. Before they can manage their stress, however, they need to decide whether they need ***professional help*** **or whether** ***self-help*** is enough. Once people decide on a source of help, regardless of the source of the help and the *stress management techniques* involved, a series of steps are involved in the *process of change.*

Professional Help or Self-Help

When trying to manage stress, it is often difficult for people to decide whether self-help will be enough or whether they should seek professional help. In practice, people usually turn to self-help instead of professional help. Sometimes professional help is necessary. Professional help is probably necessary if self-help fails or does not offer any worthwhile solution or if the problems associated with stress develop into mental disorders or physical illness.

A wide range of professionals is available to people with stress-related problems, ranging from medical doctors to mental health professionals. A medical doctor, such as a general practitioner or a specialist, is a good choice when stress leads to symptoms that may indicate physical illnesses. A mental health professional, such as ***clinical psychologist*** **or a** ***psychiatrist,*** is a good choice when stress leads to symptoms that may indicate a mental disorder. Clinical psychologists and psychiatrists along with other mental health professionals like *counseling psychologists* can also provide assistance with stress management in general, not just with mental disorders that may accompany stress. ***Other mental health professionals like marriage and family counselors, social workers, nurses, clergyperson*** may also be able to provide some assistance with stress management.

Stress Management Techniques

Countless stress management techniques have been used for stress management. These techniques usually involve ***cognitive-behavioral approaches, relaxation, exercise, diet and nutrition,*** **and/or** ***medication.***

1. Cognitive-Behavioral Approaches

Cognitive-behavioral approaches to stress management attempt to change stress-related thoughts, feelings, and actions. Cognitive-behavioral techniques traditionally have been used within the context of three types of therapies: ***cognitive restructuring, coping skills therapies,*** **and** ***problem-solving therapies*** More recently, however, the same principles have been incorporated into self-help methods.

(a) Cognitive Restructuring

The goal of cognitive restructuring is to establish patterns of thinking that are more adaptive and less stress provoking. Examples of cognitive restructuring are *rational-emotive therapy*', *rational behavior therapy*, *cognitive therapy*', *self-instructional training*, and *structural psychotherapy*

The main purpose of rational-emotive therapy is to identify irrational beliefs (i.e., stress-provoking appraisals) and reveal why they do not make sense. A unique feature of rational-emotive therapy is the philosophical emphasis of its major goals:

- Social interest
- Self-direction
- Tolerance of self and others
- Flexibility
- Acceptance of uncertainty
- Commitment to vital interests
- Self-acceptance
- Scientific thinking
- Realistic expectations in life
- Self Interest

Rational behavior therapy is essentially the same as rational-emotive therapy, but it lacks the obvious philosophical emphasis of rational-emotive therapy and focuses on *neuropsychophysiology* (psychological relevance of brain functioning) and learning theory.

(b) Coping-Skill Therapies

The goal of coping-skills therapies is to develop a set of skills designed to help people cope with a variety of stressful situations Examples of coping skills therapies are ***systematic rational restructuring anxiety-management training***, and ***stress inoculation training***

(c) Problem-Solving Therapies

The goal of problem-solving therapies is to develop general strategies for solving a wide range of problems. Problem-solving therapies are essentially a combination of cognitive restructuring and coping skill therapies.

2. Relaxation

The purpose of relaxation techniques is to reduce stress responses. Sometimes it is easy to relax just by getting a massage, listening to calming music, or admiring peaceful works of art. Similarly, simple environmental or ergonomic changes in people's lives can be relaxing by allowing their interactions with specific objects and their surroundings in general to be less strenuous. Other times, however, people have trouble relaxing and need to learn relaxation techniques. Relaxation techniques include *progressive muscle relaxation*, *autogenic relaxation*, *meditation*, the *relaxation response*, *diaphragmatic breathing*.

3. Exercise

Aerobic exercise, *weight lifting*, *yoga*, and *tai chi* are examples of forms of exercise that can help with stress. Aerobic exercise uses the large muscle groups in continuous, repetitive motions and involves increased oxygen intake and increased breathing and heart rates. Aerobic exercises include the following types of exercise:

- Running
- Swimming
- Brisk walking
- Bicycling
- Jumping rope

An exercise program aimed at improving physical fitness should include aerobic exercise 3 to 4 times a week for 20 to 30 minutes preceded and followed by a 5- to 10-minute warm-up and cool-down period, respectively .Yoga involves aspects of meditation and special physical and breathing techniques used to control bodily processes like heart rate and blood pressure. Yoga is a way of life, combining the body, mind and spirit.

4. Diet and Nutrition

Switching to a diet that is healthier,can relieve stress for people who do not have a healthy diet already, especially for people who are overweight. No dietary secrets or miracle diets can lead to long-term stress reduction (or weight loss). People just need to eat right. The following recommendations may be helpful for people who want to improve their diet:

- Eat more fresh fruits and vegetables, enough so that fresh fruits and vegetables make up 50% to 75% of your diet.
- Avoid processed foods and all foods that are stressful for the body, such as artificial sweeteners, carbonated soft drinks, chocolate, eggs, fried foods, junk foods, meat, and chips and similar snack foods.
- Try getting rid of dairy products from your diet for 3 weeks. Then, slowly add them back into your diet and see if stress responses coincide with them.
- Avoid caffeine.
- Avoid alcohol, nicotine, and mood-altering drugs.

5. Medication

Over-the-counter pain relievers are used frequently by many people to relieve the pain of some problems associated with stress. Regarding prescription drugs for stress, *amitriptyline*, an antidepressant drug, has been used to treat tension headaches. Additionally, a wide variety of prescription drugs are used to treat mental disorders and physical illnesses associated with stress. Anxiety and depressive disorders, for instance, are often treated with *antianxiety agents* and *antidepressants*, respectively. Examples of antianxiety agents are as follows:

- Hydroxyzine
- Propranolol
- Other beta-blockers

Summary

Is workplace stress always negative— Under normal circumstances, people should be able to find new balances and responses in their reactions to new situations. Stress is not necessarily a negative phenomenon and it would therefore be a mistake to concentrate only on its pathological effects. A moderate level of stress can be an important motivational factor and can be instrumental in achieving a dynamic adaptation to new situations. If health is considered as a dynamic equilibrium, stress is part of it. There is no health without interaction with other people and with the environment. Only excess of stress is pathological. Some stress is therefore normal and necessary, at work and outside it. But if stress is intense, continuous or repeated, if a person is unable to cope, or if support is lacking, stress then becomes a negative phenomenon which can lead to physical illness and psychological disorders. In a work context, it often results in inadequate adaptation to situations and people and failure to perform at an optimal level.

Learn to develop a sense of humour about yourself and your problems.

Conclusion

"Stress is not all bad" Bear in mind that an appropriate stress response is a healthy and necessary part of life. One of the things it does is to release norepinephrine, one of the principal excitatory neurotransmitters. Norepinephrine is needed to create new memories. It improves mood. Problems feel more like challenges, which encourages creative thinking that stimulates your brain to grow new connections within it. Stress management is the key, not stress elimination. The challenge in this day and age is to not let the sympathetic nervous system stay chronically aroused. This may require knowledge of techniques that work to activate your relaxation response.

"It's not what happens to you that matters, but how you take it".

Hans Selye

References

[1] Stress at work, United States National Institute of Occupational Safety and Health, Cincinnati, 1999.

[2] Guidance on work-related stress: Spice of life - or kiss of death, European Commission, Directorate-General for Employment and Social Affairs

[3] Managing stress at work: Discussion document, United Kingdom Health and Safety Commission, London, 1999.

[4] Conditions of work digest: Preventing stress at work, University of Manchester Institute of Science and Technology,UK

[5] The measurement of the total workload of men and women M. Frankensteiner, Stochholm, 1991

[6] Northwesteren National Life Insurance,Minneapolis,1992

[7] malehealth.co.uk.

[8] www.Wikipedia .com

[9] www.Yahoosearch.com

[10] www.msnsearch.com

✫✫✫

23

WORKPLACE STRESS: HOW TO MANAGE

*Anjali Garg

* Lecturer, MBA Deptt., Dronacharya Institute of Management and Technology, Kurukshetra.

Human resource is the most important asset of any organization. A healthy and committed workforce ensures increased efficiency and productivity for an organization. Quality of human resource assumes even greater significance in today's knowledge-driven business. The human capital has replaced dollar capital, and real value of company's depends more on ideas, insights and information in the heads of their employees, than on assembly line and other physical assets. In this scenario, **WTO** predicts that by 2020, 'depression' is expected to emerge as the second largest global factor contributing to increase in the number of unproductive years in an individual's life (Economic Times (a),2001). Therefore, it has become increasingly important for the organization to evolve approaches and policies that enhance the health of their employees and keep the level of work stress at its optimum.

Stress is a normal part of life and a normal part of any job. Without stress, we won't meet deadlines, strive to hit sales or production targets, or line up new clients. Meeting the demands and challenges of a job is part of what makes work interesting and satisfying, and it's often what allows people to develop new skills and advance in their careers. When stress crosses the line from normal to excessive, it can trigger physical and emotional responses that are harmful to employees and businesses alike. And unfortunately, for many people "stress" has become synonymous with "work." There have been different definitions of **stress,** the most commonly accepted definition of stress (mainly attributed to Richard S Lazarus) is that **stress is a condition or feeling experienced when a person perceives that demands exceed the personal and social resources the individual is able to mobilize.**

Workplace stress can be defined as the physiological and emotional responses that occur when workers perceive an imbalance between their work demands and their capability and/or resources to meet these demands

Stress and Worker's Performance

Stress in the workplace is not a new phenomenon, but it is a greater threat to employee health and well-being than ever before. In most work situations our stress responses cause our performance to suffer. Workplace stress has a negative impact on the business as well as the employees. The increase in job stress creates emotional, financial, and safety concerns for employers and managers. While technology has made aspects of many jobs easier, it has also added to the anxieties of office life through information overload, heightened pressure for productivity, and a threatening sense of impermanence in the workplace. In 1996, the World Health Organization labeled stress a "worldwide epidemic." Today, workplace stress is estimated to cost American companies more than $300 billion a year in poor performance, absenteeism and health costs. The signs of job stress vary from person to person, depending on the particular situation, how long the individual has been subjected to the stressors, and the intensity of the stress itself. Typical symptoms of job stress can be:

Insomnia, Loss of mental concentration, Anxiety, Absenteeism, Depression, Substance abuse, Extreme anger and frustration, Family conflict, Physical illnesses ,such as, heart disease, migraine, headaches, stomach problems, and back problems, low morale etc.

Causes of Workplace Stress

Some jobs are stressful by definition because they're physically dangerous (such as firefighting or criminal justice), involve matters of life and death (emergency functions), or are psychologically demanding (social work, teaching). But people who stamp metal or crunch numbers can also be subject to stress on the job.

Job stress may be caused by a complex set of reasons. Some of the most visible causes of workplace stress are:

- **Job Insecurity**

  organized workplaces are going through metamorphic changes under intense economic transformations and consequent pressures. Reorganizations, takeovers, mergers, downsizing and other changes have become major stressors for employees, as companies try to live up to the competition to survive.

- **High Demand for Performance**

  Increased workload, extremely long work hours and intense pressure to perform at peak levels all the time for the same pay, can actually leave an employee physically and emotionally drained. Excessive travel and too much time away from family also contribute to an employee's stressors.

- **Technology**

  The expansion of technology—computers, pagers, cell phones, fax machines and the Internet, has resulted in heightened expectations for productivity, speed and efficiency, increasing pressure on the individual worker to constantly operate at peak performance levels.

- **Workplace Culture**

  Adjusting to the workplace culture, whether in a new company or not, can be intensely stressful. Making one adapt to the various aspects of workplace culture, such as, communication patterns, hierarchy, dress code if any, workspace, working and behavioral patterns of the boss, as well as the co-workers, can be a lesson of life.

- **Personal or Family Problems**

  Employees going through personal or family problems tend to carry their worries and anxieties to the workplace. When one is in a depressed mood, his unfocused attention or lack of motivation affects his ability to carry out job and responsibilities.

- **Job Stress and Women**

  Women may suffer from mental and physical harassment at workplaces, apart from the common job stress. This can consist of unwelcome verbal or physical conduct.

Ways of Reducing Workplace Stress

Stress on the job creates high costs for businesses and institutions, reducing morale, productivity, and earnings. Clearly, it is in every employer's best interests,fiscal and otherwise,to reduce workplace stress as much as possible. Businesses can lower and prevent job stress through various ways.

Following is a list of ways in which an **organization can foster** low levels of job stress and high levels of productivity:

- Share information with employees to reduce uncertainty about their jobs and futures.
- Clearly define employees' roles and responsibilities.
- Consult your employees
- Give workers opportunities to participate in decisions that affect their jobs.
- Consult employees about scheduling and work rules.
- Make sure that the workload is suitable to employees' abilities; avoid unrealistic deadlines.
- Show that individual workers are valued.
- Offer rewards and incentives
- Praise good work performance verbally and institutionally.
- Provide opportunities for career development.
- Promote an "entrepreneurial" work climate that gives employees more control over their work.
- Cultivate a friendly social climate
- Make management actions consistent with organizational values

While organizational change comes from management, there are still many things **employees—individually or collectively**—can do to reduce workplace stress.

Stand Up for yourself -Get a job description. If your employer hasn't provided specific, written description of your job, ask for one.

Change your job- If you like where you're working but your job is too stressful ask if the company can tailor the job to your skills or move you to a less pressured slot.

Get support- Use the local, state, and federal agencies created to support workers' interests and your union, to back you up in situations that expose you to unnecessary danger, unsafe or unhealthful conditions, or undue harassment.

Get a new job- If the level of stress at your job is harming your health and your relationships, and you don't see any prospect of real change, it may be time to move on.

Eliminate Self-Defeating Behaviors- Many of employees make job stress worse with pattern of thought or behavior that keep us from relieving pressure on ourselves. Turn around these self-defeating habits, you'll find employer-imposed stress easier to handle.

Resist perfectionism- No project, situation, or decision is ever perfect, and you put undue stress on yourself by trying to do everything perfectly. Don't set unrealistic goals for yourself or try to do too much, Do your best and you'll do fine.

Clean up your act- If you're always running late, set your clocks and watches fast, if your desk is a mess, throw away the clutter; just knowing where everything is, saving time and cutting stress. Plan your day and stick to the schedule — you'll feel less overwhelmed.

Flip your negative thinking- If you see the downside of every situation and interaction, you'll find yourself drained of energy and motivation. Try to think positively about your work, avoid negative-thinking, and pat yourself on the back about small accomplishments, if no one else does.

Get time away- If you feel stress building, take a break. Walk away from the situation. Take a stroll around the block, sit on a park bench, or spend a few minutes meditating. Exercise does wonders for the psyche. But even just finding a quiet place and listening to your iPod can reduce stress.

Talk it out- Sometimes the best stress-reducer is simply sharing your stress with someone close to you. The act of talking it out – and getting support and empathy from someone else – is often an excellent way of blowing off steam and reducing stress.

Cultivate allies at work- Just knowing you have co-workers who are willing to assist you in times of stress will reduce your stress level. Just remember to reciprocate and help them when they are in need.

Find humour in the situation- When you, or the people around you, start taking things too seriously, find a way to break through with laughter. Share a joke or funny story.

Conclusion

Moderate levels of stress increase efforts, stimulate creativity and encourage diligence in one's work. Excessively high levels of stress can overload and breakdown a person's physical and mental system. Stress is an inevitable part of one's life and cannot be avoided. What can however be avoided is negative reaction to stress.

Organizations are beginning to realize the importance of stress management. The US corporate giants have incorporated health education and wellness programmes, realizing that a healthy employee is a productive employee. Stress counseling and management in India still has a low profile. It is high time,that Indian Corporate giants take steps like their Western counterparts, enabling their executives to absorb and bye-pass stress and strain in their jobs which are rapidly increasing.

References

[1] Pravaiz Talib and Mohsin Aziz, "Strategic Approach to Manage Organizational Stress: A Conceptual Model", The ICFAI Journal of Organizational Behavior, Vol V, No. 2, April 2006, pp.12-17.

[2] L. Manivannan, M G Saravanaraj and S Sumathi, "Managing Stress Among the Employees", The ICFAI Journal of Organizational Behavior, Vol. VI, No. 2, April 2007, pp.53-59.

[3] F.JohnReh, http://management.about.com/od/yourself/ht/ReduceStress05.htm

[4] http://www.helpguide.org/mental/work_stress_management.htmJobStress Management

✡ ✡ ✡

24

WHAT IS OCCUPATIONAL STRESS

* *Mrs. Suparna Singh*

* Lt Col (Dr.) MBBS, DGO.

Occupational stressors are working conditions that overwhelm the adaptive capabilities and resources of workers, resulting in acute psychological, behavioral or physical reactions. Prolonged exposure to a stressful working condition may lead to illness or disease. Although individual factors (such as coming strategies) and social resources can modify the reaction to occupational stressors to some degree it is certain working conditions that places workers at risk for developing health problems .

Job stressor commonly include job/ task demands (work overload, lack of task control), Organizational factors (poor inter personal relations), unfair management practices, discriminatory hiring practices and physical condition (noise). Additional sources of stress include financial and economic factors, conflict between work and family roles, sex specific stressors (sexual harassment), training & career development issues and poor organizational climate (values, communication, styles), etc. Stress can cause psychological (affective & somatic) responses, job dissatisfaction, behavioral (sleep problems, absenteeism) or physical (changes in BP) reactions. Prolonged exposure to job stressors, produce psychological & physical illness, such as depression and coronary artery disease. There is no evidence that a particular job stressor will result in a particular acute stress reaction or illness. Rather a range of health symptoms can be associated with workplace stressors.

Research Evidence:- One of the most frequently used models for studying effects of job stress or worker's health is job strain model. It characterizes jobs with low level of job control (or decision latitude) & high workload demands as high strain and predicts that these type of jobs will be most likely to produce symptoms and illness.

High strain jobs have been linked with psychological distress, pain and reduced physical functioning among nurses, increased sickness absenteeism and depressive symptoms among female workers in wide variety of occupations and a significant increase in blood pressures among more highly educated female white collar workers.

Low level of skill discretion/decision authority was linked to high levels of psychological distress in a sample composed primarily of male and female white color professionals regardless of the level of job demands. In other words, lack of challenge and boredom were linked with distress regardless of the amount of work the subjects had to do.

Sex Specific Occupational Stress:-_ for many years, research on occupational stress focused almost exclusively on men and consequently certain sex specific occupational stressors, including various forms of sex discrimination and difficulties combining work and family, received little attention.

Sex Discrimination:- Sex discrimination is inequitable treatment based on sex and includes discriminatory hiring and promotion practices, salary differentials between equally qualified men and women, limited career advancement opportunities and sexual harassment. In terms of hiring and promotion differences, sex determination is pervasive. Men and women agree that organizations engage in such discrimination against women but rarely against men. Women who are targets of discriminatory hiring or promotion practices report higher levels of work conflict and are more likely to consider leaving or changing jobs. Barriers to advancement to higher managerial positions - 'The glass ceiling' are also widespread, 60% reported that they had little or no opportunity for advancement. These barriers to advancement contribute to the salary differentials that exists between the sexes. Although salary gap has reduced since 1997, women still earned only 79% of what men earned. . Barriers to financial advancements and career have been linked to more frequent physical and psychological symptoms, and more frequent visits to the doctor.

Sexual Harassment - Unwanted and unsolicited verbal or physical sexual behaviors can be a severe occupational stressor with serious physical, psychological, behavioral and career consequences Fitzgerald estimated that half of all working women will be harassed at some point, during their academic or professional lives. All women are susceptible to harassment, regardless of age, social status, race or ethnicity. Targets have reported a range of psychological symptoms like depression, anxiety, fearfulness, feelings of guilt and shame, and physical symptoms such as headaches, sleep disorders and such job related outcomes as job withdrawal, negative job attitudes, involuntary job loss or career in disruption. Several studies have shown that sexual harassment is a particularly noxious stressor for women and has a significant impact on their psychology . Although a range of factors probably contribute to risk for workplace sexual harassment, sex ratio within workplace and organizational tolerance for harassment appear to be particularly important. Workplaces with a high ratio of men to women and that tolerate harassing behaviors perpetrators are unlikely to be punished, complaints are not taken seriously, reporting may trigger negative consequences, have higher levels of sexual harassment.

Combining Work and Family

70% of mothers with children under age of 18 were working in 1996. Today the employment curve for women tracks that of men, with the highest labour force participation rates during prime working years of 25 to 55. Working women still retain primary responsibility for dependant care and household chores, however women are more likely than men to have less time to address their children's needs (83% vs 22%) and are more likely to have responsibilities towards elders too.

Although fathers are spending more time with their children and on household chores than they did 20 years ago the gender gap is still significant Galinsky and Bond found that 80% to 90% of married working women reported primary responsibility for cooking, cleaning and shopping and that 2/3rd had primary responsibility for bill paying. Even when a child care or household cleaning services were used, women still have responsibility for their arrangement. Overall however employment has many benefits for women, including increased financial resources, a sense of achievement and reduced social isolation, all of which can benefit health. However when women lack sufficient child care and household help from spouses, and work in psychological demanding jobs, their health and well being may suffer.

Controlling Occupational Stress

Occupational Stress interventions can focus either on individual worker or on the work place. Individual interventions may consist of training in coping strategies, progressive relaxation or other stress management techniques.

Healthcare professionals may find it difficult to diagnose and treat, occupational stress related health problems for a number of reasons. Symptoms arising from workplace stressors are non - specific and do not constitute an identifiable syndrome. Healthcare professionals are not trained generally to inquire about or recognize Occupational Stress.

However when recognized, Occupational Stress related symptoms or illness can be successfully treated.

Most effective way of reducing occupational stress is to eliminate the stressors through organization and job redesign interventions. Organisations with family responsive human resources policies such as flexible work scheduling, family leave policies and child care assistance appear to engender higher levels of commitment and attachment among their employees regardless of the extent to which the employees actually use the programs. In summary, women are subject to the same workplace stressors and their health effects as men. However they are also subject to such specific job stressors as sex discrimination and difficulties combining work and family that may pose additional risks to their health and well being. Some strategies for reducing stressors in the workplace can be particularly beneficial for working women these range from enhancing individual coping capabilities to job and organizationally focused intervention that actually remove the sources of Occupational Stress. The latter may be particularly beneficial for employers because they improve commitment and well being among all workers and not just among the targeted populations.

"The only thing you take with you when you're gone is what you leave behind"

"The sooner we learn to take responsibility for how we respond to events and turn them into positive use of energy, the less will we suffer "

✡ ✡ ✡

25

STRESS AS I SEE IT

*Brig S. M. Sharma

* Surgeon, Commandant, MH Ambala Cantt.

Every matter animate or inanimate, in existence in space or planet is under stress at one time or other. But stress is the price which a living being has to pay for existence. Stress is significant for human beings because he can perceive it, feel it and express it. Man is prone to stress, since the time immemorial, because of his struggle to live within the environment to which he is not fully evolved or suited, unlike the animals, who are in a very advanced stage of compatible living on earth, because of higher adaptability to the changes on earth. Stress is peculiar to human beings of all ages from childhood to old age. Stress is stimulus to growth, progress; development and creativity to some extent, which can reach a breakpoint beyond certain limits of capability and capacity.

Human beings are unique because of their superior intellect, thought, configuration to translate ideas and thoughts, for transformation of matter to creativeness, and formation of newer objects. This transformation has been added from generation to generation, which has resulted in materialism and ethical and value based civilization. Man has been engaged relentlessly in pursuit of creativity through hard work, without the impact of stress or slow down. The hard work itself is the stimulus to work more and destress. A sincere hard work with dedication is impetus to long life, which is useful to society as a whole. One works most of the times for others as well. But at times, a situation comes when a person gives way, and feels unable to cope up with his responsibilities , either due to limitations of capability or due to anxiety, fear and uncertainty. Thus, stress basically means inability to achieve what is expected out of one, due to physical or mental inadequacy. Thus stress is peculiar to a individual with compromised physical, mental and spiritual well being. One individual can cope up with huge multiple responsibilities throughout his life, where as the second individual finds it difficult to do even smaller commitments. Therefore, stress is an individuals inability to stand to a commitment successfully, and the factors responsible to this may be environmental or genetic. Stress is of diverse nature; it may be due to physical stress where an individual is incapacitated due to illness or bodily weakness, or it may be due too mental outlook, anxiety, worries, domestic and social conflicts, or due to personality traits like jealousy, competition, hostile surroundings, lack of physical and social support, lack of amenities and services, or due to swallowing or accepting much more than is possible to digest. A student is under stress due to exams or studies, youth is under stress due to personal problems, habits, or due to uncertain future. An elderly is under stress due to responsibilities towards families. These situations affect the duties of an individual. A stressed individual becomes liability to himself and the society. Therefore, persons who are unreasonably or genuinely under stress require guidelines to help them out to cope up with stress.

Stress does not mean that one should not undertake the work or responsibilities entrusted to him. One should not avoid the responsibilities. One must strike a balance between body, mind and thoughts. For any person the stress lies in the mind. But one thing is certain; that one should realize one's capacity and capability to undertake the task, otherwise result will be stress, confusion, irritation and demoralization. To perform successfully, one must have a suitable and friendly environment. One can't work in a hostile surroundings. It is better to come out of such a situation and set one self free from tension and stress, rather than to be with unfriendly people and choose better and good human beings to work with.

One gets into stress and tension because of ones own deeds and works. So control your tongue, lest harm may come to you. Always speak firmly, but in gentle and polite tone. One must prioritize his work in a perfect order. Select the work and finish it meticulously, preferably case by case. Jumping to multiple tasks at the same time will lead not only to confusion, but also to imperfection, delays and ultimately loss of trust, dissatisfaction and stress. To execute tasks successfully one should choose trusted and competent team. One should be humane to his colleagues and friends. One must help others genuinely. One should relax de-stress himself by walking, exercises, praying, meditation, humor and by accommodative nature. One should not get drowned in ones own pent up feelings and emotions. Let your emotions and feelings be out and thus keep your heart and mind light. Be frank, forthright and clear in your actions and speech.Keep your time well, work within time frame, regulate your life as per the time calls for it. Fix time table for your work and routine, pleasure and leisure. Trust your subordinates and delegate responsibility. Do not be overbearing. Do not be over corrective. Learn from mistakes and never loose temper. Always receive the problems and solve them. Do not pass on responsibilities to others just to avoid them. One should de-stress by developing a hobby. One may pick up and choose a game, take interest in nature. Love for it can do wonders. Never get entangled with anything which may steal your energy, thoughts and efforts and divert your creativity towards turmoil and nothinglessness.

One must eat healthy food. One should destress by walking, sleeping and talking moderately. One must live a life full of ethics, which includes truthfulness, non violence in action, thoughts and speech. One should be above jealousy. One must respect others, especially the elders and lead life by example. Stress, to a large extent, is the result of mental incompetence and incomplete personality development. Let us work silently for the sake of justification for existence of life given to us by Nature and God, and out of the bossom of mother earth . Let this precious life, before it dissolves back into earth, be returned to it only after accomplishments for others. May it be family or society, with the aim of repaying the debt of bounty of life given to us by God. Let us lead useful happy life by serving mother earth and the nature.

Let each and every living being on this earth live like family. This is the key to peace in this world and beyond. An individual with higher goals passes through the turbulence of life with happiness and contentment, and knows not what the stress is.

"Any Living Being Who is Stable In Body And Mind Can withstand Any Storm till It Lives."

✡✡✡

26

OCCUPATIONAL STRESS

** Vijay Rohal*
*** Varun Chadha*

* Research Scholars (Tilak Raj Chadha Institute of Mgt. and Tech., Yamuna Nagar)

Introduction

As the pace at which our society operates increases, the pressures for every member of society to keep up with this pace also increases. Many of these pressures affect people through their jobs. Stress has become the "buzzword" that many people use to describe the impact that these pressures cause. In the short-term, stress can enable individuals to meet high levels of demand or pending deadlines. Prolonged stress, however, has been shown to cause illness and other conditions that can have detrimental effects on an employer's workforce.

Stress In Organizations

As Leon Warshaw noted in 1979 in his book on dealing with stress in the workplace: "Stress affects personality, modifying our perceptions, feelings, attitudes and behaviour.There are many factors that contribute to making a workplace stressful. Research clearly indicates that certain jobs are more stressful than others. For example, people who work as police officers, fire fighters, air traffic controllers, and elected officials are exposed to higher levels of stress The factors that contribute to making some jobs more stressful include: level of decision-making required; level of monitoring workers must endure; unpleasant or dangerous physical or emotional conditions; repeated exchange of information with others; and whether job tasks are generally structured or unstructured.

Understanding the factors that contribute to creating stress in the workplace can help employers begin to manage stress among the workforce.

Organizations cutting across industries were gearing up to provide employees with a stress-free healthy environment. The efforts to address this issue were more pronounced in some industries than others. Experts felt that, though stress at the workplace is a global phenomenon, professionals in some industries were more susceptible to stress than others.

Model of Occupational Stress

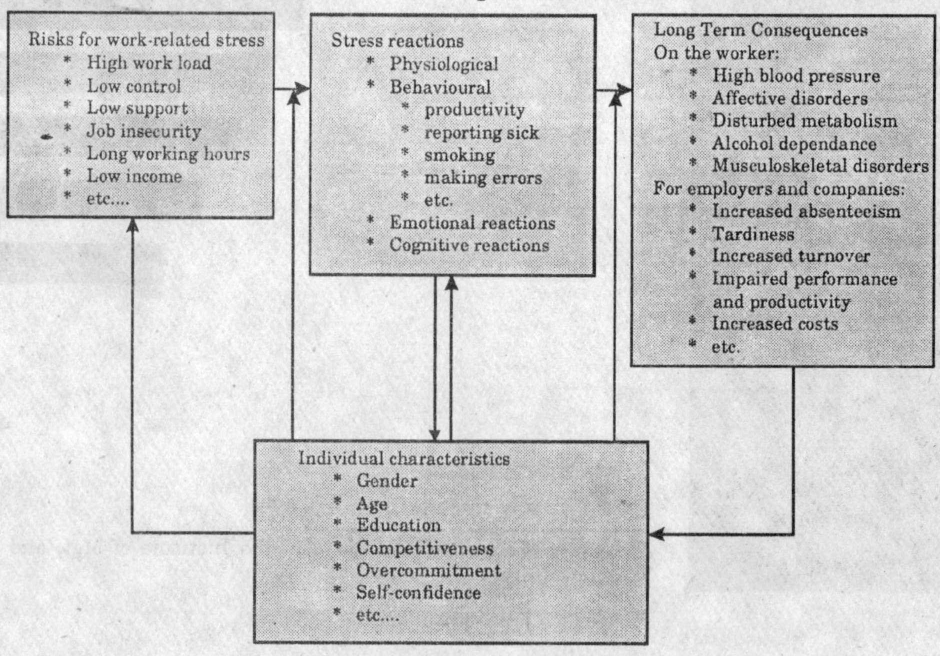

Stressors on the Job

Following are the main stressors that have been identified as those causing the most stress for the most people:

1. "Politics" in general and organizational politics in particular.
2. Too much/too little independence in performance and decision-making.
3. Responsibilities without adequate power to fulfill them.
4. Lack of adequate knowledge to fulfill assignment or make plans for self within the organizational structure
5. Lack of motivators for performance.
6. Too much or too little responsibility.
7. Too much or too little work.
8. Interruptions and conflicting demands
9. Role conflict.
10. Managing time on the job.

Job stress comes in many different forms and affects our bodies in various ways. Minor sources of stress may include equipment that won't work or phones that won't quit ringing. Major stress comes from having too much work, fearing a job layoff, or not getting along with your boss.Usually it is the major sources of stress that lead to burnout, causing people to become unhappy and less productive in their work. Job stress can affect health and home life as well. Low levels of stress may not be noticeable; slightly higher levels can be positive and challenge us to act in creative and resourceful ways; and high levels can be harmful, contributing to chronic disease.

The stress can be classified into four groups.

1. Distress **2. Euphoric stress** **3. Hyper stress** **4. Hypo stress**

The term **distress** is the most commonly accepted interpretation of the term stress. It account for all the happenings and resultant feelings of unpleasantness, losses. The opposite of distress is **eu-stress** or stress caused by experiences of over joy, over pleasantness or a windfall or sudden gain. The **hyper** stress is the situation characterize by over activities, pressure of meeting the deadlines etc. Opposite to this is **hypo** stress, indicated by lack of activity, absence of challenge and pressure for performance. Generally, executives complain about hyper stress but if possible avoid the situation of hypo stress or hyper stress. In fact, many organizations create legitimate tasks and regular systematic work routine of responsibilities. The stress is essential to reach the definite performance. Infact, excellence in any sphere of life is essentially accompanied by stress. It is a bad master, but a good servant.

Stress in IT Industry

Sensing the high stress levels among employees that lead to lower productivity and higher attrition rates, Information Technology and Business Process outsourcing firms are resorting to unconventional methods, including teaching dancing and music, to tackle and beat the stress.

Top 10 Software Companies in India

Rank	*Company*
1	Tata Consultancy Services Ltd.
2	Infosys Technologies Ltd.
3	Wipro Technologies Ltd.
4	Satyam Computer Services Ltd.
5	HCL Technologies Ltd.
6	Patni Computer Systems Ltd.
7	I-flex Solutions Ltd.
8	Tech Mahindra Ltd. (formerly Mahindra-British Telecom Ltd.
9	Perot Systems TSI (I) Ltd.
10	L&T Infotech Ltd.

Some of the leading Indian IT firms have lined up their resources so as to tackle this acute problem persisting in their organization. India's largest IT services firm, **Tata Consultancy Services** for instance, creates a balance between work and fun which is facilitated through different clubs like Theatre Club, Bibliophile Club, Adventure & Trekking Club, Fitness Club, Sanctuary Club, Music Club and Community Services Club, among others.

At **Infosys** a unique Health, Safety and Environmental Management System (HSEMS) called the 'Ozone Initiative' is equipped to make the employees happy and willing to work. **Infosys** ,on its part, has a custom-designed instrument, which assists in increasing self-awareness. Based on the response, further guidance is provided to identify ways of effectively coping with the stress. The company also conducts a series of workshops by experts. Even smaller companies like **Nucleus** and **Tulip** practise their innovative ways to keep the stress levels among employees under check. What they believe is that there is a high amount of stress among employees these days, and this is largely due to lack of interpersonal interaction among the members of the company. To counter such problems, they have a system of mentors and an 'open door' policy, where all employees are free to talk to their superiors.

Tulip has also gone the extra mile by conducting salsa and jazz classes, besides the stress management workshops.The BPO sector, with its irregular hours and strenuous working conditions, are badly hit with the stress syndrome contributing to approximately **25 to 30** per cent attrition rate among the BPOs. The BPOs have also adopted innovative methods of reducing the high attrition rates, besides the normal facilities of taxi service, and subsidised cafeterias. Gurgaon based BPO **Convergys**; to reduce the stress of its young employees, helps them continue their education even while working. Convergys also has a special Education Assistance Program that allows one to get up to Rs 24,000 of the course fee reimbursed.

Stress and Work Performance

Relationship between occupational stress and job performance! The amount of money workplace stress is extracting from the economy is estimated to be billions of dollars. Such estimates are based on the assumption that workplace stress leads to increased healthcare costs, higher rates of absenteeism and turnover, accidents, and lower levels of performance and organizational productivity. A comprehensive, research-based examination of the relationship between occupational stress and job performance presents a concise overview of the field, a clear explanation of terms and concepts, and a summary of relevant theoretical models of the stress process. the relationship between major job-related stressors (such as workload, interpersonal conflict and lack of control) and a variety of performance indices explores a number of other factors that may affect the relationship between occupational stress and job performance, including gender differences, age, personality, and job experience.

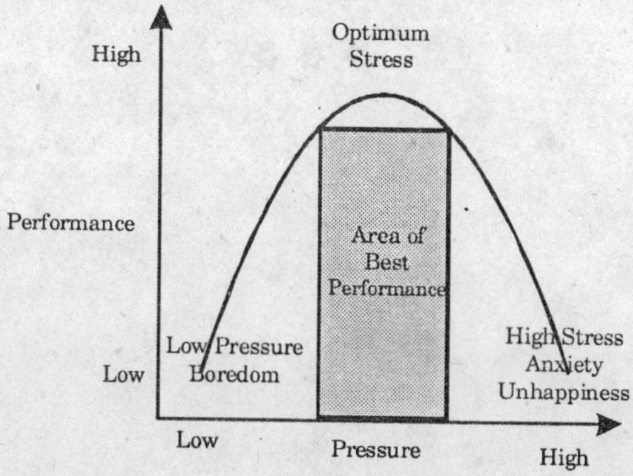

The Inverted-U relationship between pressure and performance

Conclusion

It can be said that stress can be both positive and negative, which has an impact on the employee's performance at work. If taken positively the results are positive, and if taken in negative way, may yield to disastrous results. For most of the people, lower to moderate amount of stress enables them to perform their jobs in a better way.

References

[1] www.dnaindia.com

[2] www.mindtools.com/stress

[3] www.timesofindia.indiatimes.com/articleshow/1927625.cms

[4] www.lifepositive.com

[5] www.pp.okstate.edu/ehs/links/stress.htm

[6] www.ub-counseling.buffalo.edu/stressmanagement.html

[7] www.stress-management-isma.org

[8] www.coolnurse.com/stress_mgt.htm

[9] www.stress-management-isma.org

[10] www.infosys.com/index/careere.htm

[11] www.indianitfirms.com/top.htm

[12] www.stresssesinIT.com/stress.htm

[13] HRM Review December 2007 issue, pg 42 "Stress at Work".

[14] Ashwathappa K " Human Resource Management", Tata McGraw-Hill Publication, Reprint 2007,"stress management".

[15] Robbins P. Stephen: "*Organizational Behaviour*", IX Edition Aug 2001, Prentice-Hall of India Private Limited, New Delhi PP-564.

✡ ✡ ✡